Readings in Medieval Poetry

READINGS IN
MEDIEVAL POETRY

A. C. SPEARING

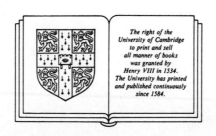

The right of the
University of Cambridge
to print and sell
all manner of books
was granted by
Henry VIII in 1534.
The University has printed
and published continuously
since 1584.

CAMBRIDGE UNIVERSITY PRESS

Cambridge

New York   New Rochelle   Melbourne   Sydney

Published by the Press Syndicate of the University of Cambridge
The Pitt Building, Trumpington Street, Cambridge CB2 1RP
32 East 57th Street, New York, NY 10022, USA
10 Stamford Road, Oakleigh, Melbourne 3166, Australia

First published 1987

Printed in Great Britain at the University Press, Cambridge

British Library cataloguing in publication data

Spearing, A. C.
Readings in medieval poetry.
1. English poetry – Middle English, 1100–1500
– History and criticism
I. Title
821'.1'09   PR311

Library of Congress cataloguing in publication data

Spearing, A. C.
Readings in medieval poetry.
Bibliography.
Includes index.
1. English poetry – Middle English, 1100–1500
– History and criticism.   I. Title.
PS260.S7   1987   821'.1'09   87-6659

ISBN 0 521 32268 5

Contents

v

Preface

This is not, then, a book intended primarily for scholars (though I hope it will contain things to interest them), and it therefore inevitably contains a certain amount of storytelling and of summary of existing views. I am particularly conscious of the latter in Chapter 6; but experience suggests that some of the general properties of alliterative poetry are still not widely understood even among readers of Langland and the *Gawain*-poet.

In earlier versions, most of Chapter 2 first appeared as 'Medieval Narrative Style' in *Poetica* 17 (1984), 1–21; part of Chapter 4 as 'Literal and Figurative in *The Book of the Duchess*' in *Studies in the Age of Chaucer, Proceedings*, No. 1 (1984) (Reconstructing Chaucer), 165–71; Chapter 7 as '*Purity* and Danger' in *Essays in Criticism* 30 (1980), 293–310; and a large part of Chapter 9 as 'Langland's Poetry: Some Notes in Critical Analysis' in *Leeds Studies in English* ns 14 (1983) (Essays in Memory of Elizabeth Salter), 182–95. I am most grateful to the editors and publishers of these journals for permission to reuse the material here. Parts of the book derive from lectures given as follows: Chapter 1 at the University of Virginia; Chapter 2 at the University of York; Chapter 3 at Yale University and at the Pennsylvania State University; Chapter 8 at the University of Pittsburgh; Chapter 9 at Groningen University. Chapter 3 was also read to Professor Frank Kermode's seminar on narrative at Cambridge, and several parts of the book have been imposed on the Cambridge English Faculty's Medieval Graduate Seminar. I am grateful for the helpful discussion and criticism they received, and hope they have benefited from it. I am also much indebted to colleagues and friends for reading and commenting on earlier drafts of some chapters: to Professor Derek Brewer for Chapter 2, to Professor Christopher Ricks for Chapter 7, to Professor Derek Pearsall for part of Chapter 9, and especially to Dr Sarah Kay for some incisive comments on Chapter 1 and to Professor John Stevens for a particularly thorough critique on Chapter 5. The remaining faults and errors are all my own; I wish I could be equally sure that the same can be said of things other than faults and errors. With a book such as this, which ranges rather widely, it is difficult to be certain that one has never presented as one's own, ideas picked up from reading or from conversation with others; if I have ever done that, I hope that the true begetters will forgive me.

Preface

In quoting from modern editions of medieval texts, I have made minor changes to spelling, removing thorn and yogh and normalizing i/j and u/v; I have also made occasional changes in punctuation, noting these only when they seemed particularly significant.

A. C. SPEARING

Cambridge
October 1986

1 · Elaborated and restricted codes

My first chapter approaches the subject of this book – medieval English poetry – in a manner which may seem doubly oblique. My chief example is a poem written in French, and my route towards it takes a large circuit through the sociolinguistic theories of Basil Bernstein. The poem is the *Chanson de Roland*, the most famous of all literary works in French from the earlier medieval period, and I begin with it for several reasons. The *Chanson* survives in seven manuscript versions, and the oldest and best of these is found in a manuscript that was written in England – the Oxford manuscript, dating from the twelfth century but containing a version of the poem from about 1100. Vernacular poetry of this type and date is still closely related in its written form to the traditions and methods of oral composition. Moreover, just as, when an orally transmitted poem was recited, it was not read aloud from a written text but was newly created from memory with the aid of a large system of stereo-typed themes and formulas, so, when a poem was written down it was not yet in a single 'correct' form: each written version has an independent existence. Thus, whatever the precise origin of the version set down in the Oxford manuscript, and whatever irrecover-able sequence of versions, oral or written, may have existed between that and the *Chanson*'s historical origin (a battle between Franks and Basques at Roncevaux in 778), the Oxford *Roland* has some claim to be considered an English poem in its own right. It may be salutary to begin a study of the expectations we can profitably bring to the reading of medieval English poetry with this reminder that, for some three centuries after the Norman Conquest, English poetry was as likely to be in French as in English. Indeed, it was three centuries after 1066 that what can now be recognized as the decisive break occurred, when Geoffrey Chaucer, in 1368, wrote *The Book of the Duchess*, a poem deeply indebted to French literary traditions and addressed to a French-reading patron, not in French but in English. In the earlier part of the medieval period, much – perhaps most – of the finest vernacular poetry of England is in French.

A second reason for beginning with the *Chanson de Roland* is that it is a superb example of a type of writing to which there is nothing fully comparable in English, either in its own time or later. (The closest similarity, as we shall see, is to be found in alliterative poems of the type discussed in Chapter 6.) It is a primary epic poem – written down and therefore doubtless differing in significant ways from oral epic poetry, but nevertheless a poem celebrating deeds of martial heroism with Homeric vigour and wholeheartedness rather than Virgilian sadness and subtlety. It represents a type of poetry to which much subsequent medieval literature in both French and English stands in a relation of modification or divergence. Expressing the ideals of a warrior aristocracy for which French was the natural language, it has no parallel in English, but it is essential for our understanding of the nature of what succeeds it in both languages.

Finally, the qualitative superiority of the *Chanson* makes it an especially useful starting-point for a study of medieval poetry in which the initial problem – one that persists to some extent throughout the medieval period – is to gain attention for characteristics that begin by seeming like deficiencies or absences when regarded in the light of the expectations appropriate to more recent writing. The power and memorability of the *Chanson de Roland* are beyond question; the problem then is, how and why does it come to be as it is? These questions are partly historical, but their fundamental purpose is to help us to recognize and respond to the work's intrinsic properties.

I begin with an example. The following passage is a single *laisse* (a group of lines forming a narrative unit and bound together by the assonance of their final syllables). Charlemagne's army is withdrawing from Spain under an agreement with the Saracens, but its rearguard, under the command of Roland with his companion Oliver, has been betrayed by Roland's enemy Ganelon, and is about to be ambushed. The *laisse* begins among the Saracens; the noise of their preparations is heard by the French and this provides a transition to the conversation of Oliver and Roland.

> Paien s'adubent des osbercs sarazineis,
> Tuit li plusur en sunt dublez en treis,
> Lacent lor elmes mult bons sarraguzeis,
> Ceignent espees de l'acer vianeis,
> Escuz unt genz, espiez valentineis
> E gunfanuns blancs e blois e vermeilz;

Elaborated and restricted codes

Laissent les muls e tuz les palefreiz,
Es destrers muntent, si chevalchent estreiz.
Clers fut li jurz e bels fut li soleilz,
N'unt guarnement que tut ne reflambeit,
Sunent mil grailles por ço que plus bel seit;
Granz est la noise, si l'oïrent Franceis,
Dist Oliver: "Sire cumpainz, ce crei,
De Sarrazins purum bataille aveir."
Respont Rollant: "E Deus la nus otreit!
Ben devuns ci estre pur nostre rei:
Pur sun seignor deit hom susfrir destreiz
E endurer e granz chalz e granz freiz,
Si.n deit hom perdre e del quir e del peil.
Or guart chascuns que granz colps i empleit,
Que malvaise cançun de nus chantét ne seit!
Paien unt tort e chrestïens unt dreit;
Malvaise essample n'en serat ja de mei." AOI.   (994–1016)[1]

They arm themselves in Saracen hauberks,
all but a few are laced with triple mail;
they lace on their good helms of Saragossa,
gird on their swords, the steel forged in Vienne;
they have rich shields, spears of Valencia,
and gonfanons of white and blue and red.
They leave the mules and riding horses now,
mount their war horses and ride in close array.
The day was fair, the sun was shining bright,
all their armor was aflame with the light;
a thousand trumpets blow: that was to make it finer.
That made a great noise, and the men of France heard.
Said Oliver: "Companion, I believe
we may yet have a battle with the pagans."
Roland replies: "Now may God grant us that.
We know our duty: to stand here for our King.
A man must bear some hardships for his lord,
stand everything, the great heat, the great cold,
lose the hide and hair on him for his good lord.
Now let each man make sure to strike hard here:
let them not sing a bad song about us!
Pagans are wrong and Christians are right!
They'll make no bad example of me this day!" AOI.[2]

My guess is that most readers will find this passage stirring; it belongs to a world remote from us, but not beyond the reach of our imaginations in its depiction of the glamour of medieval chivalry and its strong and simple heroic ethic. These qualities in fact do survive into modern life, but they have been marginalized: now, at least in peacetime, they are found most noticeably within the restricted field of team-sport, with its parade of colours and

3

emblems, its (most commonly male) comradeship, its celebration of physical prowess, of leadership and loyalty, its concern for fame. If you were able to live imaginatively *within* that field, as many schoolboys and some adults, but perhaps few readers of this book, actually do, you would come quite close to the world of *chanson de geste*. Two aspects of the passage are perhaps worth comment at this stage. One is the extreme simplicity of its syntax, especially in the description of the Saracen preparations; the fine objects, brilliant colours, loud noises, seem to be merely heaped up, conveyed in a series of simple statements, with no complexity or subordination in their linking – even the elementary conjunction *and* is frequently lacking. To put it in that way is to present the passage's style in terms of deficiency: something is absent that we expect to be present. The other aspect, most noticeable in the second half, is the nakedness of its ethical didacticism. This appears in three forms: statement of purported fact ('Paien unt tort e chrestïens unt dreit'), statement of obligation ('Pur sun seignor deit hom susfrir destreiz'), and exhortation ('Que malvaise cançun de nus chantét ne seit!'). It is not to be supposed that Roland is revealing new truths in this passage; on the contrary, he is restating what Oliver and the poem's audience already know well. In a sense, no doubt, all literature constitutes a transmission of values; but the expectation of the modern reader is likely to be that some new subtlety of insight will be added by the individual writer, and indeed that new insight is a mark of what we call literature. Again, when confronted with a passage such as this, we seem obliged to speak in terms of deficiency. In the earlier Middle Ages it may be said that the category of the literary as an autonomous sphere does not exist; 'literature' is the verbal form by which medieval culture reproduces itself, as painting is the visual form. This situation is particularly clear with the *Chanson de Roland*. The poem exists as a means of transmitting the heroic ethic; a chronicler reports that, some time before the Oxford version was composed, a song of Roland was sung by a minstrel to the troops of William of Normandy before the Battle of Hastings. The heroic poem functions in a quite literal way as a means of producing heroic behaviour; at the same time heroic deeds are thought of as the material for further heroic poems, and this thought is a further means of producing heroic conduct: 'Que malvaise cançun de nus chantét ne seit!' In principle the circle

Elaborated and restricted codes

        heroic deeds > heroic poems > heroic deeds
or
        heroic poems > heroic deeds > heroic poems
is complete and continuous. The poem is a means by which the culture imprints a certain pattern in the minds of its members. Poetry is above all memorable; and, in a world where books were scarce and literacy rare, it was through memory, shaped by constant repetition, that human culture survived.

It is here that the concepts of elaborated and restricted codes, derived from the sociolinguistic theory of Basil Bernstein, begin to become of use to us; and I shall need to take some time to expound Bernstein's views, which are perhaps better known among those concerned with education than among those concerned with literature – indeed, their unexpected relevance to literature is precisely what I want to argue. Bernstein developed his theory in a series of articles published between the late 1950s and early 1970s, most of which are conveniently collected in his book, *Class, Codes and Control*, volume 1.[3] It has been extremely influential among educationists, though often, in his view, in distorted or misunderstood forms; it has also attracted severe criticism, especially for its alleged lack of empirical support.[4] Since my purpose is to argue the applicability of Bernstein's theoretical concepts to a field quite different from that in which he developed them, this criticism, even if justified, does not necessarily affect their usefulness here.

The task of expounding Bernstein's ideas, even in the largely uncritical way I intend, is made more difficult by the fact that they have undergone considerable modification in the course of time. His starting-point in 1958 was the 'relations between social class and educational attainment' (23), and education has continued to be a central focus of his work. My concern, though, is with his views of language, which he saw from the beginning as providing the essential link between social class and educational attainment. His insistence on the crucial importance of language derives from the thought of Edward Sapir and Benjamin Lee Whorf.[5] The 'Sapir-Whorf hypothesis' (which has itself been subjected to fundamental criticism) is that one's native language has built into it, not only in its vocabulary but also, less visibly, in its grammatical structure, a set of categories which form a grid through which one perceives the world; and thus one's perception of reality is fundamentally constrained by the language one possesses. Bernstein, however, has been careful to distinguish his view from that of Whorf and his followers, because he argues that, in positing what is in effect a direct link between native language and culture, they disregard the mediation of the social structure. In his view, it is the social structure that 'generates distinct linguistic forms or codes and these codes essentially transmit the culture and so constrain behaviour' (122). This means that within a single native language there may be a number of distinct codes, corresponding to different forms of social relationship among its speakers; and indeed it is the existence of different codes within English, rather than genetic differences, that he sees as responsible for the differing educational attainment of different social classes. Thus, as he puts it, 'it is reasonable to argue that the genes of social class may well be carried less through a genetic code but far more through a communication code that social class itself promotes' (143).

The evidence which suggested this theory to Bernstein was very simple. Some of it arose from his own early work in teaching working-class day-release pupils, some from questioning of mothers about how they addressed their children. One example that he gives is as follows. A middle-class mother says to her noisy brat, 'I'd rather you made less noise, darling', and that sentence, with its carefully judged use of comparative terms (*rather* and *less*), its relatively complex syntactical structure, its indirectness and its personal appeal, will be understood by the child as the cue for an appropriate response on its part. The working-class mother in the same situation is more likely to say, 'Shut up!', which will provide the cue for a similar response on her child's part. The middle-class child will of course understand 'Shut up!' as well; as Bernstein puts it, the child 'has learnt to be able to respond to *both* statements, and *both* are differentially discriminated within a finely articulated world of meaning' (26–7). The working-class child, on the other hand, has learned to respond only to 'Shut up!', and so, 'although he may understand both, he will not differentiate effectively between the two' (27). In the order of Bernstein's work, the analysis of the two codes came first, and was followed, in the course of the 1960s, by a gradually developing analysis of the types of social structure which he saw as generating the codes. But in my exposition I shall reverse this procedure, beginning with what is causally prior, the types of social structure, and moving on to analysis of the codes.

In 1971, then, Bernstein wrote:

Elaborated and restricted codes

A restricted code will arise where the form of the social relation is based upon closely shared identifications, upon an extensive range of shared expectations, upon a range of common assumptions. Thus a restricted code emerges where the culture or sub-culture raises the 'we' above 'I'. (146)

In these circumstances, there will be less need for language to make things explicit, because speakers will have more in common with one another, more that they can take for granted. And, as Bernstein goes on to point out, though the most obvious and largest example of such a 'culture or sub-culture' may be the working class as a whole, there are likely to be many smaller groups in which the same conditions obtain. He mentions, in various of his papers, many examples, including prisoners, age-groups of adolescents, combat units in the armed services, friends or married couples of long standing, senior common rooms. All such groups will tend to employ a restricted code – restricted in that it will habitually exclude the 'verbal elaboration of individual experience' (147) – though of course the code will differ in detail for each group. An elaborated code, on the other hand,

. . . will arise wherever the culture or sub-culture emphasizes the 'I' over the 'we'. It will arise wherever the intent of the other person cannot be taken for granted. In as much as the intent of the other person cannot be taken for granted, then speakers are forced to elaborate their meanings and make them both explicit and specific. (147)

In another paper, published in 1973, Bernstein expresses the difference between the two types of social relationship in this way: in one type of culture *Difference* lies at the basis of the social relationship, and is made verbally active' in the form of an elaborated code, while in the other type it is not difference but *consensus* that lies at the basis, and this generates a restricted code (178). Or, in yet another formulation, 'A restricted code . . . is a form of speech which symbolizes a communally based culture' (152).

But how does this contrast between types of culture or subculture relate to the example given of the contrast between 'I'd rather you made less noise, darling' and 'Shut up!'? Surely both of these expressions originate within a narrow family circle where a restricted code would normally be used, regardless of the class of the family? Bernstein meets this difficulty by positing two kinds of role system, either of which may be found within the family: the personal (or open) role system and the positional (or closed) role system. He sees the positional family as characteristically, though

7

not exclusively, working-class, and as generating a restricted code. Within a positional family, the child's role and the behaviour expected of him derive from his relative position; he must do or not do certain things because he is a child ('Because I'm your father!' is the ultimate sanction), or because he is a boy, or the oldest, or the youngest, and so on. His behaviour is controlled by unquestionable principles, always relating to status rather than to personal qualities and relationships: 'Boys don't play with dolls' or 'You're too old to suck your thumb' or 'That's not the way to talk to your mother'. But normally those principles do not need to be stated at all: they can simply be taken for granted, and they will be transmitted implicitly in the structure of a language code which contains no means of questioning them. In a personal family system, on the other hand, the child's role is not closed in this way, and his behaviour is controlled by his being made sensitive to the subjective feelings of others and to his own subjective feelings.

. . . the conduct of the child is related to the feelings of the regulator (parent) or the significance of the act, its meaning is related explicitly to the regulated, to the child, e.g. 'Daddy will be pleased, hurt, disappointed, angry, ecstatic if you go on doing this', 'If you go on doing this you will be miserable when the cat has a nasty pain' . . . Control is effected through either the verbal manipulation of feelings or through the establishing of reasons which link the child to his acts.[6]

In 1971 Bernstein summed up this aspect of his thought as follows. In the positional family, or in any other closed role system (such as that of the traditional working-class culture),

. . . verbal meanings are likely to be assigned. The individual (or child) steps into the meaning system and leaves it relatively undisturbed. Where the role system is of the open type, the individual is more likely to achieve meaning on his own terms and here there is the potential of disturbing or changing the pattern of received meanings . . . Where the role system is open, the individual or child learns to cope with ambiguity and isolation in the creation of verbal meanings; where the role system is closed, the individual or child foregoes such learning.   (149)

I now turn back to consider the actual nature of the linguistic codes that these two opposed types of social relationship or role system generate. Bernstein sees one fundamental criterion for distinguishing between them, and that is the relative ease or difficulty of predicting the syntactic patterns that a speaker or writer will use. In 1962 he put it in the following terms:

Two general types of code can be distinguished: *elaborated* and *restricted*. They can be defined, on a linguistic level, in terms of the probability of predicting for any one speaker which syntactic elements will be used to organize meaning. In the case of an elaborated code, the speaker will select from a relatively extensive range of alternatives and therefore the probability of predicting the pattern of organizing elements is considerably reduced. In the case of a restricted code the number of these alternatives is often severely limited and the probability of predicting the pattern is greatly increased.   (76–7)

This is an important and powerful distinction, but it is possible to go beyond it and describe what from a literary point of view are the stylistic features of the two codes in considerably greater detail; and Bernstein did this at an early stage. It will be most useful to concentrate on the features of the restricted code because, as will be obvious by now, the elaborated code is familiar to all readers of this book: it is habitual to us as students or intellectuals, people who are in the habit of reading books about literature or reflecting theoretically on the nature of the language used by ourselves and others.

This is Bernstein's list of the characteristics of a restricted code:

1 Short, grammatically simple, often unfinished sentences, a poor syntactical construction with a verbal form stressing the active mood.
2 Simple and repetitive use of conjunctions (so, then, and, because).
3 Frequent use of short commands and questions.
4 Rigid and limited use of adjectives and adverbs.
5 Infrequent use of impersonal pronouns as subjects (one, it).
6 Statements formulated as implicit questions which set up a sympathetic circularity, e.g. 'Just fancy?' 'It's only natural, isn't it?' 'I wouldn't have believed it'.
7 A statement of fact is often used as both a reason and a conclusion, or, more accurately, the reason and conclusion are confounded to produce a categoric statement, e.g. 'Do as I tell you' 'Hold on tight' 'You're not going out' 'Lay off that'.
8 Individual selection from a group of idiomatic phrases will frequently be found.
9 Symbolism is of a low order of generality.
10 The individual qualification is implicit in the sentence structure, therefore it is a language of implicit meaning.   (42–3)

Most of these characteristics are easily grasped, but it may be worth adding a little more about numbers 7 and 8. As to 7, Bernstein goes on to explain that, when this occurs, 'the authority or legitimacy for the statement will reside in the form of the social relationship which is non-verbally present (e.g. by a parent to a child; the lower ranks of a chain of command in army hierarchy; by a leader to a gang member), rather than in reasoned principles' (45); thus any challenge to the command must be a challenge to the authority itself, not a discussion of the principles involved. And as to 8 Bernstein explains that a restricted code will contain 'a large number of idiomatic, traditional phrases from which the individual chooses' (46); he chooses from among those phrases rather than creating a personal style to mediate his individual perceptions and feelings. Readers of medieval literature will recognize here the major feature of the kind of style referred to as *formulaic* by scholars; I shall return to this point later. Last, I must mention one further aspect of the restricted code to which Bernstein calls attention in a later paper, and that is that the narrow range of syntactical patterns on which it is based means that it cannot very easily convey 'logical sequence and stress' in verbal terms. The syntax is not adequately complex to hold together a sustained sequence, with the result that

The thoughts are often strung together like beads on a frame rather than following a planned sequence. A restriction in planning often creates a high degree of redundancy. This means that there may well be a great deal of repetition of information, through sequences which add little to what has already been given. (134)

Bernstein has much to say about the kind of activity that is made possible and encouraged by the elaborated code. A crucial point, to which he comes back repeatedly, is this: 'an elaborated code facilitates the verbal elaboration of subjective intent whilst a restricted code limits the verbal explication of such intent' (108). But it is not only that an elaborated code makes it relatively easy for the user to *express* his inner states and purposes; it also encourages him to *be aware of* his own subjectivity, to conceive of and reflect on his personal identity, his selfhood. As he puts it, 'The concept of self, unlike the concept of self of a speaker limited to a restricted code, will be verbally differentiated, so that it becomes in itself the object of special perceptual activity' (132). And he later implies that, for the elaborated code speaker only, this perceptual activity can have not only the self but speech as its object, so that a 'theoretical attitude' is developed towards language itself (134). It must certainly be the case that only an elaborated code would permit the development of the concept of codes. One possible consequence, though, of these activities made possible by the elaborated code is alienation. Bernstein writes, 'Elaborated codes give access to alternative realities, yet they carry the potential of alienation, of feeling from thought, of self from other, of private belief from role obligation' (186). In literature, doubtless, such forms of alienation constitute some of the most interesting subject matter; but throughout his work Bernstein has been greatly concerned to insist that the speaker of an elaborated code does not have all the advantage on his side, and that the restricted code has its own distinct merits. 'Clearly one code is not bettter than another; each possesses its own aesthetic, its own possibilities' (135). He had earlier given some indication of the aesthetic values that might be looked for in a restricted code: 'a simplicity and directness of expression, emotionally virile, pithy and powerful and a metaphoric range of considerable force and appropriateness' (54). Unfortunately, however, Bernstein supplies few examples which might illustrate these qualities, and offers little analysis of them. He is not attempting literary criticism, and it must be added that his own written language is quite startling, even among sociologists, for its ugliness and clumsiness.

Despite this, and despite the paucity of empirical backing of which his critics have accused him, Bernstein has devised a conceptual scheme of great power, and one which proves, I believe, to have important applications for literary studies. Having offered this compressed summary of his views, I now return to early medieval literature to investigate their relevance to it. If Bernstein is right about the relation between social structure and linguistic code, it ought to be the case that, wherever a transition is found from a culture or subculture which exalts the 'we' over the 'I' to one that begins to exalt the 'I' over the 'we', a transition from restricted to elaborated code would also be found; and, though Bernstein is primarily concerned with speech, he insists that the distinction between codes is not a distinction between speech and writing, so that one might hope to find this transition exemplified in literature. It is generally agreed by historians that one such transition took place in Western Europe among the comparatively small literate class in the twelfth century (or perhaps rather in the period 1050 to 1150). The transition has been described, for example, by Sir Richard Southern as 'the emergence of the individual from his communal background', and as a process which took place in both secular and religious life. He writes:

This impulse towards individual expression was at work in religious communities in the enlargement of the opportunities of privacy, in the renewed study of the theory of friendship, of conscience and of ethics. In the secular life, it found expression in the theory of love and the literature of the passions.[7]

In more recent discussion, the conception of an emergence (or, in the title of one influential book, a discovery) of the individual in this period has been questioned, and it has been suggested that, in the religious life especially, it might be better to refer to 'the discovery of the self' – a self which was seen not as fully autonomous, but as capable of fulfilment only in relation to groups and models outside itself.[8] This may well be true, but it remains the case that this period saw a new focus on the inner landscape or subjectivity of the human being – new at least since St Augustine's *Confessions* – and that 'knowing the inner core of human nature within one's own self is an explicit theme and preoccupation in literature of the period'.[9] The sense of self was doubtless sharpened and pressed towards articulation by the increasing possibility of choice among the models, roles or groups to which people might attach themselves. Southern writes too of a change in the very image of human life: it gradually ceases to be seen as a defensive struggle from within some fortress or place that has to be guarded against dangerous adversaries, and comes to be imagined instead as an outward journey, a quest or pilgrimage towards some distant goal. And this period is one in which we begin to know something of the inner lives of a number of distinguished individuals, who possessed striking powers of self-expression: people such as St Bernard, Abelard and Heloise, John of Salisbury, whose writings bear the imprint of their personalities in a way which is extremely uncommon in the earlier medieval centuries.[10] We are considering a movement which immediately affected probably only a very small subculture, a group of people made up of the higher clerical classes and of the courtly aristocracy; and for this highly literate group, scattered over Western Europe, writing as much as speech is likely to have been the means of transmitting values.

Southern calls the chapter in which he discusses this change 'From Epic to Romance', and, as that title indicates, he sees a rough correspondence between the cultural change and a literary change – the movement from epic poems, *chansons de geste* such as the *Chanson de Roland*, to courtly romances such as those of Chrétien de Troyes. In suggesting this correspondence, he is thinking primarily of the leading motives of the works in question, rather than of the details of their styles or of the sociolinguistic codes in which they are written; but others have noticed differences in their styles which are strikingly similar to the differences between the restricted and elaborated codes as defined by Bernstein. We need to bear in mind that 'cultural change' is not a simple, once-for-all event: romances often have much in common with *chansons de geste*, and *chansons de geste* went on being copied and read long after Chrétien wrote his romances. We also need to remember that the *Chanson de Roland* cannot be taken as a perfectly typical *chanson de geste*. Nevertheless, by seeing it in this light, we may be able to grasp its expressive resources more firmly and understand more clearly what it is that they express.

I want now to consider another example from the *Chanson*, taken this time from earlier in the poem, and describing the reception by Charlemagne of a peace-mission from the Saracen king Marsilion, who has sent ten richly equipped white mules as a peace-offering. (After each line I give my own literal translation.)

Bels fut li vespres e li soleilz fut cler.
The evening was fair and the sun was bright.

Les dis mulez fait Charles establer.
Charles has the ten mules stabled.

El grant verger fait li reis tendre un tref.
The king has a tent spread in the great orchard.

Les dis messages ad fait enz hosteler.   160
He has the ten envoys lodged in it.

.xii. serjanz les unt ben cunreez.
Twelve officers have well provided for them.

La noit demurent tresque vint al jur cler.
They stay the night until it came to be clear day.

Li empereres est par matin levét.
The emperor has got up in the morning.

Messe e matines ad li reis escultét.
The king has listened to mass and matins.

Desuz un pin en est li reis alez.   165
The king has gone from there beneath a pine.

Ses baruns mandet pur sun cunseill finer.
He calls his barons to conclude his council.

Par cels de France voelt il del tut errer.   AOI.
He wishes to proceed by [the advice of] those of France in everything.

Li empereres s'en vait desuz un pin.
The emperor goes out beneath a pine.

Ses baruns mandet pur sun cunseill fenir.
He calls his barons to conclude his council.

Le duc Oger e l'arcevesque Turpin,   170
Duke Oger and archbishop Turpin,

Richard li velz e sun nevuld Henri,
Richard the old and his nephew Henri,

E de Gascuigne li proz quens Acelin,
And the brave count Acelin from Gascony,

Tedbald de Reins e Milun sun cusin,
Theobald of Rheims and his cousin Milun,

E si furent e Gerers e Gerin.
And there were also both Gerers and Gerin.

Ensembl'od els li quens Rollant i vint,   175
Together with them there came count Roland,

E Oliver li proz e li gentilz.
And Oliver the brave and noble.

Des Francs de France en i ad plus de mil.
There were more than a thousand Franks of France.

Guenes i vint ki la traïsun fist.
There came Ganelon who committed the [act of] treason.

Des ore cumuncet le cunseill que mal prist. AOI.
Now begins the council that went wrong.

Erich Auerbach, analysing the style of the *Chanson de Roland* in a
chapter of his influential book *Mimesis*, has noted particularly a
feature that we observed in our discussion of the previous passage
from the poem – its paratactic quality, the way in which it consists of
a string of simple sentences, with few or no syntactical linkings
among them. As he puts it, 'Every line marks a new start, every
stanza represents a new approach', and he adds that each stanza (or
laisse) 'appears to be a bundle of independent parts, as though sticks
or spears of equal length and with similar points were bundled
together'. He comments that the poem gives 'no analyses or
explanations' of what happens in it: 'The poet explains nothing; and
yet the things which happen are stated with a paratactic bluntness
which says that everything must happen as it does happen, it could
not be otherwise, and there is no need for explanatory connec-
tives.'[11] And Eugène Vinaver has added that the parataxis of the
Chanson de Roland is 'genuine, not contrived':[12] it is not that the poet
is deliberately offering mysteries for us to ponder, but that he
simply sees no need to make connections explicitly in his words,
presumably because the connections were already present, as part of
the assumed nature of things, in the culture out of which he wrote.
The world of the poem (like, we may suppose, the culture which

14

produced it) is one in which meaning is universal yet elusive, 'everywhere and nowhere: everywhere in the perfect clarity of the immediately and always intelligible reality, nowhere in that this reality is lived as immediacy . . . in a manner which reduces the process of knowledge to one of recognition'.[13]

In this passage we can certainly see many of the characteristics of the restricted code as defined by Auerbach. There are the short, grammatically simple sentences (lines 178 and 179 form the only complex sentence in the passage), and the simple and repetitive use of conjunctions (here, indeed, *and* and *until* are the only conjunctions used). The employment of adjectives and adverbs is certainly rigid and limited: the sun is bright (157), and so is the day (162); the evening is fair (157); the orchard is large (159); Acelin is brave (172), and Oliver is brave and noble (178); there are no adverbs at all. And perhaps we can find number 7 on Bernstein's list, the confounding of reason and conclusion, in line 167, which amounts to saying that Charlemagne consults his barons because he always consults his barons. The reason why he does so is part of the feudal and positional structure of the poet's society, and he has no need to state it, nor perhaps any means of stating it. The important relations are not personal but positional: Charlemagne is present primarily not as an individual but as king (which he is called three times) or as emperor (which he is called twice), and the barons are essentially barons, their names and attributes forming a mere catalogue. It is a self-complete world, which displays itself to us but does not open itself to us unless we are already part of it. In a line from the earlier passage – 'Paien unt tort e chrestïens unt dreit' (1015) – the closed nature of the community is defined by its opposition to another, equally closed community, which differs from it only in being opposed to it. All that is not Christian is pagan; all that is not pagan is Christian. The opposition offers no choice, and it is deadly serious. (The point may be clarified by comparison with the thirteenth-century poem in English, *The Owl and the Nightingale*. There an analogous binary opposition is found, equally closed by generic definition – owls are owls, nightingales are nightingales, and neither can become the other – but it is now used to explore alternatives: opposition has become a form of intellectual play and it is possible to envisage its transcendence on a higher level of understanding, that of Nicholas of Guildford, the judge of the cases put by the two birds.)

Southern remarks that, though the poet claimed to be writing about the time of Charlemagne, he took as his model the society of Northern France in the late eleventh and early twelfth centuries, and he adds that 'It was a masculine society, and its members were more conscious of the group to which they belonged and of their duty towards it than of their own hearts.'[14] That sounds like a perfect description of the type of culture which, according to Bernstein, ought to generate a restricted code, in which subjective intent is not made explicit. The fact that it was a masculine society may itself be significant, because Bernstein suggests that girls are more likely than boys to employ an elaborated code or at least to reveal 'a more differentiated, more individualized use of language' (161). (If this is true, it is doubtless a consequence of cultural formation rather than of nature; but it has been argued that the growth of a female audience was an important influence on the rise of romance.[15]) The style of this extract is entirely impersonal; we are not aware of any poet telling the story or offering to interpret it; the narrator is merely the spokesman of the culture's 'we', not yet an 'I' on his own account. We may not even know his name, for it is by no means clear that the 'Turoldus' mentioned in the final line of the Oxford manuscript is the poet rather than the scribe. Many of the stylistic features found in the passage under discussion have been seen by scholars as characteristics of a formulaic style developed for oral composition and oral delivery: the repetition of epithets and indeed of whole lines (as lines 165–6 are repeated more or less verbatim at 168–9) has been seen as a necessity for a poet, perhaps illiterate, who recomposes his poem each time he recites it. Without at all denying the functional utility of these stylistic features, we can also see, looking at the passage through Bernstein's eyes, that they would be positively desirable as symbolic expressions of a communally based culture. Unlike any of the few examples that Bernstein himself gives, this passage seems to me a triumphant vindication of his repeated claims for the aesthetic possibilities of a restricted code. It does not represent one of the great dramatic moments of the poem, but, in its very simplicity, it has an unparalleled strength and grandeur. The human action proceeds in a course that seems unchangeable before an unchanging natural background of day and night, mountain and orchard, and the divergences from extreme simplicity are themselves powerfully expressive. Thus the only two complex sentences – 'Guenes i vint ki la traïsun fist' and 'Des ore cumencet le cunseill que mal prist' (178–9) – use their relative constructions to cast an ominous shadow of prophecy over the peaceful scene. The future is already fixed, and no explanation is needed in terms of human intention or philosophical scheme.

Yet already, in commenting on the passage in this relatively straightforward way, I have begun to distort its immediate effect. The critical language I use belongs to an elaborated code, and it is impossible to imagine a critical language that would not do so. To translate from the restricted code of the poet into the elaborated code of any kind of critical discourse is to transform the poem into something different from what we may suppose it was for the culture that produced it. Bernstein has remarked that the restricted code is one that 'facilitates the ready transformation of feeling into action';[16] we may recall the minstrel's performance to William of Normandy's troops. The poem was undoubtedly created as a stimulus to action and a reinforcement of social solidarity, not to the kind of reflection that we call criticism. At the same time, we should no doubt resist the temptation to exaggerate the *Chanson*'s simplicity and to make it serve our own desire for a myth of heroic innocence. As it approaches its end, it becomes evident that the unquestioned heroic value-system with which it began leaves an apparently insoluble problem. The traitor Ganelon claims that his destruction of Roland was an act of personal vengeance, a just and open[17] response to Roland's malice towards him, shown in Roland's proposal that he should accept the dangerous mission to the Saracen king; and in this world of intense loyalties, there appears to be no answer to his claim. The barons beg Charlemagne to set Ganelon free, and only one man speaks out against this course. This is Thierry, a hero of quite unheroic appearance, standing outside the poem's normal descriptive formulas:

> Heingre out le cors e graisle e eschewid,
> Neirs les chevels e alques bruns li vis,
> N'est gueres granz, ne trop nen est petiz.   (3820–2)

> His body was spare and slight and slender,
> His hair was black and his face rather dark;
> He is hardly big, but neither is he too small.

Thierry's argument breaks the impasse by introducing a new consideration. Loyalty to the king should override all other loyalties, and the fact that Roland was on royal service when commanding the French rearguard against the Saracens ought to have protected him against Ganelon's vengeance. In comparison with 'Pur sun seignor deit hom susfrir destreiz' or 'Paien unt tort e chrestïens unt dreit' this argument is quite complex, and it could scarcely be expressed in paratactic form. In fact, the lines in which Thierry puts his case to Charlemagne are unusually tightly articulated (though the fact that they belong to dialogue rather than narrative must have something to do with this):

> Que que Rollant a Guenelun forsfesist,
> Vostre servise l'en doüst bien guarir.
> Guenes est fels d'iço qu'il le traït,
> Vers vos s'en est parjurez e malmis. (3827–30)

> Although Roland may have wronged
>   Ganelon,
> [The fact that he was in] your service ought
>   to have protected him in this matter.
> Ganelon is guilty inasmuch as he betrayed
>   him:
> In this he has perjured and forsworn himself
>   towards you.

Thierry is not, of course, moving on to the plane of subjectivity or of intention or of individuality; indeed he is insisting on the supreme value of the positional as against the personal; but in doing so he is distinguishing the personal from the positional, whereas the positional value-system assumed earlier in the poem has drawn its power precisely from the absence of any such distinction. Ganelon's fate has eventually to be settled in the heroic manner, by judicial combat between his champion, Pinabel, and Thierry; but when the unpromising Thierry wins, we sense that the triumph belongs to a new way of thinking, one which will demand an elaborated code for its expression.[18]

I know of no medieval works written in English that both possess some recognizable literary value and belong as completely to a restricted code as the *Chanson de Roland* does; this indeed was an important reason, as I explained, for my beginning with a work written in French. By the fourteenth century, however, we do find some English poems of merit of a type approximating to the earlier French *chansons de geste*. Such poems may be more common within the alliterative tradition; but whether or not this is generally true, one alliterative poem in particular, the *Morte Arthure*, has been widely recognized as possessing powerful epic qualities. My next example is a short passage from the *Morte*, a poem which will be considered more fully in Chapter 6; it comes at a point where King Arthur sets off in search of a giant who has been tyrannizing over the country and people near Mont-Saint-Michel.

> The Kyng coveris the cragge wyth cloughes full hye,
> To the creste of the clyffe he clymbez on lofte;
> Keste upe hys umbrer and kenly he lukes;
> Caughte of the colde wynde to comforthe hym selven.
> Two fyrez he fyndez, flawmande full hye;
> The fourtedele a furlang betwene thus he walkes;
> The waye by the welle strandez he wandyrde hym one,
> To wette of the warlawe, whare that he lengez.
> He ferkez to the fyrste fyre, and even there he fyndez
> A wery wafull wedowe, wryngande hire handez,
> And gretande on a grave grysely teres;
> Now merkyde on molde sen myddaye it semede.
> He saluwede that sorowfull with sittande wordez,
> And fraynez aftyre the fende fairely thereaftyre. $(941-54)^{19}$

Some of those lines, especially in the first part of the extract, are simple and paratactic, and a 'rigid and limited use of adjectives and adverbs' predominates (*full hye, kenly, colde, grysely, fairely*). Towards the end, though, the sentences become longer and more complex, and as a whole the passage is less redundant and repetitive and more fully organized as a causal and temporal sequence than the passages examined from the *Chanson de Roland*. As a whole, this passage does not belong to a restricted code. Although it does not convey subjectivity in a fully explicit way, it implies clearly enough a sharply defined state of mind in both the king and the widow: Arthur, as he enjoys the cold breeze on his face after the effort of climbing the crag in full armour, is more of an individual than Charlemagne was. This movement towards an elaborated code is in keeping with the content of the poem as a whole. The *Morte Arthure* is not a poem like the *Chanson de Roland*, where (until the Thierry incident at the very end) values are taken for granted and unproblematic. On the contrary, it seems to incorporate at least two different value-systems, in close enough juxtaposition to create a problematic situation. One value-system approximates to that of the *Chanson*, with its unquestioning celebration of personal loyalty and martial prowess; the other belongs to a later form of Christianity than is found in the *Chanson*, and involves compassion for the victims of martial glory and disapproval of pride in conquest and victory. As I shall argue in Chapter 6, the poet of the *Morte Arthure* had not managed to establish a balance between these two systems; it is more a matter of uneasy coexistence, a conflict within the poem not fully under the poet's control.

It is not difficult to find Middle English poems, or at least substantial passages from them, that conform more completely to a restricted code; but most of them have little or no value as literature. I shall give only one example of this kind. It is taken from the tail-rhyme romance *Sir Isumbras*, and it is part of the description of the hero near the beginning of the story.

A man he was ryche ynowghe
Of oxen to drawe in his plowghe,
   And stedes also in stalle.
He was bothe curteys and hende;
Every man was his frende,
   And loved he was with all.

A curteys man and hende he was;
His name was kalled syr Isumbras,
   Bothe curteys and fre.
His gentylnesse nor his curtesye
There kowthe no man hit discrye:
   A fful good man was he.
Menstralles he hadde in his halle,
And yafe hem robes of ryche palle,
   Sylver, golde and fee.
Of curtesye he was kynge;
His gentylnesse hadde non endyng;
   In worlde was none so fre.

A fayre wyfe then hadde he
As any in erthe myghte be;
   The sothe as I telle yow;
And manne children had they thre,
As fayre as any myghte be,
   For they were fayre ynow.   (13–36)[20]

It is true that some of the sentences in this extract are technically complex, but the thought is extremely simple, and the possibility of predicting syntactic patterns is high – indeed, after reading only a few stanzas, one feels that one could continue composing them in one's sleep. As has been written about the Middle English romances generally,

The repetition of patterns insures that the message contained will be preserved and communicated through its many oral performances, each of which provides an opportunity for distortion; and the predictability which is the product of such repetition increases the audience's agreement with the ideas offered in the narrative.[21]

Conjunctions are few and simple. The use of adjectives is certainly 'rigid and limited', with the many repetitions of undifferentiating terms of praise – *curteys, hende, fre, fayre, ryche*, along with some of the corresponding abstract nouns. There is some confounding of reason and conclusion: the children were fair because they were fair. What is being said is felt to be entirely unproblematic: the composer and his audience are evidently in total agreement that it is good to be *curteys, hende, fre, fayre*, and *ryche*, and the meanings of the qualities named by those terms are neither expounded nor questioned, for they are given in the communal world to which composer and audience both belong. The composer, adopting the role of minstrel, may perhaps be thought to give some personal stress to the admirable quality of generosity to minstrels, but 'personal' is not really the right word: he says that as a minstrel, not as an individual differentiated from other minstrels, and it is what his audience expected minstrels to say. We are made aware of no subjectivity, no 'difference': this is surely the poetry of consensus, except that it is not poetry at all.

The argument of this chapter can best be completed by a brief anticipation of material of a kind that will be discussed in more detail in several later chapters: an example of medieval poetry belonging fully to an elaborated code. By contrast with the examples considered so far, this is likely to seem 'normal' to the modern reader, because of course nearly all the literature we know is likely to belong to an elaborated code. As Vinaver has remarked about courtly romance by contrast with *chanson de geste*, 'The difficulty of defining romance lies mainly in the fact that its most important distinguishing feature is inseparable from what we normally understand by "literature".'[22] But my hope is that, by seeing this familiar kind of literature in the different context provided by this chapter so far, we shall be able to recognize more clearly what is distinctive about it, without taking it for granted. My example is taken from *The Franklin's Tale*, a product of the most sophisticated English culture of the late fourteenth century, written by a poet whose work possesses a personally distinctive style or cluster of styles in a way unknown in any earlier English writing. The passage comes from near the end of the tale, after Arveragus has told his wife Dorigen that she must keep her rash promise to become Aurelius's mistress if he could remove the rocks from the coast of Brittany. In the ensuing scene, Aurelius decides not to demand fulfilment of the promise;

and if we can envisage this scene as somehow transported into a restricted code poem such as the *Chanson de Roland*, we shall surely have to imagine the decision shown simply in action, or rather in the absence of action: Aurelius does not make Dorigen fulfil her promise. The motivation involved, the whole subjectivity of the situation, will simply be left out and there will also of course be a translation into a style simpler in syntax and rigid in vocabulary and phrasing. Instead, in the scene as Chaucer wrote it, we have a most detailed analysis of Aurelius's emotional reaction to his meeting with Dorigen and the process of reasoning which it provokes in him, a process which involves not only his own subjectivity but also the reflections in it of the subjectivities of both Dorigen and Arveragus. Correspondingly, the syntax is highly complex, winding its way from line to line, linking fluently together a whole variety of motives, facts, and speculations. *The Franklin's Tale* as a whole, far from silently accepting and transmitting communal values, brings them into conflict among themselves – *trouthe*, *gentillesse*, *franchise* – and questions and redefines them with the greatest subtlety.

> This squier, which that highte Aurelius,
> On Dorigen that was so amorus,
> Of aventure happed hire to meete
> Amydde the toun, right in the quykkest strete,
> As she was bown to goon the wey forth right
> Toward the gardyn ther as she had hight;
> And he was to the gardyn-ward also,
> For wel he spyed whan she wolde go
> Out of hir hous to any maner place.
> But thus they mette, of aventure or grace,
> And he saleweth hire with glad entente,
> And asked of hire whiderward she wente;
> And she answerde, half as she were mad,
> "Unto the gardyn, as myn housbonde bad,
> My trouthe for to holde, allas, allas!"
> Aurelius gan wondren on this cas,
> And in his herte hadde greet compassioun
> Of hire and of hire lamentacioun,
> And of Arveragus, the worthy knyght,
> That bad hire holden al that she had hight,
> So looth hym was his wyf sholde breke hir trouthe;
> And in his herte he caughte of this greet routhe,
> Considerynge the beste on every syde,
> That fro his lust yet were hym levere abyde
> Than doon so heigh a cherlyssh wrecchednesse
> Agayns franchise and alle gentillesse;
> For which in fewe wordes seyde he thus . . .   (V 1499–525)[23]

Elaborated and restricted codes

And from this moment of existential choice, at which the crucial events have taken place 'in his herte', Aurelius proceeds to a full 'verbal elaboration of subjective intent'. In this passage he has been shown not only to come to a new understanding of others through that *compassioun* that is part of the very essence of courtliness, but to reach a new awareness of himself as an individual, no longer able to rely for guidance on the unanalysed assumptions of his culture.

2 · Early medieval narrative style

I now want to look more closely at two examples of early medieval narrative poetry in English. The first, which I shall examine in greater detail, is *King Horn*, one of the earliest English romances; the second, a slightly later romance, is *Havelok*. The discussion of *Havelok* need be no more than an epilogue to this chapter, because the nature of its style is more easily recognizable than that of *King Horn*, and so I turn at once to the earlier poem.

King Horn

King Horn is found first in a manuscript dated about 1260, and the poem itself may well be somewhat earlier than the manuscript. It belongs largely to the restricted code as defined in Chapter 1, but I shall now be concerned not with the code itself and its cultural origins but with the kind of imaginative activity possible in a narrative style governed by this code. It is a common experience, I think, for readers of the earlier English romances to respond to them with pleasure and admiration while finding that there appears to be nothing to say about them as verbal structures. Their styles are so simple as to seem transparent; they dissolve under scrutiny, leaving behind only the actions narrated, not the narrative itself. In particular these narratives, and *King Horn* above all, lack the manifest figuration based on metaphor and simile to which twentieth-century readers are accustomed to respond in a conscious way when they read poetry, with the result that we are scarcely able to grasp that their verbal form is having any specific effect on us. To such narratives might be applied by analogy an aphorism by the French film theorist Christian Metz: 'A film is difficult to explain because it is easy to understand.'[1] Confronted with poems of this kind, we are in a situation like that of the average filmgoer, apparently responding directly to certain subject matter without any awareness of the artistic medium through which that subject matter is presented to him and which is shaping his response to it. The analogy is close enough, in my view, to make it profitable to employ some of the terminology of film analysis in discussing the style of medieval narrative poetry. I do so simply as a heuristic device – and, I must add, as a mere amateur in the field of film theory – in the attempt to find a way of approaching a topic that is widely felt to be extremely elusive.

When judged by the standards of post-Shakespearean literature, the style of most medieval narrative poetry is unusually simple and plain. Some reasons for this have been suggested in Chapter 1, and to them can be added that a poem such as *King Horn* was undoubtedly composed for oral delivery, and that it not only had to be understood at a first hearing but also had to be understood by listeners most of whom would have had their competence and their tastes formed by listening only. The nature of this narrative style may be thrown into relief by an illustration of the opposite extreme, taken from a much later narrative poem. Two lines will be enough to make the point:

> Those green-rob'd senators of mighty woods,
> Tall oaks, branch-charmed by the earnest stars.[2]

Those are very beautiful lines, and their beauty is certainly not just a matter of auditory pattern or 'verbal music', but derives largely from their deep and complex metaphoric texture; and that metaphoric texture makes them strikingly difficult. In what senses are the oak-trees senators of mighty woods? In what senses are the stars earnest? In what senses do the stars charm the branches of the oaks? The questions raised are endless. Keats's lines, it would seem, could hardly be understood at all by listeners if they had not already read them, or at the very least if they were not in the habit of making a close study of written texts.

In Chapter 1 I moved forward from the early Middle Ages to the age of Chaucer; in what follows I want to begin with the age of Chaucer and then retrace the path back to the period of *King Horn*. In the narrative poetry of the great age of medieval English literature, the second half of the fourteenth century, we find far less metaphor than in the example from Keats, but there is considerable use of simile – a figure of the same kind as metaphor, requiring a similar kind of mental activity, though less difficult because less compressed and more explicit. In this period, when similes are brief, they are normally familiar, and often indeed stereotyped, presumably so as not to demand too much effort of interpretation, and thereby interfere with a listener's concentration on the narrative content. Thus in a passage from *The Knight's Tale* describing the tournament organized by Duke Theseus to settle whether Arcite or Palamon should marry Emelye, we are told that the swords of the participants are 'as the silver brighte' (I 2608) and that one knight who is unhorsed 'rolleth under foot as dooth a bal' (2614). Where the material offered for comparison is less familiar, the simile is usually extended rather than compact, so that the listener will have time to take it in. A few lines after the two brief similes just quoted, Arcite is said to be as fierce towards Palamon as a Boeotian tigress is towards a huntsman if her cub is stolen from her, and Palamon is said to be as bloodthirsty towards Arcite as an African lion that is hunted or mad for hunger; and this matching pair of exotic similes is spread out over eight lines (four for each simile):

> Ther nas no tygre in the vale of Galgopheye,
> Whan that hir whelp is stole whan it is lite,
> So crueel on the hunte as is Arcite
> For jelous herte upon this Palamon.
> Ne in Belmarye ther nys so fel leon,
> That hunted is, or for his hunger wood,
> Ne of his praye desireth so the blood,
> As Palamon to sleen his foo Arcite.   (2626–33)

Such extended similes were of course seen as appropriate stylistic features of literary epic, and Chaucer's source for *The Knight's Tale*, Boccaccio's *Teseida*, is full of them. But Chaucer also uses them at quite un-epic moments, as for example in *Troilus and Criseyde* when the two lovers are in bed for the first time. Troilus clasps Criseyde in his arms, and, Chaucer says, as a startled nightingale ceases to sing when she hears a shepherd talking or some creature stirring in the hedges, and then lets her voice peal out again afterwards, so Criseyde, having overcome her initial timidity, speaks freely to Troilus:

> And as the newe abaysed nyghtyngale,
> That stynteth first whan she bygynneth to synge,
> Whan that she hereth any herde tale,
> Or in the hegges any wyght stirynge,
> And after siker doth hire vois out rynge,
> Right so Criseyde, whan hire drede stente,
> Opned hire herte and tolde hym hire entente.   (III 1233–9)[3]

This simile too is one of a matched pair; it is followed by one comparing Troilus to a man who expects death but then escapes to safety.

Chaucer's great contemporary, the *Gawain*-poet, similarly makes little use of metaphor (though perhaps a little more than Chaucer himself), and of his similes those that are at all unusual are expanded so as to avoid difficulty or misunderstanding. A good example is found in *Sir Gawain and the Green Knight* at the moment when Gawain, at the Green Chapel, waits to receive the Green Knight's axe-stroke. He flinches away from the first blow, but remains completely steady and unmoving under the second – as still as a stone, the poet says (a brief, stereotyped simile), or as still as a tree-stump that is entwined in gravelly ground with a hundred roots (a less familiar comparison, which is therefore developed in greater detail):

> Bot stode stylle as the ston other a stubbe auther
> That ratheled is in roché grounde with rotez a hundreth. (2293–4)[4]

The age of Chaucer and of the Alliterative Revival was one in which new poetic styles of a more consciously literary kind began to be employed in English. If we go back further, we find that the typical style of narrative poetry is plainer and simpler still, and we tend to be faced with the difficulty mentioned earlier: even when it appeals to us and moves us, we may be at a loss to define in what sense it is poetic, or indeed to say anything about it at all. Aristotle describes metaphor as the greatest distinction of poetry and the only sign of poetic genius,[5] and that view has been widely shared in more recent thought about poetry. By contrast, the American classical scholar Milman Parry long ago described the style of the Homeric poems in these words:

. . . this perfect narrative style, where no phrase, by its wording, stands out by itself to seize the attention of the hearers, and so stop the rapid movement of the thought.[6]

The ideal that Parry was describing is one that is realized in much pre-Chaucerian narrative, and it is essentially an ideal of transparency. The style is to be such that its existence as a verbal medium will not be noticeable: it will merely be a window, through which it will seem that we can view directly 'the rapid movement of the thought'. (With most medieval English narrative it would be more accurate to refer to the rapid movement of action and feeling, for we are not usually made aware of the presence of a thinking narrator.[7]) Yet with this narrative, as with cinematic narrative, the transparency or invisibility of the medium is really an illusion: the medium is there, and it shapes our responses even when it escapes observation or comment. In order to be able to see it at all, in order to penetrate its cloak of invisibility, its disguise of naturalness, we need, as it were, to hold the transparent medium at an 'unnatural' angle, or to run the film through, at least in our minds, at an 'unnatural' speed. That is what I shall attempt to do with the narrative style of *King Horn*.

King Horn, like most narratives of its period, whether in English or in French, is written in rhyming couplets, but in this case the lines are unusually short. They are not the normal octosyllabics of French romance or their accentual English equivalent, but lines of only two or three stresses; and this gives the narrative an oddly lyrical quality, which is heightened by its frequent repetitions of phrases and its ballad-like abruptness of movement. The story, in a much abbreviated outline, is as follows. Horn, the son of the king of Suddene, is driven into exile by Saracen pirates who kill his father. He crosses the sea to Westernesse with two friends – Athulf who is faithful, and Fikenhild who is false. There, though Horn is unknown, the king's daughter Rymenhild falls in love with him. He says he must prove himself before they can get married. He kills many Saracens, but soon the king, Aylmar, is persuaded by the malicious Fikenhild that Horn has seduced Rymenhild, and he banishes him. Horn crosses the sea again to Ireland, and there kills a Saracen giant who had earlier killed his father. The king of Ireland offers Horn his daughter in marriage, but Horn remains true to Rymenhild. He is summoned back to Westernesse, where Rymenhild is about to be married to someone else. He arrives disguised as a beggar, identifies himself by puns and other signs, kills the unwanted suitor, and is accepted by Aylmar. Now Horn returns to Suddene to attempt to win back his kingdom. While he is away, Fikenhild attempts to force Rymenhild to marry him; but Horn once more returns, disguised this time as a harper, kills Fikenhild, marries Rymenhild, and settles down as king of Suddene. In this story, as often in traditional narrative and in myth, the same motif is repeated several times in variant forms;[8] and here one consequence is that the different sections of the narrative are divided up by sea-voyages. (The usual background to knightly adventure in medieval romance is the forest; even more than this, the sea seems to symbolize the dangerous realm of chance, the source both of death and of new life, that lies outside the walls of civilization.)

Comment on *King Horn*'s style can appropriately begin with mention of two features that are not present in it and the absence of which contributes largely to its unnoticeability. The first has already been mentioned: metaphor. So far as I have been able to observe, there are no metaphors in *King Horn* – or at least (an important reservation) there are none which exist simply on the level of verbal style. There *is* a metaphor, and a very important one, but it functions structurally, or on the level of action. Rymenhild has a dream in which she goes fishing. Her net is burst by a 'gret fiss',[9] and she interprets this as meaning that she will lose the fish that she would choose for herself. Horn identifies the fish that tore the net as someone who will cause them suffering, and this turns out to mean Aylmar, whose banishment of Horn causes their separation (lines 658–64). Later, when Horn visits Rymenhild in disguise, he identifies himself to her by means of an extended metaphor in which he says that he is a fisherman who has left his net by the seashore and has now returned to see whether there is a fish in it. The fact that this metaphor originates in the ambiguous symbolism of a dream indicates how special metaphor is for the poet: it is the product of a mind working in a quite unusual way, irrational and perhaps inspired. If a pun counts as a metaphor, then the poem also contains a second metaphor on the level of action, in the form of a pun on Horn's name. Aylmar puns on it when he first learns what Horn is called:

> Horn, thu lude sune
> Bi dales and bi dune! (209–10)

And the pun is repeated in the same scene in which the disguised Horn alludes to Rymenhild's dream of fishing. She bears a drinking-horn to pour drink for the guests at the feast that is supposed to celebrate her wedding to the king who wishes to marry her, and Horn urges her to 'Drink to Horn of horne' (1145). These are, I believe, the only two figures in the poem that belong to the general category of metaphor, that is, of identification based on resemblance. It is striking that the fishing-metaphor and the pun on Horn's name should be clustered together in the same scene of the poem, a scene of disclosure and recognition, in which what was hidden is revealed. The poem's language alone is not enough to support metaphor.

Even the easier figure of simile is extremely rare in *King Horn*, and most of the few instances are similarly clustered together. They occur at the very beginning of the poem, in the initial description of the hero in his childhood:

> He was bright so the glas;
> He was whit so the flur;
> Rose-red was his colur. (14–16)

These comparisons are of course entirely familiar. Though we might expect them to be applied to a heroine rather than to a hero even in his childhood, they require no effort of interpretation, and they scarcely affect the transparency of the poem's style.

The second absence that helps to make the style of *King Horn* escape our attention is that of the narrator. He appears in the opening lines of the poem, to establish a relation with his listeners and announce his intention:

> Alle beon he blithe
> That to my song lythe!
> A sang ihc schal you singe
> Of Murry the kinge.

And he ends the poem by announcing the completion of his intention and thus the dissolution of the relation with the listeners into a generalized piety encompassing 'us alle':

> Her endeth the tale of Horn,
> That fair was and noght unorn.
> Make we us glade evre among,
> For thus him endeth Hornes song.
> Jesus, that is of hevene king,
> Yeve us alle His suete blessing!

Between the beginning and the end the narrator very occasionally mentions himself in lines such as 'Also ihc you telle may' (30), but the narratorial 'I' seems a mere grammatical convention: his role is positional rather than personal, and 'his omniscience is largely situational'.[10] The story appears to tell itself, and even the narratorial comments on it, intended to arouse specific responses in the audience – 'Al to fewe he hadde tho!' (50) or 'Of wordes he was bald' (90) – seem to have no personality behind them. The poet prefers whenever possible to dramatize rather than narrate the events of the poem. Nearly half of *King Horn* – almost 700 lines[11] – consists of direct speech by the characters; and the poet sometimes converts narrative into direct speech by having one of the characters tell another about some of the poem's events. Again, there are none of those explicit narratorial transitions that are so common in Chaucer and in later medieval narrative generally, such as

> Now wol I stynte of Palamon a lite,
> And lete hym in his prisoun stille dwelle,
> And of Arcita forth I wol yow telle.   (*Knight's Tale* I 1334–6)

There are no references to sources or even to 'olde stories' (859), no modesty *topoi* –

> Who koude ryme in Englyssh proprely
> His martirdom? for sothe it am nat I;
> Therfore I passe as lightly as I may   (1459–61)

– and no examples of *occupatio* (the listing of what is not going to be recounted) –

> And certes, if it nere to long to heere,
> I wolde have toold yow fully the manere
> How wonnen was the regne of Femenye . . .   (875–7)

In short, there are none of the devices by means of which later medieval poets, even without necessarily personalizing the narrator, make us aware of a narrator distinct from the material of the narrative, who is consciously aiming to present that material to us in one way rather than another.

In *King Horn*, then, there is nothing to suggest to us any distinction between the story itself and the way in which the story is told. This is despite the fact that, as my summary will have indicated, the narrative structure is very complicated, involving three main settings (Westernesse, Ireland, and Suddene), each of which is visited several times; eight sea-voyages; and several cross-cuts from Ireland and Suddene to Westernesse and back again. But the voyages transport us along with the characters, without the narrator's seeming to be involved; and the cross-cuts are conducted with the utmost naturalness, often being masked by an association of ideas. For example, the first cross-cut is introduced by our being told that Horn stayed in Ireland for seven years without returning to Rymenhild in Westernesse or communicating with her; and this is the cue for the narrative to turn (at line 923) to Rymenhild in Westernesse. The effect is of what in film is sometimes called 'invisible cutting'. The transitions are seamless (or rather, the seams are concealed); there appears to be simply a continuous flow generated from within the story itself, and we need to make a conscious effort to notice that a narratorial intervention has in fact occurred.

'Invisible cutting' was an ideal of the classic Hollywood film, though it was of course achieved by different means, not usually by such associations of ideas. Another respect in which the narrative technique of *King Horn* resembles that of film is in its general avoidance of summary – also a device which, by implying that someone is doing the summarizing, tends to remind us of the existence of a storyteller. It is difficult for film narrative to summarize, simply because a cinematographic representation of a certain sequence of action occupies just the same amount of time as the sequence itself. Abbreviation has to be effected by elliptical editing; and something analogous to that is preferred by the poet of *King Horn*. What he does is to divide his action up into very small units and cut rapidly from one to another, effacing himself in the process. This can properly be considered a kind of verbal equivalent to elliptical editing in the film, though it must be remembered that, whereas the film-maker at the editing stage is literally cutting up pieces of film that have already been shot, discarding the unwanted parts, and joining the remainder in a certain order, for the poet there is unlikely to be any sharp distinction between 'shooting' (i.e. imagining) and cutting. That is so, at least, unless we may think of the poet as 'cutting' the material provided by a source. There is an Anglo-Norman analogue to *King Horn* which is over 5000 lines long; the English version gets exactly the same story into only some 1500 lines, and very short lines too. *King Horn* is probably not translated directly from *Horn et Rimenhild*, but it is possible that the English poet was working from some such lengthier source and cutting it as he went along. However it came about, the narrative style of *King Horn* is very similar to that of film in its effect. Short pieces of event are joined together in series; and the joining in both cases is simply a matter of juxtaposition. Like the language of dream, the language of film is paratactic. It has no means of indicating explicitly and unambiguously the relation between one film-piece and the next or the meaning of that relation; it cannot even distinguish between *and* and *but*, still less has it any equivalent to the subordinate clause. So it is in general with *King Horn*: there is simply a sequence of briefly narrated pieces of action, with few, if any syntactical links among them, and the listeners are left to supply the connections for themselves from their understanding of the content. To take a single, striking example, Horn's first return to Westernesse to save Rymenhild from an unwanted marriage is narrated as follows:

The word of Rymenhild's wedding began to spread. Horn was in the water; he could not have come later [i.e. he came at the very last moment]. He left his ship at anchor and went to land.

> The word bigan to springe
> Of Rymenhilde weddinge.
> Horn was in the watere;
> Ne mighte he come no latere.
> He let his schup stonde,
> And yede to londe.   (1017–22)

As with the *Chanson de Roland*, in calling attention to these features of narrative style, I am undoubtedly doing something other than the poet would have expected or probably wished. If one reads the poem without making a conscious effort to be analytical, the method of storytelling becomes unnoticeable; the effect, as I have remarked, is simply of naturalness. It is worth emphasizing that 'naturalness' is not intended to imply 'realism'. The world represented in *King Horn* is highly stylized; it is a world of extremes with no middle ground between them –

> Athulf was the beste
> And Fikenylde the werste   (27–8)

– a world more like that of fairytale than like that of everyday life. (I set aside for the moment the complications introduced by the possibility that people in the early Middle Ages may have perceived their real world as being more like fairytale than we do ours.[12]) The illusion created by *King Horn* is not that the events represented are those of real life, but that there is no mode of representation intervening between us and them; or, as I put it above, that the poem is merely a transparent window through which we regard the events that make up its content.

So far this consideration of the style of *King Horn* has largely been in terms of absence; and that is how it presents itself to us so long as we assume that poetic style is essentially a matter of metaphor, or of the whole family of figures based on the resemblance of one thing to another and the transfer of meaning over this bridge of resemblance. That conception of poetic style, however, is challenged by the distinction, originating with the Russian Formalists, expounded systematically by Roman Jakobson, and developed further in relation to English literature by more recent theorists such as David Lodge, between metaphor and metonymy.[13] On this alternative view, metaphor and metonymy are generated by opposed principles or axes of language itself, metaphor being derived from similarity and metonymy from contiguity. Metonymy in this sense proves to be of greater use than metaphor in enabling us to detect the features that are present in the narrative style of *King Horn*, as opposed to those that are not. The poem's style does intervene between us and its content – how could it not? – but it does so not through figures that compare its literal content to other objects, or that substitute those objects for it, but through figures that direct us to imagine the content itself in one way rather than another. Our response is controlled by the verbal medium (its transparency is indeed an illusion), but it is controlled as our response to the events of a film is chiefly controlled, by the choice of shots and angles. It must be noted, however, that Jakobson's concept of metonymy, as the general name for the whole class of figures based on contiguity, is an enlargement of the traditional meaning of the term in rhetoric. The latter is given by the definition in the *Oxford English Dictionary*:

A figure of speech which consists in substituting for the name of a thing the name of an attribute of it or of something closely related.

An example would be the use of the word *crown* to mean 'king' or 'kingship' or, in a monarchy, 'the state'. Metonymy in this restricted sense is not at all characteristic of the style of *King Horn*. But included within Jakobson's enlarged concept of metonymy are many other figures based on contiguity, among them that traditionally known as synecdoche. The definition of this in the *Oxford English Dictionary* is:

A figure by which a more comprehensive term is used for a less comprehensive or *vice versa*; as whole for part or part for whole, genus for species or species for genus, etc.

And synecdoche, especially in the form in which the part is substituted for the whole, is a major feature of the style of *King Horn*.

The visual synecdoche in which the part stands for the whole is also an extremely common feature of the narrative style of film. A shot of two hands clasping or shaking each other may indicate that two men or two parties have reached agreement; a shot of marching feet may represent the movement of a whole army; a shot of the turning wheels and moving pistons of a locomotive may symbolize the journey of a train or of someone on board it (and this may be accompanied by what could be called the auditory synecdoche of a whistle or siren). Though visual synecdoche and the close-up shot are not the same thing, there is a strong tendency for them to be used in conjunction; if the part is to stand for the whole, then it will have to dominate our attention, and that can most easily be achieved if it occupies the whole of the screen. In considering the narrative style of *King Horn* I shall use *synecdoche* to mean the substitution of part for whole; and I find it very helpful in practice to imagine its synecdoches as close-ups in a hypothetical film. The analogy is undoubtedly less than perfect, but, precisely because we are not yet accustomed to analyse non-metaphorical narrative styles, such analogies can be useful initial aids.

I shall begin with some very simple examples. Early in *King Horn*, when the Saracens seize the boy Horn and his young companions and decide to set them adrift to drown, we are told:

> The children hi broghte to stronde
> Wringinde here honde. (111–12)

The second of these lines implies a close-up shot of hands being wrung, and this stands in place of a possible more comprehensive description of the boys' grief. Again, when Horn has grown up and is fighting the Saracens in Westernesse, we are told:

> Horn gan his swerd gripe,
> And on his arme wipe. (605–6)

That implies two close-up shots, showing first Horn's hand gripping the hilt of his sword, then the blade being wiped on his arm; and those two shots stand in place of a possible far lengthier account of his preparations for battle. They also of course imply grim determination and perhaps ruthlessness, states of mind which we infer (as in real life) from the fragments of bodily gesture. There are many cases where synecdoche is no more than a normal way of referring to a certain action. Thus, when Horn and the other boys arrive in Westernesse, the poet says,

> Of schup hi gunne funde
> And setten fout to grunde. (133–4)

To 'set foot to ground' is doubtless a perfectly ordinary, idiomatic way of referring to the action of alighting from a boat or a horse, but it is nevertheless a synecdoche, implying a shot not of the whole of the boys' bodies as they clamber ashore but of a single foot touching the ground. In yet other cases, it may be that a mode of expression which could be thought of as synecdochic is the *only* way of referring to an action. When Horn kneels to Rymenhild, the poet says that 'On knes he him sette' (383) – and how could the poet have told us that he knelt without focusing briefly on his knees?

There is clearly a danger of calling attention to what is merely commonplace, a feature of language rather than of style. It is well known that medieval literature in general tends to convey emotions through bodily gestures, to present the subjective in objective terms. (So indeed does film; given that its medium is predominantly visual, it has no choice.) On the other hand, I am convinced that we need to learn to respond more sensitively to a narrative style – a narrative imagination – which is fundamentally synecdochic, which again and again substitutes the part for the whole, and thereby gains concentration without losing rapidity and transparency. A good critic has written recently about *King Horn*:

The narrative style of the poem often seems to be a mechanical system of shorthand that we must suppose the audience could fill in. Scenic indications are so abbreviated that they seem to be notes that will be expanded upon later in the poem, but such completion never occurs.[14]

What he is describing could be understood more positively as a synecdochic style. Its potential will, I think, emerge more clearly from an examination of more extended passages, where we shall find synecdoche combined with other features of style to create powerfully imagined sequences of events.

The following passage occurs when Horn, betrothed to Rymenhild in Westernesse, arrives in Ireland under the name 'Cutberd':

> Cutberd wonede there
> Fulle seve yere,
> That to Rymenild he ne sente
> Ne him self ne wente. 920
> Rymenild was in Westernesse
> With wel muchel sorinesse.
> A king ther gan arive
> That wolde hire have to wyve:

Aton he was with the king   925
Of that ilke wedding.
The daies were schorte,
That Rimenhild ne dorste
Leten in none wise;
A writ he dude devise;   930
Athulf hit dude write
That Horn ne luvede noght lite.
Heo sende hire sonde
To evereche londe,
To seche Horn the knight   935
Ther me him finde mighte.
Horn noght ther of ne herde,
Til o dai that he ferde
To wude for to schete;
A knave he gan imete.   940
Horn seden, "Leve fere,
What sechestu here?"
"Knight, if beo thi wille
I mai the sone telle.
I seche fram bi weste   945
Horn of Westernesse,
For a maiden Rymenhild
That for him gan wexe wild.
A king hire wile wedde
And bringe to his bedde –   950
King Modi of Reynes,
On of Hornes enemis.
Ihc habbe walke wide
Bi the se side;
Nis he nowar ifunde: 955
Walawai the stunde!
Wailaway the while!
Nu wurth Rymenild bigiled."
Horn iherde with his ires,
And spak with bidere tires: 960
"Knave, wel the bitide,
Horn stondeth the biside,
Ayen to hure thu turne
And seie that heo ne murne,
For I schal beo ther bitime,   965
A Soneday bi pryme."
The knave was wel blithe,
And hiyede ayen blive.
The se bigan to throwe
Under hire wowe.   970
The knave there gan adrinke:
Rymenhild hit mighte ofthinke.
Rymenhild undude the dure pin
Of the hus ther heo was in,
To loke with hire iye   975

37

If heo oght of Horn isiye.
Tho fond heo the knave adrent
That he hadde for Horn isent
And that scholde Horn bringe.
Hire fingres he gan wringe.   980

This passage illustrates some of the points already made; it also modifies some of them. It provides good evidence of the preference for dramatization rather than narration – even Horn's initial question is given in direct speech (941–2) – and of the use of direct speech where possible to convey information that could instead have been narrated: for instance, we learn more from the messenger than we did from the narrator of the poem about the wedding proposed for Rymenhild. I mentioned that the poet generally avoided summary, but there is an example of it in the opening lines of this extract (917–20). The seven-year gap simply has to be bridged by summary: no amount of elliptical editing would have served. (A film of a somewhat old-fashioned kind might perhaps have shown the pages of a calendar being flicked over.) It may be worth pausing to note the lack of any attempt to *evoke* the passing of time, of the kind that can be found in later medieval narratives such as *Sir Gawain and the Green Knight*, with its splendid lines (500–35) on the passage of the seasons from one New Year to the next. In earlier medieval narrative there tends to be a flattening of temporal perspective, comparable with the flattening of space in earlier medieval art.

Although the style of this extract is bare, there is scope within it for certain kinds of redundancy. There is, for instance, the lyrical expression of emotion in 956–7. There is the slight stylistic elaboration of 932, with its negation of the negative to form a kind of litotes. There is even a redundant use of something like synecdoche in 959 and 975: Horn heard with his ears, Rymenhild looked with her eyes. The presence of redundancy in early narrative can sometimes be convincingly explained as resulting from its practical usefulness for a listening public; whatever words or phrases are not strictly demanded to convey meaning give the listeners a slight break, to enable them to catch up with the sequence of events. Doubtless that explanation is relevant here, but a further point to be made about such cases of redundancy is that, in traditional narrative, redundancy or pleonasm may be one of the markers of social elevation[15] and indeed of poeticality or literariness itself. Even in this pared-down, minimal narrative, words have to be shown to be available at times in abundance, words in excess of what is strictly needed, so that the sphere of the poetic may be marked off from the sphere of the actual. The real world may be dominated by scarcity (a scarcity hardly imaginable by the inhabitants of modern industrialized societies), but in the fictive world, just as there are feasts, so there can be verbal plenty on occasion, little feasts of words.

The most striking and powerful effects in this extract are matters of what I called above 'directing us to imagine the content itself' – the sequence of events, that is – 'in one way rather than another'. They may thus be thought of as lying on the borderline between poetic style and narrative technique. The cross-cutting from one location to another is drastic yet unobtrusive. The first of these 'invisible cuts' was mentioned earlier: at 921 we move from Ireland to Westernesse, as if impelled by Horn's or the narrator's thought of Rymenhild in the two preceding lines. Then when we move back to Ireland at 937, the cut is again rendered invisible by the fact that we travel with Rymenhild's messenger in search of Horn. When the messenger sets off for Westernesse again at 968, so do we; this time what arrives is only his corpse, but the journey still carries us with it.

The passage from 967 to the end of this extract has an especially cinematic effect in its movement from the drowning of the messenger to the casting up of the drowned body by the sea beneath the very wall of Rymenhild's dwelling. There is a grim irony in the way that, as Rymenhild opens the door to look for Horn's arrival, what she sees is the corpse of the messenger whom she had sent to ask for his help. A specific sequence of shots is implied. First waves tossing beneath Rymenhild's tower (967–70); then a brief glimpse of the drowning messenger. At 973 there is a close-up of the bolt of Rymenhild's door being drawn back – a striking visual synecdoche. Lines 975–6 imply a panoramic sweep over the sea, following Rymenhild's glance as she looks in vain for Horn's ship; then comes the sudden shock of the drowned man, seen clearly for the first time; and last another synecdoche, the close-up of her hands as she wrings her fingers in grief. In this laconic episode the wringing fingers are the only expression of her feelings. In a film version, the little sequence might be enclosed between two shots of Rymenhild's hands, first drawing back the bolt, then twisting in anguish. The absence of any glimpse of her face gives the sequence a powerful reticence – and that is a quality characteristic of much of *King Horn*.

My second example comes from later in the poem, when Horn has returned to Suddene, his homeland, leaving Rymenhild in Westernesse, undefended against Fikenhild's plot to marry her himself:

He com to his moder halle
In a roché walle.
Corn he let ferie   1385
And makede feste merie.
Murie lif he wroghte:
Rymenhild hit dere boghte.
Fikenhild was prut on herte,
And that him dude smerte.   1390
Yonge he yaf and elde
Mid him for to helde.
Ston he dude lede
Ther he hopede spede.
Strong castel he let sette,   1395
Mid see him biflette.
Ther ne mighte lighte
Bute fowel with flighte;
Bute whanne the se withdrowe
Mighte come men ynowe.   1400
Fikenhild gan wende
Rymenhild to schende.
To wowe he gan hure yerne;
The kyng ne dorste him werne.
Rymenhild was ful of mode;   1405
He wep teres of blode.
That night Horn gan swete,
And hevie for to mete
Of Rymenhild his make,
Into schupe was itake: 1410
The schup bigan to blenche,
His lemman scholde adrenche.
Rymenhild with hire honde
Wolde up to londe.
Fikenhild ayen hire pelte   1415
With his swerdes hilte.
Horn him wok of slape
So a man that hadde rape.
"Athulf," he sede, "felawe,
To schupe we mote drawe;   1420
Fikenhild me hath idon under
And Rymenhild to do wunder.
Crist for his wundes five
Tonight me thuder drive."
Horn gan to schupe ride,   1425
His feren him biside.
Fikenhild or the dai gan springe

Al right he ferede to the kinge
After Rymenhild the brighte,
To wedden hire bi nighte.   1430
He ladde hure bi the derke
Into his nywe werke;
The feste hi bigunne
Er that ros the sunne.
Er thane Horn hit wiste,   1435
Tofore the sunne upriste,
His schup stod under ture
At Rymenhilde bure.

Here, naturally, we find many of the same stylistic features as in the first passage. There is redundancy in 1398 ('Bute fowel with flighte'), and perhaps in 1413 – but there, though 'with hire honde' may not be strictly necessary, it is a good example of the synecdoche implying close-up, a glimpse of Rymenhild's hands flailing the water as she tries to swim in Horn's dream. Once more the chief poetic effects are of a cinematic nature, involving the selection and juxtaposition of 'shots', with the editing becoming more radically elliptical as the passage proceeds. It begins with Horn reunited with his mother in Suddene after his triumph over the Saracens; but then a single line provides the associative link to mask an abrupt cross-cut to Westernesse at 1388 – 'Rymenhild hit dere boghte' (i.e. she paid dearly for the festivities that made Horn's life merry but kept him away). In Westernesse we learn about Fikenhild's plots; and in this episode there is more narration than dramatization. Fikenhild buys supporters with gifts, he has a stone castle built on the seashore, he aims to ruin Rymenhild – and only now, after suspense has been aroused by our wish to understand this series of actions, do we learn what his goal is. At once there is another cross-cut, back to Suddene, masked by the associative link between Rymenhild's acute anxiety and the anxiety which produces Horn's prophetic dream of her death by water, and masked too, perhaps, by the growing sense of simultaneity ('That night' in 1407).

The synecdochic glimpse of Horn sweating in bed is vividly cinematic; and here perhaps I may digress for a moment. Roland Barthes, in his early essay 'The Romans in Films', notes in connection with Mankiewicz's film of *Julius Caesar* the use of sweat on the brow, often seen in close-up, as a seemingly natural yet actually conventional cinematic indication of 'moral feeling':

Everyone is sweating because everyone is debating something within himself; we are here supposed to be in the locus of a horribly tormented virtue, that is, in the very locus of tragedy, and it is sweat which has the function of conveying this.[16]

The device which Barthes is describing is of course synecdoche, though he does not name it as such; and for him, unless it is so manifestly conventional as to be 'reduced to an algebra' (which is certainly not the case in *King Horn*, any more than in Mankiewicz's *Julius Caesar*), it is an unhealthy or corrupt 'state of the sign', in its deceitful tendency 'to confuse the sign with what is signified'.[17] As such, it is for him characteristic of 'petit-bourgeois culture' or 'so-called mass-culture',[18] with its insidious attempt to make ideology appear merely natural. It is doubtless true that synecdoche could be a powerful weapon in any such attempt, but it is worth bearing in mind that this sickness of the sign was already raging like the plague in the thirteenth century, long before the coming into existence of the bourgeois world which is the object of Barthes' critique.

To return to the passage under discussion: Horn's dream is now *seen* as directly as the surrounding events in waking life; in effect it constitutes another cross-cut (an embedded or parenthetic one) from Suddene to Westernesse and back again. The dream of death by water, a hideous reversal of birth, is of course symbolic, and Horn has no difficulty in interpreting the symbolism. As with Rymenhild's dream earlier, insofar as the poem possesses any metaphoric content at all, it is on the level of represented event, not on that of verbal texture. The next cross-cut is prepared for 1425. As the narrative accelerates in response to the danger that Fikenhild will be able to carry out his intention before Horn can intervene, it also becomes more elliptical. Time is lacking to show us Horn boarding his ship; there is only the dramatic shot of him galloping towards the harbour with a party of supporters (1425–6). The available time is now reduced to a single night, in which two sets of actions are going on simultaneously: Fikenhild is persuading Rymenhild's father, leading her to his tower, beginning the wedding-feast, while Horn is sailing from Suddene to Westernesse to prevent the wedding from being consummated. The verse becomes full of indications of time: 'or the dai gan springe' (1427), 'bi nighte' (1430), 'bi the derke' (1431), 'Er that ros the sunne' (1434), 'Tofore the sunne upriste' (1436). All these phrases emphasize the *passing* of time, the inevitable coming of the critical dawn.

The sense of simultaneity found here is very rare in medieval literature. A famous later example is *Sir Gawain and the Green Knight*, where the poet conveys the simultaneity of hunting and bedroom scenes by sandwiching each scene in Gawain's bedchamber between the beginning and end of a hunt. The *King Horn* poet is following the same general method of cross-cutting here, but his task is in one way more difficult, because he has to present actions that are not only temporally simultaneous but also physically convergent. His success seems to me to reach a triumphant climax with the final 'shot' of this extract, which shows Horn's ship beneath the very tower in which Rymenhild is confined. We have not seen the course of Horn's voyage – all that has been elided – but only the frantic haste of Fikenhild's preparations; now, before Horn himself knows it, as the poet says (1435), he has arrived, and there is the unexpectedly peaceful glimpse of his ship riding at anchor next to the tower, in the first light of dawn, already there. The tower and the ship together form a powerful complex of meaning, not metaphoric but synecdochic, and an appropriate point of rest before the narrative proceeds.

Havelok

In *Havelok* too metaphor is rare (though simile is less so than in *King Horn*); synecdoche, on the other hand, is less prominent, and the most obvious manifestation of artistry and source of interest beyond the facts of the story is a continuous patterning of the poem's verbal surface. Continuous pattern, whether carved into stone or on the surface of a manuscript page or in any other medium, was a favourite taste throughout the Middle Ages, and it is found as much in verbal art as in any other medium. Medieval treatises on the art of poetry devote much attention to what they call 'figures of words' (*figurae verborum*) – matters of verbal arrangement, designed not to evoke a fictive reality but to produce decorative patterns. Such patterning would of course have a much more immediate effect on a listener, or even on someone who habitually reads by pronouncing the words to himself (probably the normal medieval situation even among the highly educated), than it would on a completely silent reader.

Havelok, dating from about 1280, has twice as many lines as *King Horn*, the lines themselves are longer, and it offers a more solid and substantial fictional world than the earlier poem. It is less lyrical, less pared-down, far more interested in material things. Like *King Horn*, it tells the life-story of a king who is dispossessed in youth and then through a series of wanderings and adventures regains his land and wins a bride; but this story is realized not in the bare symbolic landscape of fairytale, but in a world which has many connections with the everyday life of thirteenth-century England. Food and money are important; so is the work that has to be done in order to earn them, and at one point the hero's thoughts on this are presented quite explicitly:

> Swinken ich wolde for mi mete.
> It is no shame forto swinken;
> The man that may wel eten and drinken
> Thar nouht ne have but on swink long;
> To liggen at hom it is ful strong.   (798–802)[19]

We even see something of the consequences of unemployment in a world where men need to labour in order to live: Havelok has to knock competitors down in the mud so as to get work as a porter. For the *Havelok*-poet, the characters are something more than agents of the plot, and he shows them as both psychologically and thematically motivated. He displays a particularly strong interest in kingship considered as a functional political institution. The poem opens with a set-piece in praise of the ideal king, and kingship is seen throughout not in the terms of chivalric or courtly romance, as a matter of symbolic personal grandeur, but in strictly practical terms: the good king brings justice, peace and loyalty to his people, the bad king brings the opposite and causes his whole society to degenerate.

The composer of this admirably sturdy narrative gives every sign of possessing the skills of a writer trained in rhetoric. Like the poet of *King Horn*, he can produce cinematically conceived 'shots' that convey meaning without narratorial comment; for example, when Havelok and his two sisters are children, the villain Godard locks them up in a tower, starves them, and then kills the little girls when pretending to play with them, and the poet writes:

> Ther was sorwe, hwo so it sawe,
> Hwan the children bi the wawe
> Leyen and sprauleden in the blod.   (473–5)

Even there, though, we are made more aware of the narrator than we usually are in *King Horn* – it is he who is pointing out the pity of the situation ('hwo so it sawe') as well as presenting it to us – and this is generally true of *Havelok*. The poet's verse is more thickly textured than that of *King Horn*, and less often creates the illusion of transparency; at times it even has a mimetic effect, with the sound and rhythm echoing or enacting the sense. This is still not a very concentrated kind of poetry, however, and to see how it works on the level of style we need to examine a rather long passage. This first extract represents a complete scene, from about a third of the way through the poem, in which we are told of Havelok's success in a great stone-putting contest and of how this gave the idea to Godrich, the wicked regent of England, that he would make the heiress to the throne, Goldeboru, marry Havelok, and thus gain power for himself. He thought that Havelok was a mere churl; but in fact he was heir to the throne of Denmark, so that Godrich's scheme recoiled on him in the end.

> In that time al Engelond
> Th'erl Godrich havede in his hond,   1000
> And he gart komen into the tun
> Mani erl and mani barun;
> And alle men that lives were
> In Engelond thanne were there,
> That they haveden after sent   1005
> To ben ther at the parlement.
> With hem com mani champioun,
> Mani wiht ladde, blac and brown;
> And fel it so that yunge men,
> Wel abouten nine or ten,   1010
> Bigunnen there for to layke:
> Thider komen stronge and wayke;
> Thider komen lesse and more,
> That in the borw thanne weren thore;
> Chaumpiouns and starke laddes,   1015
> Bondemen with here gaddes,
> Als he comen fro the plow;
> There was sembling i-now!
> For it ne was non horse-knave,
> Thouh thei sholden in honde have,   1020
> That he ne kam thider the leyk to se:
> Biforn here fet thanne lay a tre,
> And putten with a mikel ston
> The starke laddes, ful god won.
> The ston was mikel and ek gret,   1025
> And al so hevi so a net;
> Grund-stalwurthe man he sholde be
> That mouhte it liften to his kne;
> Was ther neyther clerc ne prest
> That mihte it liften to his brest: 1030

45

Therwith putten the chaumpiouns
That thider comen with the barouns.
Hwo-so mihte putten thore
Biforn a-nother an inch or more,
Wore he yung or wore he old,   1035
He was for a kempe told.
Al-so thei stoden and ofte stareden,
The chaumpiouns and eke the ladden,
And he maden mikel strout
Abouten the altherbeste bout,   1040
Havelok stod and lokede ther-til;
And of puttingge he was ful wil,
For nevere yete ne saw he or
Putten the stone or thanne thor.
Hise mayster bad him gon ther-to,   1045
Als he couthe ther-with do.
Tho hise mayster it him bad,
He was of him ful sore adrad;
Therto he stirte sone anon,
And kipte up that hevi ston   1050
That he sholde putten withe;
He putte at the firste sithe
Over alle that ther wore
Twelve fote and sumdel more.
The chaumpiouns that that put sowen   1055
Shuldreden he ilc other and lowen;
Wolden he no more to putting gange,
But seyde, "We dwellen her to longe!"
This selkouth mihte nouht ben hyd,
Ful sone it was ful loude kid   1060
Of Havelok, hu he warp the ston
Over the laddes everilkon;
Hu he was fayr, hu he was long,
Hu he was wiht, hu he was strong;
Thorhut England yede the speke,   1065
Hu he was strong and ek ful meke;
In the castel, up in the halle,
The knihtes speken ther-of alle,
So that Godrich it herde wel
Ther speken of Havelok everi del,   1070
Hu he was strong man and hey,
Hu he was strong and ek ful sley,
And thouhte Godrich, "Thoru this knave,
Shal ich Engelond al have,
And mi sone after me;   1075
For so I wile that it be.
King Athelwald me dide swere
Upon al the messe-gere
That y shulde his douhter yeve
The hexte man that mihte live,   1080
The beste, the fairest, the strangest ok;

46

That gart he me sweren on the bok.
Hwere mihte I finden ani so hey
So Havelok is, or so sley?
Thouh y souhte hethen in-to Ynde,   1085
So fayr, so strong, ne mihte y finde.
Havelok is that ilke knave
That shal Goldeborw have!"

This passage is a good example of straightforward narrative. It tells its part of the story clearly, plainly, and with no fuss, moving steadily forward through time, with no glances back or ahead, except in the thoughts of Godrich's 'soliloquy'. It is largely concerned with physical action, and particularly with the physical prowess of the unknown champion Havelok. But the psychological dimension is filled in too, though again plainly and clearly; there is nothing problematic about the characters' motivation. A touching humility is shown to accompany Havelok's great strength, when we are told that he only takes part in the contest because his master – Godrich's cook – tells him to (1045–8). Godrich's motives, too, are made abundantly clear, in his internal monologue: he is going to keep the letter of his promise to King Athelwold, but, as is indicated by the verbal play on *hexte* (1080), meaning 'highest' but also 'tallest', it will be in a way that, he hopes, will give him power over the country. It is worth noting also the glimpse we get of those who have been winners so far, with their good-humoured astonishment at Havelok's put, their rustic laughter, and their colloquially oblique comment, 'We've been around long enough!' (1058). This is probably the moment at which the passage comes closest to detailed psychological realism; it is also the moment at which the verse comes closest to being truly mimetic – the line 'Shuldreden he ilc other and lowen' (1056) has a jostling rhythm that exactly suggests their clumsy nudging of each other. That line, though, is by no means typical of the passage; this is not essentially verse which enacts its own meaning, even though the poet is accomplished enough to convey his sense of the physical reality of the scene when he wishes. Nor is it, of course, verse which is rich in imagery: the passage contains no metaphors, and only one simile, which tells us that the stone was as heavy as an ox (1026) – a simple enough image, and one in keeping with the agricultural setting. The main effect of the verse, throughout the passage, is to weave a continuous auditory pattern around the forward movement of the narrative, so that we gain an unobtrusive and largely unconscious pleasure, line by line, from the poet's artistic mastery over the story he has to tell.

To analyse this continuous auditory pattern (as to analyse the recurrent synecdochic effects of *King Horn*) is to run the risk of misrepresenting it; it is to call attention to very small-scale phenomena, which the poet can scarcely have meant us to notice individually. In many cases, he may not have been conscious of the patterning himself – it was the expression of an instinctive mastery over a particular kind of narrative style. But, for the modern reader, the risk has to be taken if the style is to be appreciated at all. One type of patterning found here is the persistent tendency to conceive of qualities, or of classes of people, in pairs. Sometimes these pairs indicate similar or identical units, and are thus a simple form of amplification through redundancy: for instance, 'The ston was mikel and ek gret' (1025), which obviously amplifies the 'mikel ston' (1023) without adding anything significant to it; or 'Hu he was wiht, hu he was strong' (1064), where *wiht* and *strong* support each other closely even if their meaning is not exactly the same. That line is a simple example, too, of how the patterning is syntactical as well as auditory: the repeated sound, 'Hu he was . . . hu he was', is also, obviously enough, a repeated syntactical structure. Very frequently the pairs are made up of opposites or near-opposites, and they are used as inclusive formulas, amplifying substitutes for 'all' or 'everyone' or some other inclusive category. Thus we have 'Mani erl and mani barun' (1002); 'blac and brown' (1008), referring to colours of hair or complexion;[20] 'stronge and wayke' (1012); 'lesse and more' (1013); and many other instances. 'Wore he yung or wore he old' (1035) gives a simple syntactical pattern to support the semantic pairing of opposites. A simple negative transformation turns the inclusive formula into an exclusive formula, such as 'neyther clerc ne prest' (1029).

Another kind of patterning consists of the repetition of a certain word; this then arouses expectation that the word will continue to reappear, and the expectation is satisfied sometimes in an expected way, sometimes in a slightly unexpected way, when the word appears in a different grammatical form, or perhaps in a different place in the metrical-syntactical framework. At the beginning of the passage, when the various participants in the contest are being assembled, the idea of coming is frequently repeated, with various uses of different forms of the word *come*. Godrich 'gart komen'

(1001) the noblemen to make up the *parlement* with which the contest is associated, and 'With hem com mani champioun'. In lines 1012–13 there is very strong patterning, with the inclusive pairs already mentioned accompanied by identical adverb + verb:

> Thider komen stronge and wayke;
> Thider komen lesse and more.

Among those attracted to the contest were husbandmen 'Als he comen fro the plow' (1017). And finally there is a reversion to and completion of the pattern established in lines 1012–13, which associated *komen* with *thider*. This is in the lines which complete the gathering of the competitors (1019–21): everyone came, and indeed there was not even a stable-boy, even though he had a job to do already, 'That he ne kam thider the leyk to se'.

Once the contest starts there is similar extended repetition of the word *put*, 'to heave': 'And *putten* with a mikel ston' (1023); 'Therwith *putten* the chaumpiouns' (1031); 'Hwo-so mihte *putten* thore' (1033). A little later Havelok sees what is going on, 'And of *puttingge* he was ful wil' (1042). There follow '*Putten* the stone' (1044), 'That he sholde *putten* withe' (1051), 'He *putte*' (1052), 'The chaumpiouns that that *put* sowen' (1055), and 'Wolden he no more to *putting* gange' (1057). Here, naturally enough, the word *put* ceases to be mentioned; for example, in line 1061, where it might well have occurred, the poet in fact uses the near-synonym *warp*, 'threw'. Other contributions to the verbally patterned presentation of the contest are provided by the repetitions of *chaumpioun(s)* (1007, 1015, 1031, 1038, 1055) and of *(starke) ladde(s/n)* (1008, 1015, 1024, 1038, 1062), with the frequent pairing of the two perhaps implying a contrast between the established champions and the challengers who took them on. The very word *ston* is repeated several times (1023, 1025, 1044, 1050, 1061). It would be a mistake to make too much of all these verbal repetitions. When the narrative concerns people coming to a place, the word 'come' is likely enough to be repeated, and when the narrator is telling of champions and lads heaving stones it will not be surprising if those words are mentioned more than once. The point is merely that the *Havelok*-poet positively exploits the opportunities his story gives him for making verbal patterns: instead of avoiding repetitions, as children are nowadays taught when they are learning to write compositions, he intensifies them and weaves them into patterns.

Before leaving this passage, let us note how often the poet also creates parallel syntactical structures. Usually, as might be expected, they underline the meaning, but sometimes the element of pure aesthetic pattern seems to be predominant. Many of the patterns I have mentioned already have a syntactical element; here are some others. Lines 1027–30 are heavily patterned, with line 1030 exactly repeating the structure of 1028, the only difference between them being the substitution of *brest* for *kne* (the variation between *mouhte* and *mihte* is no doubt a scribal accident). The repetition here presumably involves irony, since it would hardly be expected that clerics would excel in physical strength. Later in the passage, beginning at line 1061, there is a whole series of repetitions involving phrases that begin with 'Hu he . . .':

> . . . hu he warp the ston . . .

> Hu he was fayr, hu he was long,
> Hu he was wiht, hu he was strong . . .

> Hu he was strong and ek ful meke . . .

> Hu he was strong man man and hey,
> Hu he was strong and ek ful sley.

Here the simple pattern of repetition has woven into it a more complex sequence of repetitions of *strong*, which is alternately paired with supporting qualities (*wiht* and *hey*) and with contrasting qualities (*meke* and *sley*). Towards the end of the passage there are repetitions of qualities in the superlative form (1080–1) – *hexte*, *beste*, *fairest*, *strangest* – and then of qualities (mostly the same ones) preceded by *so* – *so hey*, *so sley*, *so fayr*, *so strong*.

Such analysis of verbal patterning could easily be prolonged until it merged into the patterning which is fundamental to language itself; indeed, it might be said that the 'literariness' of the style of *Havelok* is in general no more than a foregrounding of certain necessary features of language. But instead of attempting to squeeze more out of this passage, I want to use some shorter extracts from *Havelok* to illustrate other stylistic features of early medieval narrative. One very general tendency of medieval art is a desire to be exhaustive or encyclopaedic, rather than suggestive or impressionistic. Medieval poetry is full of lists and catalogues, and one recurrent form of list in *Havelok* is that which enumerates the

thereby serves as a means of transmitting a certain conception of society.) In the above extracts there is of course some degree of variation. Extract 1, for instance, includes in its last line widows and maidens, priests and clerks, items which do not occur in the other catalogues (except that *clerkes* come into Extract 4). The other catalogues are all-male and they are almost exclusively lay: the poet's conception of society is practical and military, but when he is telling of how all the people loved their king it is appropriate that he should include women and clerics. Extract 2, in its third line, includes four family relationships among its classes; that has no parallel elsewhere. And Extracts 2 and 3 contain inclusive formulas of the kind mentioned earlier – high and low, brown and black: both of these are common throughout the poem. Apart from this, the lists are made up of the same items repeated. Moreover, the items regularly fall into certain smaller groups. Earls and barons go together, as representatives of the aristocracy; *dreng* and *thayn* are associated, as vassal or tenant and knight or earl. Knights are associated sometimes with *burgeys* (the opposite of knights in not being landed gentry), sometimes with *swains* (the opposite of knights within the manorial system), sometimes with both. These associations hold even in a catalogue such as Extract 4, where they are not made explicit in the form of syntactical links. There seems no reason, on the face of it, why the different items in this extract should not be rearranged in some other order, so long as the rhyme was retained; but in fact they are evidently held together by associative links that lie deeper than syntax. (We may note, too, that the rhyme *thayn/swain* occurs in five of the six passages.) What all this means is that passages such as these possess the advantage that belongs to genuinely formulaic poetry – that they can be taken in by listeners with little difficulty. Once such a catalogue is started, it continues almost automatically; the component items are reassuringly familiar and the response they are intended to evoke is widely understood. This leaves the poet free to decorate the given formulaic structure, either by adding new items such as sons and brothers, or by varying its syntactical structure. In dance-like figures the familiar items are grouped in twos or fours or threes, are separated by *and*s or *and of*s or *and sithen*s, or are brought together with no explicit connectives at all. As listeners we are affected by such details below the level of conscious attention; the innumerable tiny charges of pleasure add up to conscious enjoyment only when accumulated, not separately.

Before leaving *Havelok*, I wish to consider one final group of short passages. One of the qualities for which this poem has been most admired is its firm grasp on the material world, a quality probably connected with the social inclusiveness mentioned above. This firm grasp on the actual is also partly established by lists – lists of concrete objects, among which lists of different kinds of food are prominent. Here are some examples:

7. "Goddot!" quath Leve, "y shal the fete
    Bred and chese, butere and milk,
    Pastees and flaunes . . .".   (642–4)

8. Grim solde sone al his corn,
    Shep with wolle, net with horn,
    Hors and swin and geet with berd,
    The gees, the hennes of the yerd;
    Al he solde that ouht douhte.   (699–703)

9. Mani god fish ther-inne he tok,
    Bothe with net and ek with hok.
    He tok the sturgiun and the qual,
    And the turbut and lax with-al;
    He tok the sele and ek the el;
    He spedde ofte swithe wel:
    Keling he tok and tumberel,
    Hering and the makerel,
    The butte, the schulle, the thornbake.   (751–9)

10. For hom he brouhte fele sithe
    Wastels, simenels with the horn,
    Hise pokes fulle of mele and korn,
    Netes flesh, shepes and swines;
    And hemp to maken of gode lines,
    And stronge ropes to hise netes.   (778–83)

11. He bar up wel a carte-lode
    Of segges, laxes, of playces brode,
    Of grete laumprees, and of eles.   (895–7)

12. Kranes, swannes, veneysun,
    Lax, lampreys and god sturgiun,
    Pyment to drinke and god claré,
    Win hwit and red, ful god plenté.   (1726–9)

In these extracts appear first miscellaneous food, then farmyard stock, then fish, then another miscellaneous list including both things to eat and material for making lines and nets for catching further things to eat, then fish again, and last the grander food and drink at a royal feast. The predominance of fish reflects the part of Havelok's life which he spends as a fisherman. The lists do not usually aim to be anything more than lists; they simply name a series of objects, and even the *claré* in Extract 12 is praised only in the most general terms: it was good and there was plenty of it. There is no attempt to achieve the kind of sensuous evocativeness of the concrete that is sometimes found in later English poetry: nothing like Milton's

> And first behold this cordial julep here
> That flames, and dances in his crystal bounds,
> With spirits of balm and fragrant syrups mixed,[21]

or Keats's

> With jellies soother than the creamy curd,
> And lucent syrops, tinct with cinnamon;
> Manna and dates, in argosy transferr'd
> From Fez; and spiced dainties, every one,
> From silken Samarcand to cedar'd Lebanon.[22]

No, the *Havelok*-poet, like most medieval poets, is content simply to name the things, not to evoke their textures or appearances or exotic origins. But, once more, the artist's mastery over the profusion of things in his fictive world is displayed in the syntactical and metrical ordering of the nouns. In Extract 7 they are grouped into pairs, each pair turning on an *and*, but with no explicit links among the pairs. In Extract 8 there is a more complex ordering of objects: first one mentioned by itself (*korn*), then two parallel, each with its attribute linked by a *with* (*Shep with wolle, net with horn*); then two by themselves, linked with an *and*; then, linked by a further *and*, one which reverts to the 'x with y' pattern (*geet with berd*); finally, two names of birds, one standing alone, the other in its appropriate location (*The gees, the hennes of the yerd*). In Extract 9 first the pattern is established of sentences beginning with *He tok*, but with some variation in the link-words used: 'the sturgiun *and* the qual', 'the turbot *and* lax *withal*', 'the sele *and ek* the el'. Then, after a summarizing line, *he tok* reappears, but this time after the first part of its compound object: 'Keling *he tok* . . .'. In the next line comes another pair, and then in the last line the pattern of pairs of objects mentioned in a single line (repeated six times if 'Bothe with net and ek with hok' is counted) is decisively broken by a line which mentions three objects and, for the first time, gives them no explicit links: 'The butte, the schulle, the thornbake'. A different kind of variation occurs in Extract 11, where, for once, adjectives are used, and they are placed chiastically, one after its noun and the other before: 'of playces brode,/ Of grete laumprees . . .'.

Analysis of this kind might once more be continued *ad infinitum*; but I am sure that the experiment in a certain kind of close reading, conducted in this chapter, has gone on for long enough. It may well seem to have been excessively detailed, and I am aware of having imposed on the *Havelok*-poet's work a more exact scrutiny than it was designed to bear and also of having vulgarized the *King Horn*-poet's work by my own imaginative participation when, for example, I supplied tendentious or stereotyped adjectives such as '*critical* dawn' or '*frantic* haste'. The imaginary film into which I have turned extracts from *King Horn* is certainly less good than the poet's own work, and there can be no doubt that a comparably detailed reading of the whole of either poem would be intolerably wearisome if set down in print. Yet I believe that such an experiment is necessary, because we are not accustomed to the non-metaphorical styles of early medieval narrative. Faced with *Havelok*, we may notice the sturdiness but not the artistry; faced with *King Horn*, we may allow our eyes to pass over the short lines in rapid succession without having the skill to respond to the poet's appeal to our imaginations; or at best we may have a vague sense that either poem has pleased and moved us in ways we are quite unable to identify or discuss. When we become more skilled readers of such narratives, the time for close readings in print will have passed.

3 · Interpreting a medieval romance

In Chapter 2 I was concerned to see how it might be possible to respond more consciously and appreciatively to the narrative style of early medieval romances, a style often so simple and bare that it tended to escape observation. In this chapter I shall consider another early romance, still simple in style though less minimal than *King Horn*, and in this case, since it is a poem of only 600 lines, it will be possible to move on from style to examine ways in which the meaning of the whole poem may be interpreted. My example is *Sir Orfeo*, a poem probably of the late thirteenth century, which survives in three manuscripts, the earliest being of about 1330. *Sir Orfeo* belongs to the sub-category of romance known as the Breton lay. The Breton lays are short romances, which apparently have behind them musical performances by Breton minstrels. No lays in the Breton language survive, and as a literary genre the lay originates with the twelfth-century poet Marie de France, who wrote in French but may have lived in England. In English there are some half-dozen narratives that claim to be Breton lays, all of which, except for *Sir Orfeo* itself and the special case of Chaucer's *Franklin's Tale*, have surviving French sources. There are several references in medieval French poems to an original Breton lay about Orpheus, each time indicating musical performance, so it seems highly likely that *Sir Orfeo* too had a French source, though none has survived. Of the poet of *Sir Orfeo* we know nothing; as with the *King Horn* poet, he appears as narrator in a positional rather than a personal role. He may conceivably have been a minstrel, or he may have been a literary composer who wrote down (and no doubt partly transformed) what he had heard a minstrel chant.

The story he tells concerns a king of Winchester who was an accomplished harpist. His wife, the beautiful Dame Heurodis, went out one May morning and fell asleep under an orchard tree. When she woke, she behaved very strangely, screaming and tearing at her body and clothes. She was forced to go to bed and, when Orfeo came to see what was wrong with her, she explained that in her sleep

56

two knights had come to order her to speak to their king. She had refused, but then the king himself came with a great company, made her go to his palace, and told her that next day she must come to the same tree and be carried off to live with him for ever, or else she would be torn to pieces. Next day Orfeo with a thousand armed knights accompanied Heurodis to the orchard; but for all that she was snatched away by magic, no one knew where. Orfeo in his misery told his barons that he was going to dwell with wild beasts in the wilderness; he appointed his high steward to rule in his place, and when they learned that Orfeo was dead, they were to summon a parliament and appoint a new king. He departed alone, wearing only a pilgrim's mantle and carrying only his harp.

In the wilderness Orfeo lived in great wretchedness, till his body withered and his beard grew to his waist. In fine weather he played his harp, and the beasts gathered to listen. Sometimes he saw the king of fairy out hunting, but the hunt never caught any beasts; sometimes he saw knights with swords and banners, but then they vanished; sometimes he saw knights and ladies dancing to minstrelsy. One day he saw ladies hawking; their falcons slew their prey, and Orfeo, remembering that he had once enjoyed such sport, followed them. Among them he recognized Heurodis; they looked at each other without a word, but she wept to see him in such misery. Regardless of the consequences, Orfeo followed the ladies into a great rock, where he found a glittering castle. He told the porter that he was a minstrel who had come to entertain his lord, and was admitted. Inside, he saw many people who were supposed to be dead, but had really been snatched away by magic – headless, strangled, drowned, women dead in childbirth or gone mad, some apparently asleep, and among them Heurodis, sleeping under an orchard tree. In the castle hall Orfeo found the king and queen on bright thrones. He told the king that he had come unbidden to entertain him, according to the custom of minstrels, and he played his harp so beautifully that the king promised him anything he asked for as a reward. He asked to have his wife back, and the king, somewhat grudgingly, agreed.

Taking Heurodis by the hand, Orfeo returned to the normal world. In Winchester, still in his role as a poor minstrel, he took refuge with a beggar, from whom he learned that the steward was still ruling. He went to the palace as a minstrel, disguised in the beggar's clothes, and the steward invited him in, saying that, for

Orfeo's sake, every minstrel was dear to him. He played his harp, and the steward, recognizing it as Orfeo's, asked how he had acquired it. He said he had found it in the wilderness, beside a corpse killed by lions, and the steward swooned with grief. Thus Orfeo knew that he was faithful, and told him that, supposing Orfeo returned from the land of fairy with his queen, the steward would be rewarded. At this everyone realized that the minstrel was Orfeo, and he and Heurodis were newly crowned. After their death, the faithful steward became king.

Given the names Orfeo and Heurodis, there can be no doubt that this story is a version of the classical myth of Orpheus; but, if it is compared with the more familiar versions transmitted by Latin writers such as Ovid, Virgil, and later Boethius, our first thought is likely to be that it has been transformed in a number of ways. For one thing, in the course presumably of its passage through Breton culture, it has been Celticized: the dark underworld of the classical myth has become a brightly shining otherworld, the world of fairy, and the ruler of the dead, Pluto, has given way to the king and queen of the fairies. At the same time, the story has been medievalized: Orpheus has become Sir Orfeo or King Orfeo, Eurydice has become Dame Heurodis, and the world they inhabit has become one of knights and ladies, barons and damsels, hawking and hunting. The radical change in the story's ending might also be thought of as an instance of medievalization. Orpheus loses Eurydice a second time, being unable to resist looking back at her as he leads her up from the underworld, but Orfeo succeeds in regaining Heurodis from the fairies. The tragic ending becomes a happy ending, and this is certainly in accordance with medieval taste, and especially with the preferences generally embodied in medieval romance. It is worth remembering, however, that the tragic form of the Orpheus myth is not the only ancient form. It has been shown, too, that the happy-ending version was found in three eleventh-century Latin poems written by Frenchmen, and it seems likely that that was how it reached the probable French source of the thirteenth-century English poem.[1]

Another way in which the myth has been transformed is through combination with other stories. The story of the faithful steward is widespread in traditional narrative, and it has no parallel in the Orpheus myth. At the same time, the story of Orpheus himself, the king who leaves his people, is thought to be dead, and then miraculously reappears and reassumes his kingship, has been fused with the myth of the Sleeping Emperor. The Holy Roman Emperor Frederick II, for example, was widely believed to be a kind of second Messiah; his death was not believed in (he was supposed to have retired to a distant country, or to be sleeping under Mount Etna), and it was imagined that he would return to lead his people to salvation. A similar myth attached to King Arthur. From the point of view of the citizens of Winchester, and especially that of the faithful steward, Orfeo is a ruler of this type. Unlike what was foretold of Frederick II, however, he does not then live until the end of the world: the myth dissolves into practical reality as we are told of Orfeo's death and the steward's succession.

Lastly, there are various components of the classical myth that seem to survive in the medieval version as disconnected fragments, no longer related to their original functions. For example, the name Pluto, originally that of the king of the underworld from whom Orpheus has to regain his wife, reappears in *Sir Orfeo*, but only as the name of the ancestor of Orfeo's father, along with further muddled classical mythology in his mother's ancestry:

> His fader was comen of King Pluto,
> And his moder of King Juno.   (43–4)[2]

Ovid tells us that after Orpheus had lost Eurydice for the second time he renounced the love of women and became a pederast; there seems to be a faint echo of this renunciation (though not of homosexuality) at a different point in the Middle English version when, after Heurodis has been carried off by the fairies, Orfeo asserts that

> . . . now ichave mi quen y-lore,
> The fairest levedi that ever was bore,
> Never eft y nil no woman se.   (209–11)

Again, in Ovid's version Eurydice is killed by being bitten in the ankle by a snake; dangerous snakes reappear in *Sir Orfeo* ('wilde wormes', 252), but as creatures that Orfeo sees gliding by him in the wilderness. It is as though, in the course of a long process of transmission, largely perhaps oral, the Orpheus myth, along with other narrative material, has been shaken up in a kaleidoscope, and when we look at it again in the thirteenth century many of the old elements reappear, but now forming a quite different pattern.

What that pattern is and what meaning it conveys will be my

eventual concern, but first I want to consider the poetic means used to express it. The narrative style of *Sir Orfeo* possesses many of the characteristics that we have found in the *Chanson de Roland* and *King Horn*. It is plain and lacking in individualizing touches. Certain terms, usually of non-specific evaluation, are repeated again and again. When Orfeo enters the other world, he sees a *riche* castle (356) with buttresses *y-arched riche* (362); the inner towers are made of *riche* stones (371) and the whole stone-work is also *riche* (374). Orfeo's knights are *stout and grim* (184); the fairy knights are *stout and fers* (293). Orfeo in exile is described as *blac and rowe* (265) and later as *rowe and blac* (459). As in these last instances, many terms appear in stereotyped pairs, within which meaning is scarcely differentiated. The subject matter of Breton lays may be 'of wer and . . . of wo' or 'of joie and mirthe' (5–6) and the Breton composers took up their harps 'in gle and game' (19); flowers in May 'sprede and spring' (67) and sometimes the weather is 'clere and bright' (269); when Heurodis is taken by the fairies Orfeo makes 'swiche diol and swiche mon' (198); the fairy queen is 'fair and swete' (414). Like some of these, many phrases used are formulas, linked by alliteration, which are part of the common language of Middle English romance: 'bodi and bones' (54), 'noither stub no ston' (346), and so on. This poetic style represents life in superlative terms, with no means, apparently, of conveying gradation or subtle discrimination. Heurodis is

> The fairest levedi, for the nones,
> That might gon on bodi and bones   (53–4)

(and there *for the nones* is a formulaic tag included only for the rhyme) and she is described by Orfeo as 'The fairest levedi that ever was bore' (210); when Orfeo plays for the steward on his return,

> The blissefulest notes he harped there
> That ever ani man y-herd with ere.   (527–8)

Metaphor is totally lacking; and, while there are more similes than in *King Horn*, they too are familiar and stereotyped. The damsels who accompany the fairy king wear garments 'As white as milke' and ride 'snowe-white' steeds (145–6), and when hunting they are 'Gentil and jolif as brid on ris' (305). The king's crown shines as bright as the sun (152), the fairy country shines 'As bright so sonne on somers day' (352), and the precious stones of his castle shine at night 'As bright as doth at none the sonne' (372). When Orfeo returns to Winchester after his ordeal, the onlookers exclaim, 'He is

y-clongen al-so a tre!' (508). Synecdoche is less common in *Sir Orfeo*
than in *King Horn*. There it was a concomitant of the poem's
especially minimal use of words; *Sir Orfeo*'s style is somewhat less
sparse, but it uses synecdoche more selectively and perhaps more
deliberately to give emphasis to moments of drama. Thus when the
fairy king finally agrees to give Heurodis back to Orfeo, instead of
the expansive treatment that might have been expected of their
reunion after long separation, the poet gives us only a close-up of a
single hand-clasp:

> His wiif he tok bi the hond
> And dede him swithe out of that lond,
> And went him out of that thede. (473–5)

Close-ups of Orfeo's beard form an economical and graphic means
of marking the passage of time during his exile and symbolizing his
transformation from a civilized to an uncivilized state: when he is in
the wilderness,

> His here of his berd, blac and rowe,
> To his girdel-stede was growe, (265–6)

and when he returns to Winchester it has grown even longer, and
those who see him exclaim, 'Lo! Hou his berd hongeth to his kne!'
(507).

The syntax of *Sir Orfeo* generally lacks complexity, and its style is
characterized by the 'simple and repetitive use of conjunctions' that
Bernstein sees as a marker of restricted code. Certain passages,
however, possess a more complex syntax, and here, as with
synecdoche, one has the sense of a poet not totally constricted by a
sociolinguistic code but deliberately choosing between complexity
and simplicity as he judges appropriate. For example, there are
passages in which a series of sentences each containing a relative
construction is used, manifestly in order to produce a specific effect.
One such sequence occurs as part of Orfeo's response to the
distressing behaviour of Heurodis after her experience when asleep
(the relative pronouns are italicized):

> O lef liif, what is te,
> *That* ever yete hast ben so stille,
> And now gredest wonder schille?
> Thi bodi, *that* was so white y-core,
> With thine nailes is al to-tore.
> Allas! thi rode, *that* was so red,
> Is al wan, as thou were ded. (102–8)

Here the main clauses of each sentence are concerned with the present, the relative clauses with the past; the repeated relative constructions function as a means of contrasting the idyllic past with the painful present, while insisting that it is the same person, body, and countenance that have undergone the inexplicable change. An analogous but more elaborate sequence occurs later when the poet describes the difference between Orfeo's condition as it was when he was king and as it is now he is in the wilderness. Here the relative construction is repeated four times as part of a more obvious pattern of couplets beginning alternately *He that had(de)* and *Now*:

> He that hadde y-werd the fowe and griis,
> And on the bed the purper biis,
> Now on hard hethe he lith,
> With leves and gresse he him writh.
> He that hadde had castels and tours,
> River, forest, frith with flours,
> Now, thei it comenci to snewe and frese,
> This king mot make his bed in mese.
> He that had y-had knightes of priis
> Bifor him kneland, and levedis,
> Now seth he no-thing that him liketh,
> Bot wilde wormes bi him striketh.
> He that had y-had plenté
> Of mete and drink, of ich deynté,
> Now may he al-day digge and wrote
> Er he finde his fille of rote.   (241–56)

The states of kingship and exile, civilization and savagery, are realized in terms of contrasting details, but once more the past and the present are bound together by a syntax that, far from being tacitly determined by a sociolinguistic code, is part of a skilfully controlled rhetoric.

As in *King Horn*, and indeed in most Middle English romances, the characters of *Sir Orfeo* are conceived positionally rather than personally: Orfeo is husband and king, Heurodis is wife and queen, and the anonymous steward is a faithful retainer. The narrator too, as I have mentioned, functions positionally, and he is unaffected by any problematic elements in his subject matter, because he is present not as creator but as recorder of *layes* that are themselves merely reports of 'old aventours that fel while' (8). His relation to the subject matter is perfectly direct, untouched by the pretended naïveté, open criticism, or teasing ambiguity that we may have come to expect from the work of Chaucer and his contemporaries.

Like the *King Horn* poet, he prefers to let his characters speak for themselves wherever possible; but unlike him, as we have seen in the two passages discussed immediately above, he gives both their speeches and his own a manifest rhetorical organization. His purpose is evidently to induce in his listeners or readers a strong emotional participation in the events of his story. He enters into it himself with a quite unironic sympathy, and he expects the same response from us. Thus he comments on the people's reaction to Orfeo's self-exile:

> O, way! What ther was wepe and wo
> When he that hadde ben king with croun
> Went so pouerlich out of toun! (234–6)

(Here the relative clause is used once more to contrast past and present.) And about Orfeo's sufferings in the wilderness he exclaims,

> Lord! who may telle the sore
> This king sufferd ten yere and more? (263–4)

Though the inner lives of his characters are scarcely individualized, and there is little analysis of their feelings, those feelings are certainly realized by expression in both speech and gesture. Two more examples may be given, both of speeches in which extreme sorrow is expressed at a supposed loss by death. When Orfeo sees Heurodis among the ladies hunting in the wilderness but finds himself unable to exchange words with her, he does find words for his grief once she has disappeared:

> "Allas!" quath he, "Now me is wo!
> Whi nil deth now me slo?
> Allas, wroche! – that y no might
> Dye now after this sight!
> Allas! To long last mi liif,
> When y no dar nought with mi wiif
> (No hye to me) o word speke.
> Allas! Whi nil min hert breke?" (331–8)

The rhetoric of this speech is quite sophisticated, with its use of *Allas!* as punctuation, its rhetorical questions, and its personification of death. The second example is the steward's response to the report of Orfeo's death, a small-scale lament once more marked by exclamation and rhetorical question:

> "O!" quath the steward, "Now me is wo!
> That was mi lord, Sir Orfeo!

63

Allas! wreche, what schal y do
That have swiche a lord y-lore?
A, way! that ich was y-bore,
That him was so hard grace y-yarked,
And so vile deth y-marked!"   (542–8)

Within this speech the verbal and syntactical patterning is par-
ticularly elegant: note for example the varying exclamations (O!,
Allas! and A, way!) and the precise parallelism of 'so hard grace
y-yarked' and 'so vile deth y-marked' which makes possible the
compression of the final line through the omission of 'him was'.
Shortly after this comes a fine example of the expression of emotion
by gesture. When the steward understands from Orfeo's deliber-
ately oblique final speech, in which one condition is piled steadily
upon another, that it is Orfeo who stands before him alive,

Over and over the bord he threwe,
And fel adoun to his fet.   (578–9)

The falling at his master's feet may be merely a gestural formula, but
this cannot be said of the violently dramatic overturning of the table,
with the tumbling effect briefly enacted in the repeated 'Over and
over'. The poem's action ends with a final, all-embracing expression
of emotion: the reappearance of both Orfeo and Heurodis as king
and queen provokes a communal surge of joy in which we are
clearly invited to share:

Lord! ther was grete melody!
For joie thai wepe with her eiye
That hem so sounde y-comen seiye.   (590–2)

In discussing the Chanson de Roland I emphasized its function as
transmitter of the heroic warrior culture that produced it. King Horn
is less explicitly didactic and should probably be regarded as serving
a less crucial purpose in the reproduction of cultural patterns,
though the fundamental story it tells – the story of so many Middle
English romances – of the growth of a young male from childhood
to maturity, must also have fulfilled a significant social function, in
offering reassurance as to the possibility and naturalness of the
maturation process. By comparison, Sir Orfeo is perhaps something
of a luxury object, its immediate end being apparently not to
transmit a certain ethic but to express and arouse certain emotions.
The emotions, moreover, are suspended over mystery rather than
attached to the shared convictions of the poet's culture; and I want

now to say a little more about this element of the mysterious in *Sir Orfeo*. One kind of mystery belongs to emotion itself. As we have seen, emotional reticence is far from being systematic in *Sir Orfeo*, as we found it to be in *King Horn*; but the very fulness with which emotion is usually expressed makes the moments of reticence all the more striking. We saw one such moment when Orfeo, having regained Heurodis, silently took her by the hand to lead her back home; another, similarly synecdochic and perhaps even more moving in the way it limits emotional expression to silent tears, has occurred earlier when he sees Heurodis among the hawking ladies in the wilderness:

> Yern he biheld hir, and sche him eke,
> Ac noither to other a word no speke;
> For messais that sche on him seiye,
> That had ben so riche and so heiye,
> The teres fel out of her eiye.
> The other levedis this y-seiye
> And maked hir oway to ride –
> Sche most with him no lenger abide.   (323–30)[3]

The brief close-up of tears, by its very restraint, gives the strongest possible sense of feeling breaking through the barrier of enchantment, and this is supported by the understatement by which Orfeo's wretchedness is called only *messais*, discomfort.

These moments of mysterious reticence are connected with the impingement of the fairy world on the human world; and it is in the fairies, of course, that the poem's mystery centres. Their anonymous rulers in one way reduplicate the positional king/queen, husband/wife pattern of Orfeo and Heurodis, yet their situation in the work as a whole is more uncertain. It is never clear how they relate positionally to the human characters or what it is that happens to the human beings whom they carry off to their world; and this anomaly creates an effect of threatening strangeness. There is not a symmetrical relationship between human and fairy analogous to that between Christian and pagan in the *Chanson de Roland*, where each category defines and closes the other by being opposed to it; rather there is a disturbing asymmetry, as a result of which reality is no longer, as in the *chanson de geste*, immediately intelligible, and knowledge is no longer a matter of recognition. In Chapter 1 I quoted Vinaver as stating that the parataxis of the *Chanson de Roland* was 'genuine, not contrived': the poet was not intending to create mysteries, but was simply omitting connections that he saw no need to make explicit because they were an unquestionable part of his world. The *Orfeo* poet, by contrast, does seem to be intending to create a mystery, one which centres in the fairies and spreads out into the human world wherever they impinge on it. It is for this reason, above all, that *Sir Orfeo* demands interpretation; and I now proceed to consider how it can best be interpreted.

Without entering into the fundamental problems of hermeneutics that have been an especial concern of late-twentieth-century literary theory, it is possible to see that the interpretation of narrative presents special difficulties. Even those theorists who most strongly emphasize the possibility and desirability of a historical understanding of texts from the past (and I have no doubt that such an understanding is desirable to the fullest extent that it is possible) do not seem to offer much practical assistance when narratives are in question. Thus one of the most persuasive theorists of this school, E. D. Hirsch, has written as follows:

> *Meaning* is that which is represented by a text; it is what the author meant by his use of a particular sign sequence; it is what the signs represent. *Significance*, on the other hand, names a relationship between that meaning and a person, or a conception, or a situation, or indeed anything imaginable . . . Significance always implies a relationship, and one constant, unchanging pole of that relationship is what the text means. Failure to consider this simple and essential distinction has been the source of enormous confusion in hermeneutic theory.[4]

None of the examples analysed by Hirsch is a narrative, and the problem is that it is difficult to see what the 'meaning' as opposed to the 'significance' of a narrative can be other than its literal sense – and about this, with medieval narratives at least, there is rarely any difficulty. The question of what a story means normally refers to something other than its literal sense as intended by its author at the moment when he wrote it; and it is precisely this something other that concerns us.

There has been much scholarly commentary on *Sir Orfeo* (far more than on *King Horn*); some of it is illuminating, but much seems to be based on false interpretative premises, and actually to function as a barrier to the reader's response. Characteristically, we are given what appears to be an authoritative account of how the poem *would have been* understood in its own time – an account which, when scrutinized, turns out to be a substitute for the poem offered on no higher authority than the scholar's preference among a large variety of historical possibilities. (The preference of many twentieth-century medievalists turns out to be for interpretative closure based on simple didacticism.) For this reason, my method of approach will be to consider a number of kinds of interpretation which seem to me misleading, before going on to suggest another reading which, whatever its disadvantages, at least has the advantage of not claiming to be the one historically authentic possibility.

First, then, one factor that ought to affect our sense of what interpretations are likely has already been mentioned – the large element of the traditional and the formulaic in the poem's style. We cannot expect that every detail of the text, every word, every turn of phrase, will make an individual contribution directly to the overall meaning; and any interpretation which assumes otherwise is open to question. In principle, no doubt, what Roland Barthes has written is true:

> . . . a narrative is never made up of anything other than functions: in differing degrees, everything in it signifies. This is not a matter of art (on the part of the narrator), but of structure; in the realm of discourse, what is noted is by definition notable. Even were a detail to appear irretrievably insignificant, resistant to all functionality, it would nonetheless end up precisely with the meaning of absurdity or uselessness: everything has a meaning, or nothing has.[5]

But in order to determine *what* a particular detail signifies, it is necessary to take a prior decision about the framework of communication to which it belongs. An analogy may make this clearer.[6] If the text can be thought of as comparable to a piece of wood, then there may be no limit, other than the power of the microscope, to the detail in which its grain can profitably be analysed. On the other hand, if it can be thought of as more like a man sending messages by semaphore, then beyond a certain point the detail will be irrelevant to the communication; the 'grain' of the man's performance (the expression on his face, the emotional overtones of his gestures, and so on) will form no part of the intended message, and to analyse them will be profitless or even misleading. In the case of *Sir Orfeo*, if we are right in thinking that in certain respects its style is formulaic, then some of the details of that style will not have individual meanings; they will 'mean' precisely the formulaic nature of the style.

It is not the case that medieval people were incapable of reading a text closely and scrutinizing every detail of style to see what implications it had for meaning. The text of the Bible, indeed, was often read in that way, and some of the finest medieval examples of what might now be called 'practical criticism' or 'close reading' are to be found (in Latin, of course) in Scriptural commentaries. To take a single instance, St Bernard, in his great collection of sermons on the Song of Songs, goes through every verse in the greatest possible detail, meditating on the semantic implications of every word or grammatical form. In the Scriptural text he was using, chapter 1 verse 9 reads, 'Thy cheeks are beautiful as the turtle-dove's, thy neck as jewels'. He explains why these sensory terms could be addressed by God to the soul (for that was the normal allegorical interpretation of the book): 'He was able to describe her beauty as that of the face, according to the ordinary phrase, in which one, whose beauty is praised, is said to have "a sweet or beautiful face".' 'But,' he goes on,

I know not what could have been the intention in speaking of "cheeks" in the plural, yet I do not at all think that it was without an object. For it is the Spirit of wisdom who is speaking, and it is not permissible to attribute to Him a single word spoken in a faulty or even objectless way.[7]

It was worth doing practical criticism on the books of the Bible because God was their author; but God was not the author of secular romances such as *Sir Orfeo*, and so it was not thought worth subjecting them to such close scrutiny. The distinction between God's word and that of even such outstanding secular poets as Chrétien de Troyes was clear enough to serious-minded medieval thinkers. Another preacher asked,

Would he not insult a king who, having set aside the words of the king sent to him by a messenger, listened to the words of some jongleur? Thus you insult God who, neglecting His words, more readily listen to fables and tirelessly devote your attention to fictions made about Arthur, and about Erec, and about Cligés.[8]

Oddly enough, as we shall see, the distinction has seemed less clear to some equally serious-minded modern scholars.

The general point can be illustrated with three small examples. The culminating lines of the description of the fairy castle as Orfeo first sees it are:

> Bi al thing him think that it is
> The proude court of Paradis. (375–6)

An interpretation that insisted on the significance of every word in the text might well argue that here the poet intends to convey that it is not really paradise that Orfeo has found in the underworld;

indeed, it is the very opposite, hell, and 'him think' is meant to call attention to Orfeo's misunderstanding – it *seems to him* that it is paradise, but the appearance is deceptive. Yet this couplet is found in only one of the three manuscripts of the poem, while, if we turn back to near the beginning, we find a very similar turn of phrase applied in all three manuscripts to Orfeo's harping: if anyone sat and listened to it,

> . . . he schuld thenche that he were
> In on of the joies of Paradis.   (36–7)

It is difficult to imagine an interpretation of the poem in which both the fairy world and Orfeo's music are to be seen as supposed, but not real, paradises. In both couplets, I believe, the poet is using a prefabricated phrase, and it would be mistaken to attempt to squeeze such precise meaning out of it. My second example concerns another verbal parallel. When Heurodis is describing what happened to her in her sleep under the fruit tree, she says that the fairy king

> . . . schewed me castels and tours,
> Rivers, forestes, frith with flours.   (159–60)

Some 85 lines later, in the passage comparing Orfeo's former life as a king with the miseries he suffers in the wilderness, the same sequence of words occurs:

> He that hadde had castels and tours,
> River, forest, frith with flours.   (245–6)

The parallel has been noticed by at least one scholar, who writes:

. . . that the poet chose to describe the possessions of the two kings in this identical way does imply a certain attitude toward such possessions. We have already seen how fleeting and unstable are castles and towers in the mortal world; that they grace this sinister land of headless, mad, and murdered human beings only serves to cast doubt on the value of such objects.[9]

But this way of reading implies that the poet did indeed consciously *choose* to repeat one and a half lines to describe the possessions of Orfeo and of the fairy king, whereas it is far more likely that the expression was formulaic and the repetition has no special significance at all. My third example is similar. When Orfeo wishes to prevent the fairy king from carrying out his threat to take Heurodis away, he accompanies her, fully armed,

> And wele ten hundred knightes with him,
> Ich y-armed, stout and grim. (183–4)

About a hundred lines later, among the sights Orfeo sees in the wilderness, occurs the following:

> And other while he might him se
> As a gret ost bi him te,
> Wele atourned, ten hundred knightes,
> Ich y-armed to his rightes,
> Of cuntenaunce stout and fers. (289–93)

The parallel has been noted by another critic, who writes:

No reasonably careful reader would fail to note that Orfeo had a thousand knights... with him in his attempt to prevent the disaster... and that these had been "stout & grim".[10]

But such poems were not written, we may suppose, for careful readers, but primarily for listeners, who would expect them to be made up of familiar phrases, and would not expect parallelisms of phrase to carry a special weight of meaning. Any interpretation of *Sir Orfeo* which loses touch with the relatively formulaic quality of its style will be suspect.

It is manifest that a non-Christian supernatural realm plays a far more central part in *Sir Orfeo* than it does in the *Chanson de Roland* or in *King Horn*; and it is in this area – the fairies, their underground world, their power over human beings – that the obvious mysteries and problems of interpretation lie. Both *Roland* and *Horn* tell stories that we can easily suppose might have been understood in their time as history; most modern readers of *Sir Orfeo* have assumed that the same was not true of that poem. A rare exception is Doreena Allen, who has noted the possible relevance of the ancient Celtic belief – one that still survives in modern folktales – that

... many, perhaps most, of those who were thought to die were in reality no more dead than Orfeo's stolen Heurodis. In their last agony they too had been carried off, body and soul, by the triumphant *sidhe* [fairies], and a lifeless changeling, a cunningly fashioned image of wood or straw, left in the place of each.

It could thus be imagined that for 'a Gaelic or Breton storyteller, . . . one who believed, as his countrymen did for centuries, that death might be no more than an illusion and a deceit,' the Orpheus legend lent itself to fundamental reinterpretation. The death of Eurydice would simply disappear from the story, because 'For those who held the fairy faith, it mattered little whether counterfeit death or undisguised abduction befell a man or woman.'[11] The suggestion is attractive, but it goes no further than to suggest how the story of *Sir Orfeo* might have come to acquire its present form, by passing through the hands of one or more storytellers who actually believed in fairies and their power to 'take' human beings. The poet of *Sir Orfeo*, was not 'a Gaelic or Breton storyteller'; he was an Englishman of the late thirteenth century who wrote not far from London, and there is no more reason to suppose that he 'held the fairy faith' than that Marie de France or Chrétien de Troyes did. The mystery of the fairies cannot be dissolved by this means.

Most interpretations of *Sir Orfeo* have been based on the no doubt correct assumption that its poet was a Christian who did not literally believe in fairies or that many supposedly dead people were not dead really. What then did he intend to convey by his story? In terms of what concepts did he intend it to be understood? The historical possibilities are almost limitless in number, but I shall mention only two that have been brought forward, both in relation to one particular element in the story: Orfeo's abandonment of his people and his self-exile. The ten years Orfeo spends in the wilderness have puzzled K. R. R. Gros Louis. He points out that there is no indication that he has gone there to search for his wife, yet neither does he impulsively 'rush into the wilderness in a fit of emotional despair', for he makes careful arrangements for the government of the kingdom during his absence. Gros Louis concludes that we must be intended to understand that 'The ten years he spends in the wilderness constitute a kind of penance', in which he 'undergoes a kind of purification', and that as a result of this

Orfeo receives a gift of grace – Heurodis is returned to him; . . . because he accepts the loss of his wife and does not challenge the authority of the gods, they are merciful and return Heurodis to him.[12]

This is doubtless a meaning that a medieval version of the Orpheus myth perfectly well could convey, except that it would surely need to offer some interpretation of 'the gods' (who, indeed, have no explicit part at all in the action of *Sir Orfeo*). But it could do so only by offering some commentary on the narrative or, at the very least, by incorporating within it terms meaning penance and purification, humility and grace. A brief comparison with *Sir Gawain and the Green Knight* may be helpful. That too is a poem that contains a mystery (the Green Knight, his magical powers, his double identity, the purposes he serves). But the poet leaves no mystery about the moral and spiritual issues at stake in Gawain's dealings with the Green Knight or with the lady who is the Green Knight's wife in his other role as Sir Bertilak. The values involved range widely across the spectrum, from those that seem universally human to those that belong to a specific culture – courage and cowardice, loyalty and treachery, *curtesye* and *vylaynye* – but what they have in common is that they are named, often repeatedly, in the text of the poem. If we are at all interested in 'what the author meant' (and we would surely be unwise not to be, though we might also wish to say that the poem meant more than its author knew), then we are given plenty of explicit indications in his own words. Such indications are much rarer in *Sir Orfeo*.

This is not to say, of course, that *Sir Orfeo* is not concerned with values. It is, but its values, so far as we can judge them in the absence of explicit indications, are closer to the universally human than to the culturally specific end of the spectrum. (Perhaps there have been some cultures which have thought cowardice preferable to courage or treachery preferable to loyalty; but they have been the exception rather than the rule, if only because societies based on such preferences are unlikely to have much staying-power.) *Sir Orfeo* celebrates love, courage, and loyalty: the love of Orfeo and Heurodis, the loyalty of the steward, the courage shown by Orfeo in entering the underworld, in passing the ghastly collection of figures 'taken' by the fairies (that 'kind of Madame Tussaud's or Bluebeard's Chamber of Horrors', as one critic has put it[13]), and finally in facing and outwitting the fairy king. If we do not insist, with Gros Louis, on importing into the poem culturally conditioned values that are not mentioned in it, Orfeo's self-exile is perfectly comprehensible in simple human terms. A man might really give up his normal position in society, and become a tramp or a drop-out, in despair at the mysterious loss of his dearly loved wife, and he might perfectly well make arrangements before he does so for someone else to carry out his duties in his absence. We do not *need* to find some unexpressed metaphysical significance in all this, unless the storyteller himself tells us to do so.

One group of interpretations of *Sir Orfeo* has gone further than this, and has taken the entire story to be an allegory with a deliberately hidden Christian significance. A somewhat extreme example is the interpretation proposed by David L. Jeffrey in the following terms:

Interpreting a medieval romance

Could it be that the poet meant us to see in his story ourselves lost under the *ympe-tre* to the power of death, and Orfeo as the Christ ("He that hadde had castels and tours" – l.245) who leaves paradise, going to lowly estate and another tree in order to win us back ("Al his kingdom he forsoke" – l.227)? If so, might that give tongue to the language of adultery and marriage used by Orfeo and Heurodis at the crisis of their separation, or later add motive to her weeping at his lowly estate (l.327), his descent into the realm of death through a rock (l.348), and the harping which harrows hell? Could the metamorphosis of the old story be due to seeing this imagery extended in Orfeo's successful return, and in the testing of the faithful steward who for the sake of his Lord Orfeo is hospitable, so recognizes the harp, and is thus enabled to become a king with his King?

The tentative form in which this interpretation is expressed is appropriate, for the truth is that, despite its vaguely medieval air, it is no more than a subjective fantasy woven around the medieval poem. The story of almost any romance will offer similar parallels to the Christian story of redemption and salvation, and the quotations from *Sir Orfeo* that Jeffrey adduces plainly have no specifically religious implications. When he goes on to suggest that the exclamation of Orfeo's people upon his return as a ragged beggar, 'He is y-clongen al-so a tre!' (508), might mean 'He is stricken as to a tree' and thus contain an allusion to Christ's crucifixion, it can only be said that he has completely lost touch with the language in which the poet wrote.[14]

It is certainly true that in the Middle Ages some stories were generally accepted to possess allegorical or typological meanings. This was particularly common with Biblical stories: the Song of Songs, as we have seen, was normally read as telling of the loving relationship between God and the soul (or the Church or the Blessed Virgin); the story of Jonah was seen as an Old Testament foreshadowing of Christ's role as prophet to the gentiles and harrower of hell; and so on. Such interpretations might be so widely accepted that they could be merely alluded to rather than directly stated; thus in *Patience* the *Gawain*-poet makes Jonah imagine, when he is commanded to preach to the Ninevites, that they will crucify him.[15] Medieval readings of classical mythology were also sometimes allegorical, and the story of Orpheus was certainly among those most frequently read in such terms. In the most widely known version of the myth, Orpheus loses his wife by breaking his promise not to look back at her as he is leading her up from the underworld, and already in the sixth century, in Boethius's *De consolatione philosophiae*, he was seen as a type of the man who, 'when he has almost gained spiritual enlightenment, looks back to material concerns, and thereby "loses all the excellence he has gained"'.[16] A later medieval retelling of the story, Robert Henryson's *Orpheus and Erudices*, concludes with a *moralitas* that refers to Boethius's version and to the influential commentary on it by Nicholas Trivet and explains that Orpheus means the intellectual part of the human soul and Eurydice the lower, emotional part. The concealed meaning of the whole story is thus a warning about the human readiness to succumb to sin:

> Bot ilk man suld be war and wisely see
> That he bakwart cast noucht his myndis ee,
> Gevand consent and dilectacion
> Off wardly lust for the affection;
> For than gois bakwart to the syn agayn
> Oure appetite, as it before was slayn,
> In warldly lust and sensualitee,
> And makis reson wedow for tobe.   (620–7)[17]

A number of scholars have felt that some such meaning must be implied in *Sir Orfeo*. In medieval commentaries on Ovid's version of the myth, Eurydice tends to be seen as standing for human passion, or sensuality, or *naturalis concupiscentia*, while Orpheus is sometimes interpreted as the human soul, sometimes as Christ, who descended into the underworld to bring the soul to salvation. According to both Virgil and Ovid, what caused Eurydice to be carried to the underworld was that she was bitten by a snake; and in the very influential *Ovide Moralisé*, of about 1300, Eurydice is identified with Eve and the snake with Satan. (Henryson, in his moral allegory, says the snake was 'dedely syn/ That poysons the saule wyth-out and in' [441–2].) Most modern commentators on *Sir Orfeo* seem to agree that the poet's presentation of Heurodis is so unequivocally favourable that the poem cannot easily be fitted into the pattern of allegories that make Eurydice represent some low, material or sensual aspect of humanity; but one exception is Penelope B. R. Doob, in her study of madmen in medieval literature, *Nebuchadnezzar's Children*. Doob calls attention to the fact that Heurodis first encounters the fairies and then is carried off by them when she is relaxing in a Maytime garden; she affirms that in the Middle Ages 'walking about in gardens was often interpreted as a sign of moral fault' and goes on to suggest that Heurodis's

. . . enjoyment of natural beauty . . . seems to indicate her forgetfulness of other obligations; her love of sensual pleasures; her tendency, in short, to the spiritual sin of sloth, the most deceptive of sins since it often seems to be no sin at all.[18]

Here, as it seems to me, we encounter an obstacle of the sort that well-intended and well-informed scholarship is all too apt to put in the way of our reading of medieval poems. I cannot see the smallest sign that the English poet represents Heurodis's behaviour as sinful. Going into gardens or orchards and enjoying the delights of spring is an idyllic and natural occupation as represented in secular romances; a severe reader – a monk, let us say, judging by the standards of monastic asceticism – might well see such activity as exemplifying sloth, but then such a reader would be highly unlikely to waste his time on the equally slothful activity of reading or listening to *Sir Orfeo*. The fact that a certain interpretation is put on one version of a story in learned Latin commentaries is undoubtedly worth knowing, but it is not sufficient to compel us to interpret in the same way a quite different version in a vernacular language. Knowledge is better than ignorance, but unless we know what to do with it it may be equally dangerous.

A less obviously implausible allegorical interpretation is proposed by J. B. Friedman, who suggests that the fairy king should be seen as standing for Satan. He points out that some medieval manuscript illuminations of the Orpheus myth show Eurydice lying *under a tree* being attacked by Satan, and he argues that

It seems most probable . . . on the basis of both commentaries on and illustrations of Eurydice, that the *Orfeo* poet had a conception of her which *required* her to be attacked by Satan.

Satan, he says, was often thought to appear at noon – he was identified with the 'noonday devil' of Psalm 90 – and *undrentide*, the time when Heurodis is snatched away (lines 65 and 76), and also the time when Orfeo in the wilderness sees the fairy hunt appear (line 282), could mean noon. Friedman concludes,

If we assume that the author did *not* know an allegorical version of the story of Orpheus and Eurydice or the convention of Satan's noonday appearance, the "vndrentide" abduction of Heurodis remains inexplicable.[19]

Once more, I do not think we should be too ready to accept this suggestion, learned and ingenious though it is. For one thing, the allegorical interpretation of the Orpheus myth seems to have belonged to the scholarly world. It was, for example, less widely known than the typological interpretation of Jonah, which could be seen represented pictorially in many churches; and I cannot recognize any unmistakeable allusions to Satan in *Sir Orfeo* comparable to

Jonah's fear of crucifixion in *Patience*. (Many things happen at noon besides the appearance of the noonday devil; and, given the vagueness of correspondence between canonical hours and hours of the clock, it is not even certain that *undrentide* means noon in *Sir Orfeo*.) The author of *Sir Orfeo*, though a poet of some skill, was far from being a classical scholar; he tells us at the beginning of the poem that Orfeo's father was descended from 'King Pluto' and his mother from 'King Juno' (43–4), whereas it was known to the learned that Orpheus's mother was the muse Calliope and his father either Apollo or the wine-god Oeagrus (and this genealogy was also given an allegorical interpretation). Again, the *Orfeo*-poet solemnly assures us that Thrace is the same as Winchester (49–50). We are given no reason to suppose that he had been reading the learned mythographers of his time, or even that he was capable of reading them. Moreover, if he had been reading them, he would have found them giving not a single allegorical interpretation of the Orpheus myth, but numerous conflicting interpretations. Indeed, one commentator on the myth, the twelfth-century William of Conches, notes these divergences, and argues that it is perfectly normal that, 'treating of the same book, various authors arrive at different interpretations'. The same point is made in the fourteenth century by the great commentator Pierre Bersuire, who collects together a whole variety of interpretations of classical myths.[20]

These facts have important implications, for modern medievalists commonly defend allegorical readings of medieval narratives on the grounds that they are in accordance with medieval traditions of interpretation; whereas in fact medieval commentators on ancient texts, whether classical or Biblical, are frequently more modest, claiming not to be disclosing the one true meaning of the stories they are concerned with, but to be applying their ingenuity and imagination in order to discover *possible* meanings which will be edifying for their own contemporaries. Even if the poet of *Sir Orfeo*, despite appearances, had been learned enough to read the commentators on Ovid, he would have found them offering many different interpretations of the story of Orpheus; and he could have chosen among these, or indeed he could have disregarded them completely, as Chaucer, for all his learning, was later to disregard the available allegorical interpretations of the stories he retold from Ovid and other classical sources.[21] The truth is, I believe, that we, as readers of medieval narratives, are in a position similar to that of the medieval mythographers. We are faced, as they were, with texts from the past which we find moving and memorable; they were faced with, say, Ovid's *Metamorphoses*, we are faced with, say, *Sir Orfeo*. If the texts we are faced with include explicit indications of the concepts or typological parallels in terms of which their authors intended them to be interpreted, then it is obviously our first task to go as far as we can along the lines they indicate; but if such indications are absent, it is not our first task to try to find out what other medieval writers thought about the same story, and to claim that that is its only true meaning. We have a greater liberty than that. We may well wish to consider other medieval interpretations of the same story, but we shall have to ask ourselves whether those interpretations are apt to the text with which we are concerned. Let us return for a moment to Friedman's suggestion that we must see the fairy king in *Sir Orfeo* as Satan. His argument was that 'If we assume that the author did *not* know an allegorical version of the story of Orpheus and Eurydice or the convention of Satan's noonday appearance, the "vndrentide" abduction of Heurodis remains inexplicable.' But then it may be precisely the point of the poem that the abduction should be inexplicable. If we set about explaining it, by identifying the fairy king with Satan, we deprive the tale of just that irreducible mystery that gives it its lasting power.

The essence of what is represented in *Sir Orfeo* seems to be a confrontation between human beings and a totally inexplicable external force. That force cannot be defined fully as either evil or good; the fairy land beneath the ground that Orfeo visits is full of the hideous shapes of those seized by the fairies and supposed to be dead, with Heurodis among them, and yet it is also described in paradisal terms with an admiration that there is no reason to interpret as ironic. Again, the fairy king utters bloodcurdling threats to Heurodis about how she will be torn to pieces if she does not come with him, and yet when Orfeo sees the fairy king and queen on their thrones they too are seen admiringly as blissful, bright, fair and sweet:

> Than seighe he ther a semly sight,
> A tabernacle blisseful and bright.
> Ther-in her maister king sete
> And her quen, fair and swete:
> Her crounes, her clothes schine so bright,
> That unnethe bihold he hem might.   (411–16)

The fairies are represented as remote, unearthly beings, appearing only in sleep or in the wilderness, and yet when Orfeo dares to approach the fairy king in his palace he finds that he can bargain with him, and the king's 'I wish you joy of her!' when he realizes that he has been outwitted by the ragged minstrel sounds a convincing note of human irritation:

> The king seyd: "Seththen it is so
> Take hir bi the hond and go:
> Of hir ichil thatow be blithe!" (469–71)

All these contradictions may remind us of the *Gawain*-poet's presentation of the Green Knight, as a being who is both man and giant, both elegant and monstrous, both the genial host and the terrifying challenger. In the case of the Green Knight, nothing is to be gained by attempting to pin him down, as some scholars have done, and defining him as a devil, or Christ, or a vegetation god. He is what he is, what the poet has uniquely created him to be; that is why we read the poem in preference to theological or anthropological treatises. The same applies to the fairies in *Sir Orfeo*; they are part of a brilliant imaginative creation, fascinating and disturbing, and we do the poem no service at all by attempting to reduce them to some more familiar and manageable concept.

And yet we cannot help interpreting the literary works we read, especially if they do not incorporate a commentary on their own narrative. Northrop Frye has written that

> . . . all commentary is allegorical interpretation, an attaching of ideas to the structure of poetic imagery. The instant that any critic permits himself to make a genuine comment about a poem . . . he has begun to allegorize.[22]

I shall end this largely negative chapter on a more positive note, by outlining an interpretation of *Sir Orfeo* which, in this rather loose sense, could even be described as allegorical. I must emphasize, though, that my claim is not that this is *the* meaning of the poem, the meaning intended by its author or demanded by historical understanding, and that all other interpretations are false. Like other great stories, the story of Orpheus has many versions but, beyond the literal sense of its narrative forms, no fixed meaning; what it has is the power to generate meanings, meanings which, as William of Conches perceived, will be different for different readers and different ages. The great stories are not closed books but open texts.[23] I do not say, this is what the author of *Sir Orfeo* meant it to mean, because he has not said what he meant it to mean; and, by leaving his story without an interpretation, he has left us free to devise our own.

The poem implies a minstrel performance (this is true whether such a performance was a historical reality or only part of the fiction the poet created). It is also a story *about* minstrelsy. The hero is a minstrel-king, and his sole weapon is his harp, the one civilized object that he takes with him into the wilderness and that is not thereby subsumed into the realm of nature. He abandons *kirtel, hode, schert* and shoes (229–32), and his beard reverts to the wild state, but, though he hides his harp in a hollow tree (267–8), it does not lose its power to impose the civilized virtues on those who hear it played. Obviously enough, one advantage of this story for the real or imagined minstrel performer is that it gives opportunity for the glorification of his own art. It is a story of the triumph of minstrelsy over seemingly insuperable obstacles, and one in which the great test of a ruler's worth seems to be whether he enjoys minstrelsy and is generous to minstrels – like Orfeo himself, the faithful steward, and even the fairy king. The story can be expected to suggest to the audience that they too should be generous to its performer. But, beyond this, minstrelsy can be seen as having an important symbolic function within the poem. It is presented as a magical harmonizing and civilizing power, which enables Orfeo, like the classical Orpheus, to enchant even wild beasts; and we have seen that it is also given paradisal associations. The link between music and a cosmic order that has its origin in heaven is profoundly traditional; it goes back to Plato, it is found in Boethius, and it is found too, I cannot deny, in medieval commentaries on the Orpheus myth. To take a single example from English poetry a century later, the narrator of Chaucer's *Parliament of Fowls* tells us that in the heavenly landscape of his dream

> Of instruments of strenges in acord
> Herde I so pleye a ravyshyng swetnesse,
> That God, that makere is of al and lord,
> Ne herde nevere beter, as I gesse.   (197–200)

But against what is this heavenly power directed in *Sir Orfeo*? In the classical Orpheus myth it is death, but in *Sir Orfeo*, despite the views of some scholars, it seems clear that this is not so. The underworld of the poem is not Hades, the land of the dead, but a realm of those who are 'thought dede, and nare nought' (390). As the barons remind the steward near the end, when he faints at the false news that his master is dead, 'It nis no bot of mannes deth' (552). They are right, and when Orfeo and Heurodis do eventually die, and the steward succeeds as king, there is no suggestion that they are not really dead. What has happened to Heurodis earlier is something other than death. Among the supposed dead in the underworld there are two mentions of those who were taken in madness – 'sum lay wode, y-bounde' (394) and

> Wives ther lay on child-bedde,
> Sum ded and sum awedde   (399–400)

– and there is a constant association in this poem between the fairy world and psychological derangement or disintegration.[24] Heurodis first sees the fairies in her sleep, that is, when the mind is not under rational control; she then behaves as if she were mad, shrieking, tearing at herself, and looking at her beloved husband as if he were her enemy; and her two accompanying maidens tell the squires and knights 'That her quen awede wold' (87).[25] At this stage nobody else sees the fairies; that is, to a modern way of thinking, which draws the bounds between the subjective and the objective differently and more sharply than is normal in medieval romance, they might be merely subjective phenomena. But then Orfeo too, as it were, goes mad, at least in a symbolic way, by entering the wilderness and casting off the trappings of civilization; and it is only then that he too sees the fairies. His behaviour is like that of Chrétien's Yvain in Le chevalier au lion, when he realizes that he has broken his promise to his wife and she has rejected him: he temporarily loses his identity, and the wilderness is (as we might put it) an objective correlative to the wildness of the mind as reason loses control of it. Similarly, in a later English work, the heath and the storm are correlatives to the madness of King Lear. Lear, like most of Shakespeare's plays, inherits the symbolic landscape of medieval romance, in which the court or city is the outward expression of civilization, the wilderness or forest is that of civilization's opposite, and the garden is an ambiguous synthesis of the two, a place which may be either paradisal or treacherous.

For the twentieth-century reader, then, Sir Orfeo can be read as a poem about psychological disintegration and how it can be overcome by the healing power embodied in music. The association of music with healing, and especially with the healing of mental disorders, is also traditional. One of the best-known cases was David's use of his harp to heal the madness of Saul; and David and Saul are sometimes compared as harpist-kings in medieval commentaries on the Orpheus myth.[26] As far back as Ovid, the music of Orpheus's lyre protects him against the attacks of the mad Ciconian women for so long as it can make itself heard above their howling. But I do not wish to argue that the poet was influenced by either of these cases, neither of which he mentions. It is sufficient that music was widely used in medieval practice as a way of alleviating or curing madness. The encyclopaedic *De proprietatibus rerum* notes that the madman 'schal be gladed with instrumentis of musik'; and this was widely understood.[27] The same conception of music as a cure for madness can be found later throughout Shakespeare's work: for example, in *King Lear*, where Cordelia and the doctor hope to cure the king's 'Untuned and jarring senses' by means of music, or in *The Tempest*, where Prospero describes what the Shakespearean stage-direction calls 'solemn music' as 'the best comforter/ To an unsettled fancy'. The underworld of *Sir Orfeo* can be seen as the dark side of the human mind, that 'half-world' of night that Macbeth speaks of (a world that in Shakespeare is still suspended between objective and subjective), where 'Nature seems dead, and wicked dreams abuse/ The curtain'd sleep'.[28]

Part of the danger of 'wicked dreams' lies in their attractiveness; that the same is true of some forms of psychological disorder is witnessed by Virginia Woolf, who wrote in her diary after recovering from one of her bouts of illness that 'the dark underworld has its fascinations as well as its terrors'. This is not just a chance association; there is a terrible similarity between Heurodis's farewell to her husband when she is first summoned to the other world and Virginia Woolf's last letter to her husband before madness drove her to suicide.

> Allas, mi lord Sir Orfeo!
> Seththen we first to-gider were
> Ones wroth never we nere,
> Bot ever ich have y-loved the
> As mi liif, and so thou me;
> Ac now we mot delen ato
> – Do thi best, for y mot go.   (120–6)

. . . I am doing what seems the best thing to do. You have given me the greatest possible happiness. You have been in every way all that anyone could be. I don't think two people could have been happier till this terrible disease came. I can't fight any longer. I know that I am spoiling your life, that without me you could work . . . If anybody could have saved me it would have been you.[29]

The intangible dark powers, within the mind for us, outside it for the poet, may assert themselves inexplicably at any moment, in tension or relaxation, setting a barrier between the subject and normality, absorbing him or her into an alternative world, glittering dangerously beneath the apparently solid ground. Cure is possible; but what the poem seems to suggest is that it is possible only if the healer has the love and the courage to be willing to go through madness himself, to commit himself, naked and vulnerable, to the wilderness and to the other world and its central citadel. The modern Orfeo is not the orthodox Freudian psychoanalyst, who is careful to remain detached from the patient's suffering, but the ideal psychotherapist postulated by R. D. Laing, who shares lovingly in the experience of his patient, and who 'has both quite exceptional authority and the capacity to improvise'.[30] The poem is ultimately optimistic, for Orfeo has the endurance and the ingenuity, both activated by love, to rescue Heurodis and restore them both to a normality that seems no less secure than before, a familiar world in which loyalty, the basis of the social order, remains intact. Seen in these terms, *Sir Orfeo* is about a kind of therapy; at the same time it is itself therapeutic, in giving its audience an implicit understanding of how human courage and cunning can suffice to overcome powers and dangers that we do not fully understand.[31]

In sketching this interpretation of *Sir Orfeo*, I have done no more than suggest one kind of meaning which it might have for our own time. I have not, of course, cracked the code of the poem; what I have done, at best, is to indicate one way into it, by allegorizing it, translating its rich and complex imaginative code into a conceptual code that is far more impoverished but may be more accessible. That is approximately what medieval commentators did when confronted with Biblical and classical myths. The ideal next stage would be to do what medieval romance-writers did, and incorporate my interpretation of the story in a new poem, thereby translating the conceptual back into the imaginative. (I have in mind the successive reinterpretations through rewriting of the story of the Grail or of Tristan and Iseult from the twelfth century onwards.) That, however, would demand powers that I do not possess.

4 · Early Chaucer

The last two chapters have been concerned with narrative poems of a kind that are likely to have been known to Chaucer – it has even been suggested that he may at one time have been the owner of one of the manuscripts in which *Sir Orfeo* survives[1] – and that certainly seem to have shaped the English verse style he inherited.[2] Chaucer himself in his mature work, after he had encountered and absorbed the major poetry of the early Italian Renaissance, moved beyond the tradition of Middle English romance to produce poems of greater dignity and complexity of style and larger philosophical scope – a sequence beginning with *The Parliament of Fowls* and including *Troilus and Criseyde*, the closing stanzas of which will be considered in Chapter 5. This was a major transformation, and it was to have momentous consequences for the future of English poetry;[3] but in the present chapter I shall consider two poems from the earlier period when Chaucer was still writing in the accentual four-stress couplets of *Havelok* or *Sir Orfeo* and could still have been seen as the direct heir of the makers of such relatively simple narratives. The poems are *The Book of the Duchess* and *The House of Fame*; and in them already we can recognize a smaller but still distinct transformation, for even (perhaps indeed especially) in the former, which dates from as early as 1368, there is a courtly conception of love and a courtliness of style not fully paralleled in any earlier narratives in English.[4] Having created courtly narrative in the native language in the 1360s and 1370s, Chaucer went on in the 1380s so to extend this new courtliness that by 1387 a contemporary could refer to him as 'the noble *philosophical* poet in English'.[5] The singular noun indicates what appears to be true – that the task was performed unaided.

The House of Fame

Although *The House of Fame* is later than *The Book of the Duchess*, it contains in its first book a section which is particularly closely related in style to the English romances, and I shall therefore begin with the later of these two 'pre-philosophical' poems. Its exact date is uncertain, but it is probably from the middle 1370s; it must certainly be later than Chaucer's first visit to Italy in 1372–3, for it contains the first literary response to his reading of Dante, a poet of far grander ambition and achievement than any that Chaucer could have encountered in English or French, and one who offered him an exhilaratingly and disturbingly new model of what a vernacular poet could be. It may have been Chaucer's inability to come fully to terms with this new idea of poetry and of the poet that led him to leave the *House* unfinished. The first clear traces of Dantean influence are to be found at the end of the first of its three books, with the descent of an eagle (derived from Canto IX of the *Purgatorio*) which carries the dreaming poet up to the heavens; and then in the proems to Books II and III we can see Chaucer engaged in a complex struggle to appropriate some of the most distinctive features of Dante's elevated style and vision.[6] But the 350 or so lines of Book I before the descent of the eagle and after the leisurely introductory discussion of dreams form an example of relatively straightforward narrative. These lines are a much abridged retelling of the story of the *Aeneid* as represented in a temple of Venus in which Chaucer finds himself in his dream – a version focused appropriately, for a medieval courtly poet, on the love-affair of Aeneas and Dido. Here we encounter once more the fast-moving four-stress couplets of *Havelok* and *Sir Orfeo*, lacking in metaphor but rich in those comparatively simple figures of words that produce repetition and variation in sound and syntax. The surface of the poem is covered in a thin but continuous verbal pattern, composed of many of the same devices that we found in *Havelok*. There are, for example, formulaic pairs and simple catalogues, often linked by alliteration, such as 'Lord and lady, grom and wench' (206), 'Hir lyf, hir love, hir lust, hir lord' (258), and 'For had he lawghed, had he loured' (409). Slightly more complex, but still easily within the range of the *Havelok*-poet, are patterns such as the repetition of the words *and* and *moo* in the initial description of the temple of Venus, so that they appear in a variety of different positions within the overall metrical and syntactical frame:

> In whiche ther were *moo* ymages
> Of golde, stondynge in sondry stages,
> *And moo* ryche tabernacles,
> *And* with perré *moo* pynacles,
> *And moo* curiouse portreytures,

> *And* queynte maner of figures
> Of olde werk then I saugh ever. (121–7)

It was no doubt inevitable that in his earlier work, even when he was translating from other languages, Chaucer should owe a large stylistic debt to his anonymous English predecessors. Indeed, a narrative style as fluent as that of *The House of Fame* or *The Book of the Duchess* must have been grounded in a tradition of writing in the poet's native language; it could not have derived solely from writing in other languages. And in this part of the *House* there is almost no sign of any attempt to imitate in English the stylistic features of Chaucer's actual sources (which are chiefly Books I and IV of the *Aeneid*, with some details taken from Book VII of Ovid's *Heroides*). Perhaps the sole exception is the first sentence of the story of Aeneas, which is translated almost verbatim from the famous opening sentence of the *Aeneid*:

> I wol now singen, yif I kan,
> The armes and also the man
> That first came, thurgh his destinee,
> Fugityf of Troy contree,
> In Itayle, with ful moche pyne,
> Unto the strondes of Lavyne. (143–8)

Significantly, this is the only part of the story specifically described as 'writen' in the temple (142) rather than depicted in some other way; and even here Chaucer inserts the modest 'yif I kan', far more suited to a humble medieval storyteller than to the epic elevation of Virgil. After this, Chaucer abandons any endeavour to adapt Virgil's high style and richly complex hexameter verse to the jaunty rhythm and simple syntax of English couplets; though in the proems to Books II and III, as I have mentioned, he makes a different attempt, with the aid of Dante, to come to terms with the classical sublime.[7]

In general, indeed, the element of verbal patterning in these early Chaucerian narratives seems less noticeable than in, say, *Havelok*. Chaucer's verbal art is more reticent than that of the *Havelok*-poet; he certainly does not aim for the kind of ostentation represented by the passage near the beginning of *Havelok* where rhyme on the same sound is kept up continuously for 19 lines. Chaucer would doubtless have thought such simple displays of technique old-fashioned, perhaps even vulgar; his goal seems to be a more urbane style, or one more closely related to that of courtly conversation, in which emphasis is subtle rather than drastic.[8] An impression of casualness and lack of effort may be given; if so, that is no doubt part of the intended artistic effect. It is worth noting that in the proem to Book III he claims not to desire that, 'for maistrye,/ Here art poetical be shewed' (1094–5) and that 'I do no diligence/ To shewe craft' (1099–1100). The context is one of authorial modesty, but all the same what he is saying is not that he does not possess 'art poetical' or 'craft' but that he does not wish to display them. The task of art, a century later than *Havelok*, can be to conceal itself behind the appearance of artlessness.

Another new factor has come into play in the course of that century. As we have seen, in *Sir Orfeo* and in *Havelok* the essential structure was that of romance, the unidirectional movement through time of a linear narrative, however elaborate the patterned surface. In Book I of *The House of Fame* the material is still that of romance; as in *Sir Orfeo* a story of classical origin has been recomposed in medieval terms. Chaucer is much closer to specific classical written sources and to a historical understanding of classical culture than the *Orfeo*-poet was; but he medievalizes the *Aeneid* all the same. He sees it as a tale of knights (226, 455) and ladies, refers to Demophon as 'duk of Athenys' (388), exclaims of Theseus 'The devel be hys soules bane!' (408), and addresses Venus as 'my lady dere' (213). The complex narrative structure of the *Aeneid* is simplified: what medieval rhetoricians called the *ordo artificialis* of epic is reshaped into the *ordo naturalis* generally preferred by the romance-writers, so that the order of narration coincides with the chronological order of events.[9] In Chaucer's version the story comes out strongly in Dido's favour; the great issues of Rome's political destiny, which for Virgil offer a teleological justification for Aeneas's behaviour, entirely disappear, and the story becomes one of personal love and *trouthe*. Aeneas's failure in these respects is deeply culpable: he is blamed as one of a long line of male betrayers, and Dido deserves our sympathy not only as an individual victim but as a representative of women's suffering at the hands of men.

In these ways, Chaucer's early version of Dido and Aeneas (like his later version in *The Legend of Good Women*) has the effect of a short courtly romance with a marked feminist bias. But in one important way the romance material has been transmuted into a totally different form, which is no longer that of elementary linear narrative. The whole story is related by Chaucer according to the pictorial record of it which he sees in the temple of Venus in his dream. After the opening sentence 'writen on a table of bras' (142), the events of the story are generally described as *grave(n)* but once as 'peynted on the wal' (211). They are perhaps to be imagined as polychromatic carvings; but the exact nature of the artistic medium is less important than the fact that they are already depicted before being narrated. The result of this is that the forward movement is transferred from the narrative itself to the dreamer, who 'sees' first one event and then another in a story which has been frozen into pictorial form. The emphasis on seeing is found particularly in lines 151–264 and lines 433–73. These sections of Book I are permeated with phrases such as 'First sawgh I . . .' (151), 'And next that sawgh I . . .' (162), 'And I saugh next . . .' (174), 'Ther sawgh I grave(n) . . .' (193, 212, 253), 'Tho sawgh I grave . . .' (433, 451), and so on. And even when seeing and carving themselves are not being mentioned, the syntactical form of these sections is such as to force us to keep in mind that it is not the story that is in control but the dreamer's gaze as he looks at the pictures of it. The verb 'saw' is normally followed by 'how' – how this happened, how that happened, how such-and-such followed. (The word 'how' is used in this way nearly 30 times in the *Aeneid* section.) By this means, even on the level of syntax, the actual story is relegated to subordinate clauses, dependent on verbs of seeing.

One consequence is that the dreamer-narrator is noticeably separated from the story, and himself gains an increased prominence as a commentator on it; I shall return to this shortly. The consequence that concerns me here is the overall pictorialism, the dominance of the visual sensibility, of which there are many other signs in the book. Thus the temple in which the dreamer initially finds himself can be identified as dedicated to Venus because he recognizes its iconography, meaning conveyed by a code of visual images:

> . . . wel wyste I
> Hyt was of Venus redely,
> The temple, for in portreyture
> I sawgh anoon-ryght hir figure
> Naked fletynge in a see,
> And also on hir hed, pardee,
> Hir rose garlond whit and red,
> And hir comb to kembe hyr hed,
> Hir dowves, and daun Cupido
> Hir blynde sone, and Vulcano
> That in his face was ful broun. (129–39)

A strong colour-sense is at work in this passage, too, beyond what is necessary for iconographical understanding. When Venus later comes into the actual story, disguised in human form as a huntress, the conception is once more that of gratuitous pictorial beauty:

> And a knyght highte Achaté
> Mette with Venus that day,
> Goynge in a queynt array
> As she had ben an hunteresse,
> With wynd blowynge upon hir tresse.   (226–30)

Immediately one can 'see' the rippling texture of her hair as it might have been depicted in medieval sculpture or painting.

It is characteristic of late-medieval narrative to be dominated by the pictorial, and *The House of Fame* is already moving towards that further stage of late-medieval pictorialism, the detailed verbal description of a pictorial representation of a scene or story. Instructions and models for verbal description are a common feature of medieval rhetorical works, and indeed the *ars poetica* (Chaucer's 'art poetical') seems often to have been conceived as essentially an art of description: Horace's 'ut pictura poesis' was taken quite literally, and conversely terms such as 'colour' and 'paint' were regularly applied to rhetorical embellishment, as when Chaucer asks (rhetorically!)

> What shulde I speke more queynte,
> Or peyne me my wordes peynte
> To speke of love?   (245–7)

Thus Johan Huizinga, noting this tendency, comments that 'One of the fundamental traits of the mind of the declining Middle Ages is the predominance of the sense of sight, a predominance,' he tartly adds, 'which is closely connected with the atrophy of thought'. Whereas in actual pictures we are not fatigued by the 'boundless passion for details'[10] (because there the general effect of a mass of detail can be taken in by the eye almost instantaneously), in poems the details have to be accumulated one after another, strung out in time, and the effect can be of a loss of energy, an encyclopaedism bought at the expense of wearying stasis.

In *The House of Fame*, however, there is no question of stasis, even though the carved strip-cartoon that is being described cannot, if taken literally, be imagined to move. There is a dynamic forward movement, but now it is located in the activity of a narrator who eagerly takes his audience on a kind of conducted tour of the static forms in the temple. One reason why this is possible may be that Chaucer, unlike the authors of *King Horn*, *Havelok* , or *Sir Orfeo*, was writing for an audience for whom the story he was telling already existed in other, *written* versions with which his own challenged comparison. (Hence his explicit references, unparalleled in earlier English narratives, to 'Virgile in *Eneydos*/ Or the *Epistle* of Ovyde' [378–9] – a point to which I shall return.) The story itself, then, may be of less crucial importance, whereas the method of telling it may have come to be of greater moment. The medieval textbooks of *ars poetica* take it for granted that the *materia*, the subject matter of a poem, is already fixed, and that the 'poetizing' activity belongs to the teller, who decorates it with descriptions, speeches invented for the characters, moral reflections, illustrative *exempla*, and so on; and this is exactly what happens in Book I of the *House*. Dido is given a substantial *compleynt* about Aeneas's infidelity (300–10, 315–60); Chaucer inserts a lengthy passage of *exempla* of men's betrayal of women's trust, illustrated from classical legend (388–426); every so often he throws in a proverbial saying, such as 'Hyt is not al gold that glareth' (272) or 'he that fully knoweth th'erbe/ May saufly leye hyt to his yë' (290–1) or 'But that is don, is not to done' (361); and so on. In general the effect of these additions is not just to decorate the narrative locally but to manipulate it so that it will convey certain themes. Among these I have already mentioned the personalization (and hence depoliticization) of the whole story and the partisanship of women as against men, both taken so far that Dido's sufferings seem infinitely more important than the founding of Rome. To this might be added a general emphasis on pity – both the *routhe* that women show to men, little though men deserve it, and the pity that we are invited to feel for Dido in her sufferings, aroused by devices as simple as a narratorial 'allas' (183, 265, 268, 370) or a 'Loo, was not this a woo and routhe?' (396). (The taste for pathos is again somewhat typical of the later Middle Ages.) A third theme of some importance is that of fame or reputation, which serves ultimately to link Book I to the remainder of the poem. This is treated directly in the part of Dido's *compleynt* in which she laments the loss of her 'name' (345–60), and is implied more indirectly in Chaucer's criticism of his sources for having transmitted too noble a view of Aeneas.

What happens in addition is that Chaucer dramatizes that prominence of the teller which is an underlying assumption of the *artes poeticae*. In the earlier English romances, as we have seen, the narrator is little more than a grammatical hypothesis or empty position. In *The House of Fame*, far from being absent, he constantly thrusts himself forward, prominent even in the modesty of 'yif I kan', and in a sense he may seem to have become the central figure of the whole poem. That indeed is implied by the fiction of the dream, for dreamers must be at the centre of their own dreams, and in a dream-poem what happens must inevitably consist entirely of the experiences of the dreamer-narrator. On the other hand, this does not necessarily mean that the question 'Who is the narrator?' can have a single definite answer. He seems at times to be used to dramatize not just the general role of 'poet' as implied by the *ars poetica* but certain aspects of Chaucer's own situation as poet. In Book I he steps forward to apologize for his inability to speak about love from personal knowledge and to explain that if he did he would risk boring his audience:

> What shulde I speke more queynte,
> Or peyne me my wordes peynte
> To speke of love? Hyt wol nat be;
> I kan not of that faculté.
> And eke to telle the manere
> How they aqueynteden in-fere,
> Hyt were a long proces to telle,
> And over-long for yow to dwelle. (245–52)

Here we recognize one version of the pose Chaucer often adopts in his courtly poems, of the man who must write about love (because in courtly circles that is in theory the only possible subject of poetry) but who can do so only by reporting what he finds in books (or, as here, pictures), because he lacks any personal experience of love. There is of course no reason to suppose that this was Chaucer's real-life situation; whereas later in *The House of Fame*, when he reaches Fame's palace and is asked whether he seeks fame for himself, he answers with an expression of sturdy self-reliance and a reference to his own art that at least sound more authentic:

> Sufficeth me, as I were ded,
> That no wight have my name in honde.
> I wot myself best how y stonde,
> For what I drye, or what I thynke,
> I wil myselven al hyt drynke,
> Certeyn, for the more part,
> As fer forth as I kan myn art. (1876–82)

Again, in the proems to Books II and III, he adopts a Dantean style and attitude that imply a much grander conception of poetic inspiration than appears elsewhere in the poem. But the point is not that one of these passages may be genuine self-expression and the others not – perhaps they were all poses, we can never know for certain – it is rather that they do not fit well enough together to be envisaged as expressions of a single narratorial personality. The prominent presence of 'the narrator' or 'the dreamer' serves other purposes than those of characterization or self-expression.

One such purpose is to call attention to the literary procedures being used, in a way which creates a sense of critical detachment from what is being done – detachment both from the old story and from the techniques by which it is being presented. Thus, to take a simple example, one of the proverbs with which the narrative is embellished is presented as follows:

> Therfore I wol seye a proverbe,
> That "he that fully knoweth th'erbe
> May saufly leye hyt to his yë" –
> Withoute drede, this ys no lye. (289–92)

Or again Dido's *compleynt* is identified as such in a narratorial interruption near its beginning –

> In suche wordes gan to pleyne
> Dydo of hir grete peyne,
> As me mette redely (311–3)

– and then once more when it is complete:

> But that is don, is not to done;
> Al hir compleynt ne al hir moone,
> Certeyn, avayleth hir not a stre. (361–3)

We may have been moved to pity by Dido's speech, yet we are not to forget that it is an example of poetic craftsmanship. The last remark adds to the sense of detachment, by pointing out that, however effective the *compleynt* as a literary device, it had no influence on the following events of the story.

Such narratorial mannerisms, common in Chaucer's work throughout his career, are often seen either as means of characterizing the narrator (as naïve, pedantic, clumsy, incapable of understanding the story he is telling, and so on) or as means of ironizing the entire text. I have already indicated that the former explanation is unconvincing; and the second explanation also seems unsatisfactory, since it attempts to neutralize the emotions aroused by the story: if Dido's lament is framed in irony, we should surely fall into a trap were we to find it moving. It may be more satisfactory to think of such mannerisms as calling attention to the textuality of the poem, and also to its intertextuality – that is, to its existence within a field of texts, on its difference from which it is dependent for its own meaning.[11] Such awareness is not part of earlier English narratives: thus *Sir Orfeo* seems open to interpretation as a poem about the power of minstrelsy or poetry itself, but it contains not a single allusion to its own literary status or literary antecedents; whereas in *The House of Fame*, as one recent writer has put it, 'the ambiguous universe of Eros . . . coincides with the world of literature'.[12]

This is true not only in Book III, in which Chaucer sees the great writers bearing on their shoulders the fame they have given to their subject matter, but already in Book I. Here it might be supposed that the pictorial form taken by Chaucer's 'source' would conceal its textual origins; but in fact it is not long before the latter make themselves felt. Along with the constant repetition of the verb 'to see', we find Aeneas's family fleeing from Troy 'That hyt was pitee for to *here*' (180), and the same line is repeated with reference to what Creusa's spirit instructed Aeneas to do (189). Dido's lengthy *compleynt* lacks even the pretence of pictorial form, and the narratorial interruption of it quoted above alludes to this fact when it adds a parenthetic 'Non other auctour alegge I' (314) – for it is easier to believe that such an elaborate speech derives from a written authority than from a picture seen in a dream. The actual authorities for Chaucer's account are mentioned in the *occupatio* with which he refuses to give details of Dido's death by suicide or her dying speech and letter:

> And al the maner how she deyde,
> And al the wordes that she seyde,
> Whoso to knowe hit hath purpos,
> Rede Virgile in *Eneydos*
> Or the *Epistle* of Ovyde,
> What that she wrot or that she dyde,
> And nere hyt to long to endyte,
> Be God, I wolde hyt here write. (375–82)

We noted above a similar excuse for not going into detail about the amorous relations between Aeneas and Dido – that it would be tedious to do so – and the result is a version of their story that modestly draws back from discussing its two best-known and most sensational elements, passionate love and suicide! At the same time we are made aware that Chaucer's version has meaning only within an intertextual field composed of other versions that recount what he conspicuously omits.

The activity of the narrator continues to call attention to textuality and intertextuality as the story proceeds. The list of *exempla* of men's falseness to women is introduced as being what 'men may ofte in bokes rede' (385) (and it does indeed derive from the *Heroides*); its last line refers again to what 'the book us tellis' (426). Finally, in the increasingly rapid summary of the closing stages of the pictorial *Aeneid*, we are referred to an even larger field of texts for further information about the material of Book VI. Aeneas visited the underworld,

> And every turment eke in helle
> Saugh he, which is longe to telle;
> Which whoso willeth for to knowe,
> He moste rede many a rowe
> On Virgile or on Claudian,
> Or Daunte, that hit telle kan.   (445–50)

This is Chaucer's earliest reference to Dante, to whom he owed so much for his understanding of the ways in which vernacular poetry could go beyond the possibilities implied by the English romances. Here the Italian poet figures as one of a number of literary authorities on the underworld and its punishments, and the intertextual field that they jointly represent assumes almost physical form in the glimpse of the 'many a rowe' of verse of which it is made up. Here perhaps intertextuality is felt to be a burden; but in general the willingness of later medieval poets to acknowledge that they are not in a full sense the 'creators' of their works is far from being the restriction that it may appear to the modern reader. It is the Romantic and post-Romantic poet and the classic novelist who are burdened with the obligation of an impossible originality and troubled by the guilt of a derivativeness they dare not acknowledge. Chaucer and some of his contemporaries and successors have no hesitation in admitting that they are only the latest of many retellers of old tales, and the admission frees them from the web of texts even as it incorporates them in it, for it enables them to stand as humble yet critical commentators on their many sources. The untroubled energy of Chaucerian narrative surely owes much to the freedom that comes from the acknowledgment of intertextuality.

The Book of the Duchess

The Book of the Duchess is Chaucer's earliest datable poem; its occasion is generally agreed to have been the death of John of Gaunt's first wife, Blanche, Duchess of Lancaster, an event which occurred in September 1368, and the poem was probably written rather rapidly within the next few months.[13] A crucial aspect of Chaucer's difference from his English predecessors is his self-consciousness about his activity as a poet, and it was perhaps this self-consciousness which led him to take up at the very beginning of his writing career the fashionable French form of the poem set in a dream.[14] Dreams and poems are both types of fiction, the former composed by all of us, the latter only by the gifted few; and an important function of the dream-poem seems to have been as an attempt to make a place for fiction in the medieval world. Such an attempt was necessary because, in medieval thought, fiction tended to collapse into feigning, stories to be reduced to lies. The status of dreams was ambiguous, for they might be seen either as irresponsible and deceptive fantasies, caused by physical or psychological disorders, or (just possibly) as visions of truth, in which the mind, under some superior influence, glimpses what cannot be perceived by the waking eyes. The first 58 lines of The House of Fame offer a survey of the variety of medieval views of the cause and reliability of dreams, without arriving at any conclusion; and indeed this very uncertainty was necessary for Chaucer's purpose if the dream was to be an effective analogue to the poem. The Book of the Duchess is a dream-poem, and it is Chaucer's earliest attempt to use this uncertainty as a means of defining and defending poetic fiction.

In the Book Chaucer represents himself as suffering from insomnia. To pass the night he reads a volume in which

> were written fables
> That clerkes had in olde tyme,
> And other poets, put in rime
> To rede and for to be in minde,
> While men loved the lawe of kinde. (52–6)

This collection of stories from pagan antiquity is evidently Ovid's Metamorphoses, for in it he reads the tale of Ceyx and Alcyone. The tale itself includes a dream, sent to Alcyone by Morpheus, the god of sleep, to bring her news of her husband's death; and this will eventually give Chaucer the idea that he might pray to Morpheus to send *him* to sleep, and will also influence the content of his dream. Quite apart from its causative function, Alcyone's dream offers a striking paradigm for the use Chaucer himself was later to make of dreams. When Ceyx fails to return from a sea voyage, Alcyone prays to Juno to send her knowledge of his fate (and thus already fiction and true vision are intertwined, for within this pagan fiction Alcyone asks for 'som *certeyn* sweven' [119] about her husband). The dream is Juno's answer, and it has its origins in the darkness and silence of the Cave of Sleep; it rises, as we would say, from the unconscious mind. It is itself only a fiction: Alcyone seems to see her husband, but Chaucer makes it as clear as Ovid did that she really sees a 'dreynte body' (195) – a corpse animated by the art of Morpheus. And yet what the dream image tells her is true: Ceyx is drowned, and when she wakes his body will be found cast up by the sea. Alcyone's dream is a fiction which nevertheless reveals the truth, and in this way it offers a model for the general defence of fiction as Chaucer was to undertake it in this and other dream-poems.

To conceive of poetry as fiction – that is, as the use of language to construct imitations of life – is only one way of defining it, and not the way that was commonest in the Middle Ages. The other chief definition of poetry, and one that was then commoner, is as a distinctive, aesthetically appealing or 'creative' use of language: poetry seen as eloquence or figurative discourse, a form of language marked by certain features of style.[15] This conception of poetry has a no less distinguished ancestry than the other, especially in treatises on rhetoric, and in the Middle Ages it was embodied in many of the *artes poeticae*, which were interested not in the relation of poetry to truth but in its existence as a texture of tropes and figures. (Of course, these two conceptions of poetry, as fiction and as figurative discourse, are not entirely separate. One large class of figures – a class often seen as the most distinctively poetic – is that represented by metaphor; extended metaphor is allegory, and allegory can be regarded as a form of fiction. In the defences of poetry offered in the Italian *Trecento*, such as Petrarch's coronation oration and Boccaccio's *De genealogia deorum*, it is precisely their allegorical nature that is said to make secular fictions of value. This however does not seem to have been Chaucer's view: hence his preference for the 'wonderful' dream [*Book* 277, *House* 62] as opposed to the systematically allegorical vision as the model for the poem.)

Half a century ago it was already clear that there was a very substantial overlap between the precepts of the Latin *artes poeticae* and the practice of the French courtly poetry that provided the sources and models for *The Book of the Duchess*. We know, as it happens, that Chaucer was acquainted with Geoffroi de Vinsauf's *Poetria nova*, because he quotes from it in *Troilus and Criseyde* and alludes to its author as 'Gaufred, deere maister soverayn' in *The Nun's Priest's Tale*; but he did not have to rely on any such works as sources of eloquence for his earliest poetry. 'There was no need for him to open the textbooks. His first lessons in rhetoric could be found in the pages of Machaut and the *Roman de la Rose*.'[16] Furthermore, within the system of courtly assumptions that formed the framework of Chaucer's earliest poetry, there was the closest possible connection between poetic eloquence, love, and nobility of birth. The courtly culture took three things for granted: that the subject matter of poetry was love; that such poetry could be written only out of *sentement* or *felynge*, the personal experience of love (thus Chaucer modestly distinguishes between 'Ye lovers that kan make of sentement' [*Prologue to the Legend of Good Women* F 69] and himself who can write 'of no sentement' but only 'out of Latyn' [*Troilus* II 13–14]); and that such experience was attainable only by those of gentle birth. Chaucer's Squire, as seen through the admiring eyes of the Franklin, is the ideal embodiment of this threefold connection: he is *gentil* by birth and behaviour, he tells of love in its most refined form, and, as the Franklin assures him, when tactfully bringing his tale to an end (for *gentil* eloquence about love is not necessarily endlessly interesting),

> So feelyngly thou spekest, sire, I allow the!
> As to my doom, ther is noon that is heere
> Of eloquence that shal be thy peere . . .   (*Tales* v 676–8)

And yet, if such poetry was to be truly eloquent, it would be governed by a paradox: it would be a way of expressing the *sentement* which was its source, but it would also be a way of not expressing it. The *sentement*, the love experience itself, resists expression. As the Franklin says about Aurelius, the fictional counterpart to the pilgrim Squire in his own tale, he had loved Dorigen for over two years, to the point of distraction and despair, and yet

> . . . no thyng dorste he seye,
> Save in his songes somwhat wolde he wreye
> His wo, as in a general compleynyng.   (v 943–5)

'In his songs he would somewhat *conceal* his sorrow in the form of a general lamentation.'[17] As John Stevens has remarked, citing the passage in which these lines occur,

The courtly love-lyric is, perhaps in essence, an enigma – a riddling, or dark, way of conveying your thoughts to someone who is, or pretends to be, your lover.[18]

There is a sense, no doubt, in which all poetry is a concealment of its personal origins, and, as Harold Bloom has suggested, the poetic trope is analogous to the Freudian defence, a way of warding off 'unpleasant truths concerning dangers from within';[19] but the technique of concealment is especially appropriate to the medieval courtly lyric of love, and it is explicitly taught by the *artes poeticae*.

In the traditional image, which Geoffroi de Vinsauf repeats several times, poetic style is a garment:

Materiam verbis veniat vestire poesis.

Let poetic art come forward to clothe the matter with words.[20]

The garment must be appropriate to the person who wears it, but the primary purpose of garments is, of course, to conceal the body. Their primary purpose, yes, but it must be added that in civilized societies garments are designed not only to conceal but to reveal partially and indirectly. That ambiguity of function is no doubt the reason why garments form such an apt and time-honoured metaphor for poetic eloquence; but for my present purpose it will be helpful, and not, I think, misleading, to focus on eloquence's function of concealment. Much of the stylistic technique taught by the rhetoricians is inappropriate to the relative ease and transparency of vernacular poetry in French or English; indeed it is often possible only in a language as highly inflected as Latin. The techniques of amplification, however, form a major part of the doctrine of the *artes poeticae*, and these can be used in English or French as readily as in Latin. Amplification, in its medieval sense, implies at the very least the deferral of literal statement, and the eight means of amplification that Geoffroi de Vinsauf expounds are ways either of concealing the literal meaning or of deferring it. They are: variation (*expolitio*), periphrasis (*circumlocutio*), comparison (*collatio*), apostrophe (*apostrophatio*), personification (*prosopopeia*), digression (*digressio*), description (*descriptio*), and statement by contraries (*oppositio*). How many of these Aurelius used we cannot of course be sure, but comparison was certainly among them, for in his 'layes,/ Songes, compleintes, roundels, virelayes' he sang of how he

> . . . langwissheth as a furye dooth in helle;
> And dye he moste, he seyde, as dide Ekko
> For Narcisus that dorste nat telle hir wo. (v 947–52)

(These comparisons with characters from classical mythology might have sounded odd in medieval vernacular love lyrics, but Chaucer imagines *The Franklin's Tale* as taking place in pagan antiquity.) And the passage in which Aurelius finally discloses to Dorigen that he has fulfilled the condition set in her rash promise (that she would love him if he made the black rocks round the Breton coast disappear) is a masterpiece of deferral: a speech of 28 lines (1311–38) using compliments, parentheses, circumlocutions, and other delaying tactics to hold back the literal statement that 'the rokkes been aweye' until its very last words.

By the time Chaucer wrote *The Franklin's Tale*, the courtly style was well established in English, largely as a result of Chaucer's own efforts. *The Book of the Duchess*, on the other hand, may well be the first fully courtly poem in the English language; and it begins with a first-person *compleynt* of exactly the kind that one might suppose Aurelius's *compleintes* to have been. The speaker of the poem laments that he is unable to sleep, and that as a result he has 'felynge in nothyng' (11); his mind is dominated by 'sorwful ymagynacioun' (14) and 'fantasies' (28), and he is suffering from 'melancolye' (23) and fear of dying. This prologue purports to derive from a personal experience of some kind, but expresses it by means of an amplification that conceals its cause. If we are to read it in the spirit of courtly eloquence, we must assume that this 'sicknesse/ That I have suffred this eight yeer' (36–7) and the 'phisicien but oon' (39) capable of curing it are both figurative rather than literal; but we have no idea who the physician is or what experience it is that is described as a sickness. The 'sorwful ymagynacioun' helps to explain why the speaker goes on to have a dream, and the reference to melancholy, the black humour, explains why the dream should concern a man in black; but we never learn for certain what literal *entente* or what real-life or feigned human situation underlies this texture of literary figuration.

In view of this it may surprise us to find that the person who introduces himself by means of this courtly *compleynt* turns out to be oddly literalistic in his attitudes for most of the remainder of the poem. But Chaucer's original audience (whoever they were) would probably have been less surprised, for they would not have expected consistency in the characterization of the narrator. There is, I believe, a real discrepancy in consciousness, though not in theme, between the prologue and what follows. No more here, probably, than in *The House of Fame* was Chaucer concerned to establish complete coherence on the level of narratorial consciousness.[21] At any rate, it seems never to occur to the narrator of the *Book* to interpret the Ovidian story that he reads in any but the most literal terms. The story is 'a wonder thing' (61), and he feels a naïve sympathy for Alcyone, quite as if she were a real person:

> Such sorowe this lady to her tok
> That trewly I, which made this book,
> Had such pittee and such rowthe
> To rede hir sorwe, that by my trowthe
> I ferde the worse al the morwe
> Aftir, to thenken on hir sorwe. (95–100)

He goes on to see the classical legend as offering useful guidance for his own situation in real life; it is true that he 'ne knew never god but oon' (237), but he still thinks it worth offering Morpheus a very solid and luxurious feather-bed,

> Of down of pure dowves white, . . .
> Rayed with gold and ryght wel cled
> In fyn blak satyn doutremer,
> And many a pilowe, and every ber
> Of clothe of Reynes, to slepe softe –
> Hym thar not nede to turnen ofte (250, 252–6)

– if only he will bring him sleep. All this he will do for Morpheus, or Juno, 'Or som wight elles, I ne roghte who' (244). His literalism is such that he evidently does not grasp that for anyone other than a pagan 'Morpheus' can only be a figurative expression meaning 'sleep'; and the literalism is made more convincing by colloquial touches in his language, such as that jaunty 'I ne roghte who'.

By the time his vow to Morpheus has been rewarded and the main section of the poem has begun – a dream about which again he can say no more than that it is 'wonderful' (277) – Chaucer is firmly fixed in the role of literalist. As the first-person of a courtly poem, he must necessarily speak in an adequately courtly style, but the amplifying devices he employs are in general those compatible with literalism. His descriptions of the singing birds that wake him into his dream ('They ne spared not her throtes!' [320]), of his dream bedroom, of the hunt that he hears passing by and then joins in the forest, and of the forest itself, are enthusiastically enumerative, offering a breathless surplus of detail that we cannot help attributing to naïveté. 'Flora and Zephirus' (402), like Morpheus, are for him no symbolic fictions but real beings, 'They two that make floures growe' (403), and his digression about 'Argus the noble countour' (435) has a similar confiding informativeness. There is, it is true, one richly figurative passage, which combines metaphor and personification to tell us how the earth

> . . . had forgete the povertee
> That Wynter, thorgh hys colde morwes,
> Had made hyt suffre . . .   (410–12)

but, in the context of general literalism, even that passage comes to seem intended by its speaker literally rather than figuratively. This is, admittedly, no more than a subjective impression, though it is one that I know others to share; but what happens next turns out to confirm it.

Chaucer finds 'A wonder wel-farynge knyght' (452) dressed entirely in black leaning against an oak tree. He hears him utter a pitiful lament, and politely engages him in conversation, to try to discover the cause of his unhappiness. The remaining two-thirds of the poem is occupied by this conversation, from which it emerges that the knight has lost his lady and – but this information is not disclosed until the very end of the poem – that the cause of his loss was her death. The knight describes at length his own grief and the course of his successful courtship of the lady, his 'goode faire White' (948), whom he praises in the most superlative, yet by no means entirely abstract, terms; and it is clear that the knight is John of Gaunt and 'White' is Blanche, both translated into the dream-realm of idealizing fiction. Once the black knight is introduced, one cannot fail to be conscious of a contrast between his eloquence, which is persistently figurative, and the dreaming Chaucer's literalism – a contrast coinciding with and strengthened by that between the knight's high social status and the dreamer's lower rank:

> Loo, how goodly spak thys knyght,
> As hit had be another wyght;
> He made hyt nouther towgh ne queynte.   (529–31)

Most readers of Chaucer have a general but elusive sense of lower social rank attributed to his narratorial self, and this perhaps begins to emerge in his work from the point in *The Book of the Duchess* at which he encounters this 'wonder wel-farynge knyght'. However this may be, the knight's language is at once established as a courtly rhetoric that serves to 'wreye/ His woo' rather than to express it directly and literally. The first words of his that the dreamer hears are 'a lay, a maner song,/ Withoute noote, withoute song', forming a *complaynte* (471–2, 487). It begins with an *oppositio*:

> I have of sorwe so gret won
> That joye gete I never non. (475–6)

In itself this is no different from amplifying devices used by the dreamer, as when he describes the knight as 'Ful pitous pale, and nothyng red' (470); but the *complaynt* at once rises to more radically figurative utterance, in the form of an *apostrophatio* addressed to a personification:

> Allas, deth, what ayleth the,
> That thou noldest have taken me,
> Whan thou toke my lady swete . . .? (481–3)

Jonathan Culler has described apostrophe as 'the pure embodiment of poetic pretension',[22] for it is a figure which implies that the poet has power to change reality, by conferring life on what is inanimate and summoning it to his presence; and it is surely not by accident that this is the means of poetic amplification that Geoffroi de Vinsauf discusses at greatest length and illustrates most elaborately (*Poetria nova*, lines 263–461). Among his examples is an apostrophe addressed to death (lines 386–96). As might be expected from the relatively modest aims of English poetry before Chaucer, such amibitious figures were then rare;[23] here the figure acts precisely to conceal the speaker's literal cause of grief, and, as far as the dreamer is concerned, it evidently does so successfully, for he persists in failing to understand what this cause is.

In what follows, the knight continues to speak figuratively, while the dreamer, for all his ready sympathy, continues to understand him literally. The knight's figurative eloquence defines his superior social status, and the dreamer's misunderstandings motivate the knight's continuing amplification; but, more important, we gradually come to see that the effect of the knight's eloquence is to conceal his cause of grief *from himself*. Where Aurelius dares not disclose his grief to Dorigen, the knight dares not contemplate the literal fact of his lady's death and so invents ever ampler garments of *poesis* to hide it from himself. It is precisely the need for avoidance of literal truth that produces the poetry of *The Book of the Duchess*. The knight uses an extraordinary profusion of tricks of concealment and postponement. His first extended speech alone (lines 560–709) is crammed with rhetorical figures. It incorporates numerous classical and learned allusions, which by explicit or implied *collatio* move attention away from his own literal situation; when they take a negative form, it is particularly clear that their function is to avoid the literal truth:

> May noght make my sorwes slyde
> Nought al the remedyes of Ovyde,
> Ne Orpheus, god of melodye,
> Ne Dedalus with his playes slye;
> Ne hele me may no phisicien,
> Noght Ypocras, ne Galyen.   (567–72)

('Ne hele me may no phisicien', along with many other touches, points to an analogy between the knight and the dreamer in his waking life, suffering from a sickness that but one physician could cure. From the point of view of a naturalistic dream-psychology, the knight can be seen as a projection of the dreamer himself; more important, for our purpose, is that they are both locked in a sickness which stands no chance of cure until it can be figured out or unfigured.) The same speech personifies not only death but Sorrow and Fortune. The personification of Sorrow, with which the knight identifies himself, indicates particularly clearly how the habit of figuration may constitute a resistance to the overcoming of grief:

> For whoso seeth me first on morwe
> May seyn he hath met with Sorwe,
> For y am Sorwe and Sorwe ys y.   (595–7)

The knight wishes to become fixed in the posture of a personification; what can Sorrow ever do but be sorrowful? He employs the figure called *frequentatio* for a similar purpose, exhaustively elaborating different aspects of the idea that his happiness has been transformed into misery:

> My song ys turned to pleynynge,
> And al my laughtre to wepynge,
> My glade thoghtes to hevynesse . . .   (599–601)

and so on for another 16 lines.

The knight's long *descriptio* of Fortune presents her in terms of paradox. A six-line simile compares her to a scorpion (636–41), thus

taking us even further away from what has really happened. The
knight explains how he has played a game of chess with Fortune,
and she has treacherously taken his *fers* (queen) and checkmated him;
and the dreamer conspicuously fails to understand this beautiful but
deceptive allegory. Many famous people in antiquity, he says, have
killed themselves for grief as the knight seems to threaten to do (and
the fact that the examples the dreamer mentions are all women may
be meant to imply tactfully that such an act would be effeminate),
but, he goes on,

> But ther is no man alyve her
> Wolde for a fers make this woo. (740–1)

The dreamer's literal-minded misinterpretation calls unmistakeable
attention to the figurative element in the knight's discourse; and that
it is a misinterpretation the knight at once points out:

> "Why so?" quod he, "hyt ys nat soo.
> Thou woste ful lytel what thou menest;
> I have lost more than thow wenest." (742–4)

The dreamer asks the knight to explain, and this leads him to tell the
story of his love for 'goode faire White'.

In this section of the poem too the knight continues to use the
figures of courtly poetry. He willingly became thrall to Love, paid
him tribute, did homage to him, and prayed for his favour (764ff.).
At the time when 'Yowthe, my maistresse,/ Governed me in
ydelnesse' (797–8) he chose love as his 'firste craft' (791). Fortune,
that 'false trayteresse pervers' (813), brought him to meet a fair
company of ladies. One of them outshone the others as the summer
sun the other planets (821–9). Love brought it about that he took
counsel from nothing but her look and his own heart (835–41). Her
hair was 'lyk gold' (858), and 'the goddesse, dame Nature' (871)
made her eyes open and close. To all the other personifications is
added even 'Dulnesse', which was afraid of her (879). When he
comes to describing the lady, the knight begins with an impossi-
bility-topos, saying that he lacks 'both Englyssh and wit' (898) to
reveal the truth about her face; but he then embarks on the most
elaborate *descriptio* imaginable. It is hardly necessary to analyse it in
detail, but it is full of similes and metaphors. Her throat resembled 'a
round tour of yvoyre' (946). Her courtly conversation was such that

> she was lyk to torche bryght
> That every man may take of lyght
> Ynogh, and hyt hath never the lesse. (963–5)

She was 'chef myrour of al the feste' (974), and when she was absent the company was 'As a corowne withoute stones' (980). In the knight's eyes she was indeed 'The soleyn fenix of Arabye' (982). Once the *descriptio* is over, amplification continues unabated. The lady was not accustomed to set her suitors impossible tasks: the knight mentions seven places that she did not order them to visit. In response to the dreamer's suggestion that she seemed the best of ladies only to one who saw her through her lover's eyes, the knight angrily (but not quite to the point) says that he would have loved her whatever the circumstances, and mentions 15 people and places, mostly classical, to enforce his point. The dreamer nervously assures him that his good fortune has been comparable to 'shryfte wythoute repentaunce' (1114), and the word *repentaunce* moves the knight to mention three famous traitors to whom he is not comparable. So he continues, sprinkling his discourse with further references to Tubal, Pythagoras, Nature, the ten plagues of Egypt, and Cassandra.

Without going into more detail about the knight's extraordinary display of eloquence, it may be useful to attempt to summarize its purposes. Three seem to me prominent. One is to compare the literal truth to something else, which thus temporarily takes its place. A second is to foreground the verbal structure, so that eloquence itself is admired, and the magnificence of the garment of words distracts attention from what it covers. And a third is to postpone the moment at which the knight has to give a straightforward answer to the dreamer's request to 'discure me youre woo' (549). There is thus an increasing tension as the dream dialogue proceeds between covering and discovering, between delight in the copiousness of the knight's discourse and anxiety at the evasion of the *sentement* that underlies it. The knight himself expresses his awareness of the evasive function of amplification in anxious rhetorical questions – questions which are themselves amplifying devices. 'But wherfore that y telle my tale?' (1034), he asks, and again, 'But wherfore that I telle thee?' (1088). The question *wherfore?* has ultimately to be answered.

As we get nearer to the end of the knight's tale, the texture of figuration gets somewhat thinner. He repeats the first of the songs that he composed to express his love, and this lyric – composed, like all other courtly songs in courtly theory, 'Of my felynge' (1172) – is notably simpler and more literal than the one the dreamer heard him repeating when he first saw him. The later stages of his narrative show more signs of *abbreviatio* than of *amplificatio*. His purpose now is 'To telle shortly ryght as hyt ys' (1239), and he neither conceals nor postpones the monosyllabic 'Nay' (1243) which is the lady's answer to his equally laconic first plea to her to accept his love – 'I seyde "Mercy!" and no more' (1219). After the last delaying comparison of his sorrow with that of

> Cassandra, that soo
> Bewayled the destruccioun
> Of Troye and of Ilyoun,   (1246–8)

days and years pass in scarcely more lines: 'And thus I lyved ful many a day, . . . So hit befel, another yere . . . And thus we lyved, ful many a yere' (1252, 1258, 1296). At last, in response to the dreamer's inescapable 'Where is she now?' (1298), comes a final wriggle of evasion –

> That was the los that here-before
> I tolde the that I hadde lorn   (1302–3)

– and then the bald truth: 'She ys ded!' (1309). And immediately the elaborate structure of figure and fiction that constitutes the poem can be unbuilt: the black knight can be released from his rhetorical role as a personification of sorrow, and at the same time the dreamer can be released from his no less constricting role as an uncomprehending literalist. Chaucer engages in a figurative play of puns on Lancaster, John, and Richmond, restoring the knight to his true identity as John of Gaunt, who was Earl of Richmond before his marriage to Blanche and gained the title of Duke of Lancaster by marrying her. And Chaucer finally restores himself to his true role as poet, vowing to 'put this sweven in ryme' (1332).

In an article from which I have learned much, David Aers has suggested that *The Book of the Duchess*

. . . explores the way that poetry, perhaps all art, inevitably "beautifies" even the most harrowing experience, and in its search for rhetorical form . . . transforms anguish out of recognition.[24]

That is a valuable insight, but it also needs to be recognized that the 'beautification', which I have tried to identify more specifically as rhetorical figuration, is itself a necessary part of the process of coming to terms with painful experience. The knight needs to exhaust all the strategies of evasion, needs too to understand (or at

Readings in Medieval Poetry

least to enable us to understand) that his purpose is to evade – 'But wherfore that y telle my tale?' – before he can come to acknowledge the literal truth. He is ultimately able to say 'She ys ded' because there is nothing else left for him to say. The possibilities of figuration must be used, and used up, until only the literal is left; and it is, of course, only in the context of the figurative that the literal possesses its full rhetorical power. In *The Book of the Duchess* Chaucer, having perhaps been the first to create a poem in English that possessed the eloquence of the French courtly tradition, also went a little further, setting eloquence in the context of truth and truth in the context of eloquence.

5 · Narrative closure: the end of *Troilus and Criseyde*

The endings of literary works are sensitive points, and the end of *Troilus and Criseyde* has been the subject of particularly widespread discussion and controversy. This is Chaucer's most ambitious single work, and as to his careful planning of it there could be no doubt, even if he had not quoted, as the first of its five books is coming to an end, a passage on the subject of advance planning not found in his chief narrative source, Boccaccio's *Filostrato*, but translated from Geoffroi de Vinsauf's *Poetria nova*:

> For everi wight that hath an hous to founde
> Ne renneth naught the werk for to bygynne
> With rakel hond, but he wol bide a stounde,
> And sende his hertes line out fro with-inne
> Aldirfirst his purpos forto wynne.   (I 1065–9)[1]

Yet it has been widely felt that the end of the *Troilus* is an unsatisfactory conclusion to the work as a whole: it seems to be a patchwork job, turning nervously from one topic and tone to another, adding to the story told in the *Filostrato* an account of the ascent of the hero's soul to the heavens taken from a different work of Boccaccio's, and finally giving emphatic expression to a Christian orthodoxy that apparently negates much of the human and literary substance of what precedes. In my view, too much of the discussion of this ending has been based on the assumption that concepts such as *werk* and *purpos* must imply oneness (as though every room in the house to which Geoffroi and Pandarus refer had to be made of the same materials and serve the same purpose); so that to justify the ending it is thought necessary to claim, as one of its defenders puts it, that 'Troilus's love and death and heavenly reward form a unity'.[2] The effectiveness of an ending can be vindicated without making a claim as extreme as that; and I believe it will be helpful to begin by considering more generally some of the problems of ending a literary work, and some ways in which medieval English romances end, before proceeding to consider in more detail how the end of *Troilus and Criseyde* is actually achieved.

If endings are sensitive points, it is partly because, like beginnings, they mark the boundary between the work and the world. A central theme in twentieth-century social anthropology has been the significance of boundaries, whether material or conceptual.[3] In real buildings, doorways are nearly always specially marked, with emphatic frames, porches, pediments, architraves or other architectural features, or just painted a different colour from the rest of the woodwork; that many such markings are also functional (supporting the wall above the door or providing shelter for those entering or leaving) heightens rather than contradicts their symbolic significance. Crossing the threshold is an act of special importance, as the common use of this idea as a metaphor serves to demonstrate, and there are many ceremonial acts and references connected with threshold-crossing: first-footing, carrying the bride over the threshold of the marital home, and so on. If we move from the material to the categorical, we find that in all societies the boundaries between the major stages of human life are felt to be of special importance, and are marked by social ceremonies: birth, coming of age, marriage, and death are only the most important. The boundaries themselves are places of new possibility, excitement, and danger; behaviour associated with them is governed by special rules. The same is true of conceptual boundaries such as those between God and human being, human being and beast, man and woman, or, in the animal world, between one species and another; there is a tendency for mythologies and religious ceremonies to focus on such boundaries and the rare, sacred or obscene transgressors of them. Or, to descend to the humble realm of books, the beginning and end of a modern printed book are marked unmistakeably not just by the covers but by expensive blank fly-leaves and by a title page and 'The End'. One indication, indeed, of a new sense of the integrity and dignity of the vernacular literary work which develops in the course of the later Middle Ages in England is the more emphatic marking of beginnings and ends, and of the work's internal divisions, with titles, headings, and other symbolic decorations. The most splendid of the Chaucer manuscripts, such as the Ellesmere *Canterbury Tales* and the Corpus Christi *Troilus*, illustrate this admirably, with their transference to vernacular and secular works of the systematic ceremonial *ordinatio* that had long been characteristic of religious works in Latin.

In a culture dubious, as that of Chaucer's time still was, about the

Narrative closure: the end of *Troilus and Criseyde*

status and value of fiction, literary beginnings and ends have a special sensitivity, because they mark the thresholds of an imaginative area whose claim to exist at all is hard to justify in terms of the age's official system of thought. The dream was used, by Chaucer and other poets, as an ambiguous category to contain fictional invention without committing the poet either to claim that it was a symbolic reflection of inspired truth or to admit that it was no more than empty fantasy. The beginning is difficult because of the need to justify the very existence of a poetic fabrication, and I have suggested elsewhere that the unusually elaborate introduction to *The Book of the Duchess* might be seen as a 'mediation between everyday reality and the world of imagination', a kind of slow condensation of the fiction out of the empty air.[4] But the end is difficult too, and the longer the poem the more difficult, because the end is not merely a boundary: it is expected somehow to complete or sum up the meaning of the whole. The end is the goal, the purpose of the entire work – the word *ende* has both meanings in Middle English as in modern English. In Book II of *Troilus and Criseyde* Pandarus, that expert on the planning of speech and behaviour, explains his own methods to Criseyde as he craftily reveals what he has to tell her about Troilus's love for her:

> Nece, alwey, lo, to the laste,
> How so it be that som men hem delite
> With subtyl art hire tales forto endite,
> Yet for al that, in hire entencioun,
> Hire tale is al for som conclusioun.
>
> And sithen th'ende is every tales strengthe,
> And this matere is so bihovely,
> What sholde I peynte or drawen it on lengthe
> To yow that ben my frend so feythfully? (II 255–63)

'Th'ende is every tales strengthe': yet for many modern readers the endings of narratives have seemed a weakness rather than a strength, because of their obvious and necessary artificiality. What Conrad calls 'the desire for finality, for which our hearts yearn', is granted by narratives, but the more fully it is granted, the more the narrative diverges, on this view, from reality:

No end, in reality, is ever final in the way "The End" of a novel or film is. Even death is not an end – biologically, historically, or in any sense that one takes the word. Such a term marks out plot, the story-as-discoursed. It is strictly an artifact of composition, not a function of raw story-material . . .

Hence, as another critic has written,

Even ending a story at all – ending in the sense of tying up all the loose ends of plot, settling the destinies of all the characters – even this comes to seem like a falsification of reality.

And a third remarks that 'the endings of many novels . . . often resemble a *tour de force* simply because the book must come to an end'.[5] The assumption underlying these statements is that the narrative aims ideally to offer a total analogue to experiential reality, and that its necessary failure to do this is a source of stress. Moreover, the high valuation of the literary work as an autonomous fictional 'world' which has been characteristic of both classical and Romantic and post-Romantic thought about literature leads to another problem with endings. The end must be justified by criteria internal to the narrative itself: it must emerge from inside the work, as the satisfactory completion of its intrinsic pattern or development:

. . . the end of a play or novel will not appear as an arbitrary cut-off if it leaves us at a point where, with respect to the themes of the work, we feel that we know all there is or all there is to know.[6]

'*All* there is or *all* there is to know' – it is difficult to see how this requirement could be fulfilled with a work of any complexity (or perhaps, given the irremediable richness and polyvalence of language, with any work at all). And if it is further demanded that the end shall itself be the keystone, the stroke which makes us recognize the completeness and significance of what it completes, in order to achieve closure 'in the sense of a climax of plot and meaning together',[7] then the writer becomes the victim of impossibly inflated expectations. It has been argued that the aesthetic principles of medieval scholasticism, defining beauty as a 'combination of clarity and fitness of proportion', imply of a poem that 'the excellence of its form will above all be apparent in the artistic inevitability of the ending to which it draws'.[8] Traces of such a conception can be found, to be sure, in the thought of Dante about lyric poetry: he defines a song as 'the *completed* action of one who artistically puts words together into a harmonious whole'.[9] But the song is essentially a small-scale work, and Dante's aesthetic, for all its origins in scholasticism, belongs to the Renaissance rather than the Middle Ages. On any scale larger than the lyric, perhaps only God could do what these exalted theories demand of the human artist.

Narrative closure: the end of *Troilus and Criseyde*

In the Middle Ages the analogy between the poet and God is not commonly found; it seems to be generally taken for granted that literary structure is arbitrary, and that endings will be achieved by the imposition of accepted conventions external to the substance of the work itself. For the medieval *artes poeticae* structure or *dispositio* is only a relatively minor aspect of the art, and beginnings and endings are dealt with in what now seems a somewhat mechanical way, as a matter of specific devices such as proverbs and *exempla*. Endings receive particularly slight treatment. Matthieu de Vendôme in his *Ars versificatoria* explains in a few sentences that a conclusion is 'an appropriate ending of a poem that completes its overall design' and that it may be achieved by 'a recapitulation of ideas', 'an emendation of the work', 'a plea for indulgence', 'a display of boasting', 'an expression of gratitude' to the Muses, or (he adds) by accident, if the author dies before finishing his work – and this is better called *terminatio* than *conclusio*. Jean de Garlande in the *Parisiana poetria* mentions endings achieved by recapitulation, by an example containing a similitude, or by a proverb, and also those such as the conclusions of Virgil's *Eclogues* and Statius's *Thebaid* derived *a licencia*, that is from whatever pleased the poet – a peculiarly unilluminating concept. Geoffroi de Vinsauf in his *Documentum de arte versificandi* says briefly that an ending may be achieved by reference back to the body of the work, by a proverb, or by an *exemplum* (by which he means an extended metaphor); and in the *Poetria nova*, though describing and illustrating various ways of beginning, he says nothing at all about endings.[10] If medieval theory is so weak in this area (evidently not seeing endings as liable to be difficult or problematic), it is unlikely to have given Chaucer any help in bringing *Troilus and Criseyde* to an end. It may be helpful instead to turn to poetic practice, and to see how some typical Middle English narratives actually conclude. A survey of the ends of some of the better-known Middle English romances – works, as we have seen, of a kind that Chaucer himself is likely to have been familiar with, and that certainly provided the initial matrix of his narrative style – makes a useful preliminary to an analysis of the closing stanzas of his own most ambitious romance. The differences are not always so great as might be expected.

There are several different types of romance story in Middle English,[11] but the climax of the story very frequently consists of the reconstitution of a state which existed at the beginning but has subsequently been lost. Perhaps the commonest such reconstitutions are one or both of these: the reunion of separated members of a family and the regaining by the central character or characters of an earthly position and status of which they have been unjustly deprived. Such events plainly create a sense of satisfying completion and, in the latter case, of the working out of earthly justice. Reunion and restoration are frequently celebrated by a ceremonial act of feasting and/or crowning, which expresses publicly a change of status and thus marks a boundary in the narrative events justifying the end of the poem that recounts those events. Even more emphatic, the end of the story is nearly always marked by one or both of two occurrences that form crucial boundaries in the individual life – marriage (or sometimes the reunion of a separated husband and wife) and death. The former, as might be expected, is an extremely common conclusion. Horn marries Rymenhild; Gamelyn marries 'a wyf bothe good and feyr' (898);[12] the Squire of Low Degree marries the King of Hungary's daughter; Lybeaus Desconus receives his lady as a bride from Arthur; Le Bone Florence de Rome marries Tyrrye; Havelok and Goldeboru, Orfeo and Heurodis, Launfal and his fairy lady, Ywain and Laudine, are all reunited. But, given the strong tendency for the Middle English romance to have a happy ending, it is striking how often death is also mentioned alongside reunion, coronation, or marriage – death, the most final boundary of all in the individual life.

The death is sometimes that of the villain, and in this case it contributes to the enactment of earthly justice and is greeted with robust pleasure. At the end of *Octavian* the wicked queen's suicide is met with laughter; at the end of *Amis and Amiloun*, Amiloun's wife, who is about to remarry, is imprisoned on bread and water till she dies, and the poet adds, 'Who therof rought, he was a queede' (2483);[13] at the end of *Athelston* the traitor is hanged, and the poet comments in the poem's closing lines,

> Now Jesu, that is hevene-kyng,
> Leve nevere traitour have betere endyng,
> But swych dome for to dye. (810–12)[14]

But more often the poem does not end before the hero's triumph and happiness are also ended, like all things human, by death. Sir Isumbras is reunited with his three sons and crowns them all kings, but then, we are told,

> They lyved and dyed in gode entente,
> Her sowles I wote to hevenn wente,
> Whenne they dede ware.　　　　　(790–92)[15]

Sir Gowther reigned long as an emperor, but then died as a saint, at whose shrine many miracles occur. After Horn and Rymenhild's success, the poet bluntly remarks,

> Nu ben hi bothe dede;
> Crist to hevene hem lede!　　　　　(1523–4)

After Gamelyn's marriage, he died,

> And so schal we alle, may ther no man flee:
> God bringe us to the joye that ever schal be!　　　　　(901–2)

Orfeo and Heurodis were newly crowned, 'And lived long afterward'; their death is not actually mentioned, but it is certainly implied because the next line is, 'And seththen was king the steward' (596). The English translator of Chrétien's *Yvain* adds to his source the assurance of a happy ending for 'Lunet and the liown' as well as for the hero and his wife, but he also adds that their happiness lasts only 'Until that ded haves dreven tham down' (4025–6).[16]

The finality of death is thus very frequently called on to strengthen the effect of narrative closure. As some of the above quotations show, mention of the hero's death is often accompanied by a prayer that his soul may be conducted to eternal joy; and prayer in general, linking the poet and his audience in a communal *we*, is almost invariably the speech-act performed by the closing lines of a Middle English romance. Occasionally the prayer is for divine protection in this life:

> Jesu Criste in Trinité,
> Blesse and glade this cumpany,
> And ore us halde his hande. (*Sir Amadace* 838–40)[17]

Sometimes it is of a very general kind:

> Jesus that is of hevene king,
> Yeve us alle his suete blessing!　　　(*King Horn* 1529–30)

> Jhesus, that ys Hevenekyng,
> Yeve us alle hys blessyng,
> And hys modyr Marye!　　　(*Sir Launfal* 1042–4)[18]

> God graunt ous alle wele to fare!　　　(*Sir Orfeo* 604)

> God gyff us grace well to fare!　　　(*Sir Degaré* 995–6)[19]

But more often, as with the prayer for the hero, the closing prayer is for salvation: a prayer that we may *wone* or *bide* with God in the next life. A few examples must stand for many:

> Jesu that settes yn thy trone,
> So graunte us wyth the to wone
>   In thy perpetuall glorye!   (*Emaré* 1033–5)[20]

> Jesu lorde, hevyn kynge,
> Graunt us all thy blessyng,
>   And yn hevyn to abyde!   (*Octavian* 1789–91)[21]

> Jesu Cryst, Goddys son,
> Gyff us myght with hym to won,
>   That lord that is most of meyn.
>   (*Sir Gowther* 748–50)[22]

> Bot Jhesu Criste for his grete grace
> In hevyn-blis grante us a place
> To bide in, if his wills be.
> Amen, amen, par charité.   (*Ywain and Gawain* 4029–32)

Or, what amounts to the same thing:

> Jhesu Cryst our Savyour
> And hys moder, that swete flour,
> Graunte us alle good endynge.   Amen.
>   (*Lybeaus Desconus* 2128–30)[23]

Last I must mention three other elements commonly forming part of the conclusions of Middle English romance. One is some kind of retrospective summary of the story. This may be extremely bald –

> Thus ended syr Isumbras,
> That an hardy knyghte was,
>   In sorowe allthowgh he wore   (*Sir Isumbras* 793–5)

– but in the more seriously moral romances it will usually not just sum up the events but give some indication of their general meaning:

> Thus syr Gwother coverys is care,
> That fyrst was ryche and sython bare,
>   And effte was ryche ageyn;
> And geyton with a felteryd feynd,
> Grace he had to make that eynd
>   That God was of hym feyn.   (*Sir Gowther* 739–44)

> Forthy schulde men and women als
> Them bethynke or they be false,
>   Hyt makyth so fowle an ende.
> Be hyt nevyr so slylye caste,
> Yyt hyt schamyth the maystyr at the laste,
>   In what londe that evyr they lende.
>   (*Le Bone Florence de Rome* 2176–81)[24]

Narrative closure: the end of *Troilus and Criseyde*

The other two elements both involve a kind of reflexivity, because they call attention in one case to the story that is now being completed and in the other to the poet who is completing it. It may simply be affirmed that the story has reached its conclusion –

> Her endeth the tale of Horn,
> That fair was and noght unorn;
> Make we us glade evre among,
> For thus him endeth Hornes song   (*King Horn* 1527–30)

> And thus endyth thys romance gode
>   (*Le Bone Florence* 2185)

– or that nothing more is to be told or discovered of the characters:

> Seththe saw hym yn thys lond noman,
> Ne no more of hym telle y ne can,
>   Forsothe, wythoute lye.   (*Sir Launfal* 1036–8)

> Of tham na mare have I herd tell
> Nowther in rumance ne in spell.
>   (*Ywain and Gawain* 4027–8)

The story may be defined as belonging to a particular genre (this is especially common with the romances that call themselves Breton lays), and the definition will normally imply or be accompanied by some claim to authenticity:

> . . . As testymonyeth thys story.
> Thys ys on of Brytayne layes
> That was used by olde dayes,
>   Men callys "Playnt Egarye".   (*Emaré* 1029–32)

> This is wreton in parchemeyn,
> A story bothe gud and fyn
>   Owt off a lay of Breytyn.   (*Sir Gowther* 745–7)

> Pope Symonde thys story wrate,
> In the cronykyls of Rome ys the date,
>   Who sekyth there he may hyt fynde.
>   (*Le Bone Florence* 2173–5)

> Yn Rome thys geste ys cronyculyd, ywys;
> A Lay of Bretayne callyd hyt ys,
>   And evyrmore schall be.
>   (*The Erle of Tolous*, 1218–20)[25]

In passages such as these, it is worth noting, it is the source of romance, rather than the romance itself, that has attributed to it the dignified status of a written document; but the mere reference to writing seems to imply a detachment from the story, which is no longer present as a narrative experience, in course of being told, but has become a completed physical object, 'wreton in parchemeyn'. It also, of course, implies an author – not an inventor of the story, to be sure, but at least a re-teller who copied it down or consulted its alleged source, and who can now refer to the completed work as 'thys story' or 'thys geste'. As we saw in Chapter 2, even the narratorial 'I' can be virtually absent from a Middle English romance, and the great majority of the romances are anonymous. In certain cases, however, the poem's 'I' is given some degree of definition as it reaches its end. In one rare instance, from Chaucer's own time, the speaker of a would-be fashionable narrative even names himself as its maker: 'Thomas Chestre made thys tale' (*Sir Launfal* 1039). A more interesting case is that of *Havelok*; and a somewhat fuller look at the ending of this romance, with its skilful use of a combination of closural devices, can bring this survey to a conclusion.

The story of *Havelok* ends with the usual boundary events. The villain Godrich is burned to death; though Havelok has married Goldeboru at an earlier stage, there is a wedding all the same, indeed a double one, because Havelok gives his friend Grim's two daughters in marriage to his allies the earl of Chester and Bertram; and Havelok is publicly crowned in England, with great festivity. There he and Goldeboru reign for 60 years; and there is a strong emphasis on their mutual love that seems to anticipate Chaucer's treatment of marital harmony in *The Franklin's Tale* and elsewhere:

> He lovede hire, and she him so,
> That neyther other mihte be
> Fro other, ne no joie se
> But-yf he were to-gidere bothe;
> Nevere yete ne weren he wrothe,
> For here love was ay newe . . .   (2969–74)

They had 15 children, all of whom were kings and queens (thus crowning is again implied); and the poet comments, in a *sententia* that, like the passage on marital love, brings out the work's thematic significance, 'Him stondes wel that god child strenes' (2983). Then comes a ten-line passage, consisting of a single sentence, which summarizes the course of the story as a passage from youth to maturity and once more calls attention to its thematic dimensions (rightful possession, treachery, revenge), while at the same time defining it as a *gest* now completed (*al thoru, everilk del*), spoken by the poet (*ich*) and received by his listeners (*ye*):

> Nu have ye herd the gest al thoru
> Of Havelok and of Goldeborw;
> Hu he weren boren, and hu fedde,

> And hou he woren with wronge ledde
> In here youthe with trecherie,
> With tresoun and with felounye;
> And hou the swikes haveden tiht
> Reven hem that was here riht,
> And hou he weren wreken wel,
> Have ich seyd you everilk del.　　　　　　　(2984–93)

Finally there is a further eight-line sentence, syntactically highly complex (perhaps indeed to be regarded as a continuation of the previous sentence), which reinforces the reflexive emphasis on the poem itself (*the ryme*) but in addition foregrounds the figure of its maker. He is not named, though it seems as though he could well have been, but the closing prayer for salvation now relates not to the hero but to the poet: we are invited to reward the night-time labour of literary composition (envisaged as something quite other than the supposedly instinctive skill of the minstrel) with our pater-nosters:

> Forthi ich wolde biseken you
> That haven herd the rime nu,
> That ilke of you, with gode wille,
> Seye a pater-noster stille,
> For him that haveth the ryme maked,
> And ther-fore fele nihtes waked,
> That Jesu Crist his soule bringe
> Bi-forn his fader at his endinge.　　Amen.　　(2994–3001)

To turn from the end of *Havelok* to that of *Troilus and Criseyde* is to move on a whole century, and to enter a cultural world of more spacious dimensions, influenced in important ways by Chaucer's contacts with the Italian *Trecento*. The very scope of the *Troilus* makes ending it a more difficult, problematic and interesting task; but, as we shall see, Chaucer still uses many of the closural devices for which the Middle English romances provided models.

Where does the end of *Troilus and Criseyde* begin? In one sense the whole poem is a preparation for the end which is forecast in the opening stanza:

> The double sorwe of Troilus to tellen,
> That was the kyng Priamus sone of Troye,
> In lovynge how his aventures fellen
> Fro wo to wele, and after out of joie,
> My purpos is, er that I parte fro ye . . .　　　　(1 1–5)

Chaucer has a 'purpos forto wynne' (1 1069) which governs his whole procedure; *Troilus and Criseyde* is a more carefully pondered and planned work, a work more architectural in design (with its five books forming a great classical pediment, sweeping up from Troilus's first sorrow of unrequited love to his joy in fulfilled love and down again to his second sorrow of love betrayed), than any earlier romance in English. Yet there remain throughout the poem traces of conflicting purposes, which enrich as well as confuse this grand design. In the proem to Book IV Chaucer seems to indicate that he is approaching the end of his task,

> For how Criseyde Troilus for-sook –
> Or at the leeste how that she was unkynde –
> Moot hennes-forth ben matere of my book,   (IV 15–17)

and he prays to the Furies and to Mars,

> This ilke ferthe book me helpeth fyne,
> So that the losse of lyf and love y-feere
> Of Troilus be fully shewed heere.   (IV 26–8)

Whether or not Chaucer did once intend that the fourth book should be the last, the poem from this point on seems riven by opposing impulses to tell and not to tell (a situation in some ways analogous to that we found in *The Book of the Duchess*). There is a desire to bring the design to its intended conclusion; but there is equally a desire to defer as long as possible the narration of such painful matter as Criseyde's betrayal of Troilus and his 'losse of lyf and love y-feere', without which the conclusion cannot be reached. In the proem to Book V, the end is once more ominously anticipated –

> Aprochen gan the fatal destyné
> That Joves hath in disposicioun,
> And to yow, angry Parcas, sustren thre,
> Committeth to don execucioun;
> For which Criseyde moste out of the town,
> And Troilus shal dwellen forth in pyne
> Til Lachesis his thred no lenger twyne   (V 1–7)

– and halfway through this book it seems as though a conclusion is imminent, for the insertion of formal portraits of Diomede, Criseyde and Troilus (V 799–840) gives the impression that a point of rest has been reached from which the heroine and her two lovers can be definitively surveyed. But she remains poised between them, and the narrative continues for a thousand lines more, lines largely occupied with the painful definition of human unhappiness. Where in this final section the end proper can be said to begin is an almost arbitrary decision, but as good a choice as any is line 1744, immediately after the last speech of any of the characters.

Narrative closure: the end of *Troilus and Criseyde*

The end of *Troilus and Criseyde* is different in kind from that of *The Book of the Duchess* or any of Chaucer's other dream-poems. In a dream-poem, the overall narrative is a first-person account of events stated to have happened to the poet, whether waking or dreaming, and the poet is truly free to shape the end as he chooses, subject only to any real-life occasion to which the poem alludes. (The black knight has to confess that his lady is dead, because Blanche really was.) But the story of *Troilus and Criseyde* is deeply embedded in the supposed history of the Trojan war, and was itself almost certainly regarded as historical by Chaucer and his public. The story was well known, possessing an outline that was fixed and could not be altered. Chaucer's chief source, the *Filostrato*, was unknown to his public at large; and though this was of course a modern work, Chaucer's pretence throughout the poem is that he is a historian (hence his invocation of Clio, the muse of history, in the proem to Book II) who is translating his story 'out of Latyn' (II 14) from authentic classical sources. (Evidently determined to deceive, he names as his chief source the non-existent 'Lollius'.) Chaucer had considerable freedom in matters of detail, and it was certainly possible for him to add elements that were not present in the story as generally known: an obvious example is the ascent of the hero's soul to the heavens after his death. What was not possible was for him to compose an ending which would contradict what was generally known – that Criseyde, separated from Troilus by the exchange of prisoners, succumbed to the attentions of Diomede and never returned to her first lover, and that Troilus died in battle. Not till a century later was Robert Henryson able to escape from the profound medieval reverence for the *auctoritee* of what was 'wreton in parchemeyn' in 'the cronykyls of Rome' or elsewhere, and to invent an alternative ending – and even he had to pretend that he had found 'ane uther quair' than Chaucer's *Troilus* as a written source to justify the changes he made.[26]

The story of *Troilus and Criseyde*, then, had to end in a certain way; but the end of the poem is not the same as the end of the story. Here it may be useful to draw on a distinction which has been implicit in some of the discussion of narratives in earlier chapters but which has been made more explicitly in recent theoretical analyses, that between *histoire* and *discours*. Deriving from the work of E. Benveniste on verb tenses, the distinction has subsequently been widely discussed and applied in various ways. Fundamentally it is a distinction between a sequence of events, real or imaginary (*histoire*), which could in principle be narrated in a variety of different media (film, oral report, novel, even mime or ballet) and in an infinite number of different ways; and any specific discursive presentation of those events (*discours*).[27] *Histoire* is not identical with 'plot', as that term is normally used, since it includes *all* events feigned to have occurred, including inner events such as the characters' thoughts and feelings. Thus in the preceding discussion of how romances end, events such as marriages, coronations, feasts and deaths, and also the characters' responses to such events, belong to the order of *histoire*, while statements that the story is over, that it is chronicled in such and such a place, that the poet has burnt the midnight oil in composing it, and so on, belong to that of *discours*. It must be said at once that in *Troilus and Criseyde* the process of narration is so complex that this theoretically necessary distinction cannot always be sustained in practice. Jonathan Culler has written that

narratological analysis of a text requires one to treat the discourse [i.e. *discours*] as a representation of events [i.e. *histoire*] which are conceived of as independent of any particular narrative perspective or presentation and which are thought of as having the properties of real events.[28]

If this is so, certain parts of *Troilus and Criseyde* present the difficulty that the events of the *histoire* are not always free of a contradiction or indeterminacy not normally postulated of real events. Thus at v 176–89 we have to believe both that Criseyde, almost fainting with grief, did not hear more than a few words of what Diomede said to her and that she heard enough and was alert enough to reply to his words with elaborate courtesy; while at III 1555–82 Chaucer simply declines to tell us what Pandarus does to Criseyde for which she forgives him.[29] Again and again, indeed, Chaucer on the level of the *discours* calls on his readers or listeners to use their own imaginations to resolve indeterminacies and apparent contradictions in the *histoire* and even to share with him in its production. This extraordinarily rich and complex technique of storytelling seems to defy any attempt at total 'narratological analysis'.

It can be said, nevertheless, that the end of the *discours* constituted by *Troilus and Criseyde* as a whole is not the necessary end of the complicated *histoire* of which it is a verbal manifestation. Troilus dies, it is true; but the outcome for Criseyde is unknown, as indeed is the fate of Troilus in the after-life; and the siege of Troy, with which all these events are bound up, remains unsettled. The ending of the *discours* here reveals itself to us as the product of an act of will on the poet's part rather than as the inevitable outcome of the underlying *histoire*. Once Criseyde's betrayal of Troilus has been confirmed beyond any further question, and he has himself come to understand that this is so, he wishes only to die:

> And certeynly, with-outen moore speche,
> From hennes-forth as ferforth as I may,
> Myn owen deth in armes wol I seche,
> I recche nat how soone be the day.   (v 1716–19)

His wish for death is matched by the poet's wish (or perhaps we could say, the wish of the text itself) for conclusion; but Troilus's death cannot itself provide a 'natural' and immediate ending to the *discours*. For one thing, the story has been told in such a way that we have never wanted to believe that Criseyde could betray Troilus or that Troilus could have loved so devotedly a woman who would not be faithful to him; for another, though Chaucer began by announcing that his *purpos* was 'The double sorwe of Troilus to tellen', his poem has in fact been the story of Criseyde as well, and Criseyde has functioned not merely as the object of Troilus's love but as an autonomous subject, a centre of consciousness and value in her own right.[30] Indeed, where Chaucer differs from most medieval courtly poets, and certainly from the writers of earlier versions of this story, is in evoking 'love' not as the individual possession of pleasure or happiness but as *shared* experience, mutuality – a value for which, as we have seen, *Havelok* provides a striking precedent in its celebration of married love. (Chrétien's *Erec* is a comparable example in French.) Criseyde's ultimate *untrouthe* is an offence against mutuality, and Chaucer's compassionate treatment of it has strongly implied that it was committed only because she was alone, physically separated from Troilus; Troilus's heroic *trouthe*, which makes it impossible for him to 'unlove' Criseyde 'a quarter of a day' (v 1698) even when he knows that she has deserted him, is the sustaining of an imaged mutuality even in separation and solitude. This in turn leads to problems of metaphysical scope: Troilus's anguished address to a God 'that oughtest taken heede/ To fortheren trouthe' (v 1706–07) yet who does not intervene to prevent or right the *untrouthe* that has occurred, is the culmination of a strand of philosophical questioning that runs throughout Chaucer's poem and that derives largely from Boethius rather than Boccaccio. Troilus may be a pagan, unable to ascend from God's justice to his mercy, but the Christian God too *is* Truth, 'And trouthe thee shal delivere, it is no drede'.[31] The issues raised by these elements in the body of the poetic *discours* cannot be laid to rest by the hero's death. There is by now an overwhelming desire for conclusion, which leads the poem from the incomplete pagan *histoire* to the completeness of the Christian faith and from Troilus's unloved solitude to the community of those who share the love of God and his mother; but the means of achieving this end can hardly be simple, natural or inevitable.

From line 1744 onwards, the *discours* of *Troilus and Criseyde* does not run smoothly, but is divided into a number of discrete sections, giving the effect of a series of attempts to find a way of ending the work. The storyteller is hastily dismantling the house he has built, setting his material in a variety of different perspectives, until finally he finds the only one which is possible for a medieval Prospero once the charms of his pagan history are all o'erthrown – that of the normal end of the Middle English romance, prayer. I say 'the storyteller', but I should make it clear that I do not find it helpful here, any more than in *The Book of the Duchess* or *The House of Fame*, to think of the *histoire* as narrated by a stable and fully characterized 'persona' clearly distinguishable from the poet. The latter approach has come almost to be taken for granted, especially in American readings of *Troilus and Criseyde*; its chief disadvantages seem to me to be two. First, it simply transfers the notion of organic unity from the tale to the teller: regarding the individual self as a stable and consistent substance, by a strange paradox it applies that view of the self even more rigorously to a subject named in the poem only as 'I' than it does to those shifting and varying selves named 'Troilus', 'Criseyde', 'Pandarus', and so on. And second, its practical consequence has been a whole series of totally subjective readings of the poem, since the only certain thing it tells us about the narrator is that what he says must be something different from what Chaucer means.[32] I shall normally refer to the storyteller of *Troilus and Criseyde*, then, as 'Chaucer' – meaning by that the Chaucer constructed in writing, from whom different readers may well deduce different Chaucers behind the writing.

I shall consider the sections of the ending piece by piece. First comes a single stanza summarizing what has happened, and defining it as what had to happen, something sadly typical of events in this earthly world:

> Gret was the sorwe and pleynte of Troilus;
> But forth hire cours Fortune ay gan to holde.
> Criseyde loveth the sone of Tideus,
> And Troilus moot wepe in cares colde.
> Swich is this world, who-so it kan byholde;
> In ech estat is litel hertes reste;
> God leve us forto take it for the beste.   (1744–50)

This helpless resignation, with its ghost of a prayer for patience, would make one way of ending the poem, though perhaps it might be felt to be intolerably unemphatic, if not banal; but in any case we have not yet heard what came of Troilus's vow, in his final speech, that he would take vengeance on Diomede in battle if he could (1702–5). And so Chaucer returns to the *histoire*:

> In many cruel bataille, out of drede,
> Of Troilus, this ilke noble knyght,
> As men may in thise olde bokes rede,
> Was seen his knyghthod and his grete myght;
> And dredeles, his ire day and nyght
> Ful cruwely the Grekis ay aboughte,
> And alwey moost this Diomede he soughte.
>
> And ofte tyme I fynde that they mette
> With blody strokes and with wordes grete,
> Assayinge how hire speres weren whette;
> And God it woot, with many a cruel hete
> Gan Troilus up-on his helm to bete.
> But natheles, Fortune it naught ne wolde
> Of oothers hond that eyther deyen sholde.   (1751–64)

Here the *histoire*, as recorded in 'thise olde bokes' and thus not to be altered by a medieval poet, fails to supply a possible heroic climax to the poem, in the form of Troilus's triumphing in battle over his rival in love. That climax too would surely be banal, in a poem so little concerned with physical prowess and so much with the quality of human feeling; moreover, the repetitive language of these stanzas, whether deliberately or not, implies the uninterestingness of the whole concept of martial triumph – 'cruel bataille . . . Ful cruwely . . . cruel hete', 'out of drede . . . dredeles', 'knyght . . . knyght-hod', 'grete myght . . . wordes grete'. Fortune, constantly frustrating human purpose, declines to provide a climax that, on reflection, would be an unsatisfying betrayal of the enterprise undertaken in the *discours*.

And Chaucer goes on to remind us and perhaps himself that his original *purpos* had to do not with epic prowess but with love:

> And if I hadde ytaken forto write
> The armes of this ilke worthi man,
> Than wolde ich of his batailles endite;
> But for that I to writen first bigan
> Of his love, I have seyd as I kan –
> Hise worthi dedes, who-so list hem heere,
> Rede Dares, he kan telle hem alle i-feere – (1765–71)

For deeds of valour, if those are what you want, turn to Dares Phrygius, supposed historian of the Trojan war from the Trojan point of view. Here we have something more complicated than the references to chronicles at the end of other romances: Chaucer has referred throughout the poem to his sources and the various difficulties they have given him, but now he is distinguishing one generic form of *discours* from another, and in doing so both foregrounding himself as poet and making us aware of the range of literary choices with which he has been faced.

What follows may seem an almost embarrassing lowering of tension, as, having reminded us of the unalterable *histoire* and of the variety of *discours* in which it might be expressed, he continues downstage, moving out of the fiction to address one part of his audience (or, if you prefer, assigning his audience a certain role within the fiction):

> Bysechyng every lady bright of hewe,
> And every gentil womman, what she be,
> That al be that Criseyde was untrewe,
> That for that gilt she be nat wroth with me:
> Ye may hire gilt in other bokes se,
> And gladlier I wol write, if yow leste,
> Penelopes trouthe and good Alceste.
>
> N'y sey nat this al oonly for thise men,
> But moost for wommen that bitraised be
> Thorugh false folk; God yeve hem sorwe, amen!
> That with hire grete wit and subtilté
> Bytraise yow; and this commeveth me
> To speke, and in effect yow alle I preye,
> Beth war of men, and herkneth what I seye. (1772–85)

Perhaps, with an actual court audience in mind, Chaucer really had to apologize to ladies for writing of an unfaithful heroine (particularly since earlier versions of the story had invariably presented it in antifeminist terms); perhaps this was only a way of finally disentangling himself from the treatment of Criseyde without narrating what happened to her after her *untrouthe*. In any case, the effect within the poem is complex. There are many other versions of the story of Criseyde (and they all represent her as unfaithful, so that Chaucer can scarcely be blamed for that); there are also many other stories about women, and Chaucer professes that he would gladly write of women's *trouthe*. The specific allusion is undoubtedly to *The Legend of Good Women*, his next major work, in the prologue to which he represents himself as being commanded by Alcestis to write a kind of anti-*Troilus*, a collection of stories which would show the sufferings of faithful women betrayed by men. (Penelope is not in fact among them, but then the *Legend* is unfinished.) The playful deference to courtly listeners, and especially to ladies, is a regular part of Chaucer's social style in his courtly poetry; here, while seeming to acknowledge however reluctantly that Criseyde *was* treacherous, it also enables him to hint that she too may have been among the 'wommen that bitraised be' – betrayed, for example, by being exchanged for Antenor (himself a famous male traitor), despite Hector's claim that 'We usen here no wommen forto selle' (IV 182). The lightness of tone in these two stanzas is typically Chaucerian in its reluctance to risk the monotony of 'high seriousness' even on the most sombre occasion; but it also has its specific work to do here, in distancing us from the world of the story and building up around us that other world, more familiar and less threatening, in which the story is being told.

And now Chaucer turns still more emphatically from the past to the present and even to the future, from Trojan history to his book and its fate in the perspective of literary history.

> Go, litel boke, go, litel myn tragedye,
> Ther God thi makere yet, er that he dye,
> So sende myght to make in some comedye;
> But litel book, no makyng thow n'envie,
> But subgit be to alle poyesye,
> And kis the steppes where as thow seest space
> Virgile, Ovide, Omer, Lucan and Stace.

> And for ther is so gret diversité
> In Englissh and in writyng of oure tonge,
> So prey I God that non myswrite the,
> Ne the mysmetre for defaute of tonge.
> And red wher-so thow be or elles songe,
> That thow be understonde, God I biseche,
> But yet to purpos of my rather speche –   (1786–99)

The sense that an end has been reached is strongly given by this presentation of the work as a 'litel boke': no longer a text in course of composition, no longer a mere script for performance, but a poem artistically complete, physically complete too as an object and now detachable from its maker – who is left free perhaps to write other books of the different kind envisaged in the stanza addressed to ladies. Chaucer shows unprecedented boldness, for a medieval English poet, in defining his little book as a *tragedye* (a rare and learned word) and in seeing it as having a place, however humble, in the tradition established by the classical poets. They belong to a pagan past that, throughout the *Troilus*, he has seen in the Renaissance manner as distant yet accessible through stylistic imitation (by contrast with, for example, the complete assimilation of classical mythology to a medieval setting in *Sir Orfeo*). Now, for the very first time, the work of a poet writing in English is envisaged as following in the footsteps of Homer, Virgil, and the others. And Chaucer's book, like theirs, will have a future too: it will go down to posterity, as part of a literary history beyond his control, and he can only pray that it will be correctly transmitted and understood. It is one of the great paradoxes of this new idea of the vernacular text as *poyesye* that, having fixed its form as best he is able, the maker has no choice but to relinquish it to the mercies of future copyists and readers.

The complex of thoughts in these two stanzas, I have argued elsewhere, makes Chaucer, if not what Dryden called him, 'the father of English poetry', at least the originator of the *idea* of English poetry and thus the father of English literary history.[33] But there is also an unspoken connection linking this passage with its context as part of the ending of the poem. Chaucer prays that God may grant the maker of the *Troilus* 'er that he dye' the power to compose a *comedye* to match it. The poet's coming death, glimpsed here, parallels the coming death of Troilus; but it is also bound up with the poem's future life. The condition of the poem's life for future readers or listeners – a life which in one sense will also immortalize the poet, becoming his monument[34] – is precisely that the poet should die; the poem's freedom to go forth into the world of reading and interpretation requires that its maker should no longer be able to control it by his living presence. And Troilus's future life also depends on his present death. The links are not precise or logical, but they are strongly suggestive, working away beneath the surface to give this section of the poem a power to move in excess of its explicit meaning.

The final line of the last stanza and the first of the next acknowl-

edge that Chaucer has been digressing from the story of Troilus, to
which he now returns:

> The wrath as I bigan yow for to seye
> Of Troilus the Grekis boughten deere;
> For thousandes hise hondes maden deye,
> As he that was with-outen any peere,
> Save Ector in his tyme as I kan heere;
> But weilawey, save only Goddes wille,
> Despitously hym slough the fierse Achille.　　(1800–06)

What might have been the culminating event of the *histoire*, the
hero's death, seems almost an afterthought; and it is accompanied by
the last of several reminders in the poem that Troilus was not the
greatest warrior of Troy, but only the second best. This qualifi-
cation of the superlative claims normally made by romances for
their heroes is part of *Troilus and Criseyde*'s 'historical' realism. Here
it adds to the sense of anticlimax, of a rejection of the expected
closural force of the hero's death.

The three stanzas that follow introduce yet another perspective
into this consciously discontinuous ending, and perhaps the most
surprising and even disturbing one of all:

> And whan that he was slayn in this manere,
> His lighte goost ful blisfully is went
> Up to the holughnesse of the eighthe spere,
> In convers letyng everich element;
> And ther he saugh with ful avysement
> The erratik sterres, herkenyng armonye
> With sownes ful of hevenyssh melodie.
>
> And down from thennes faste he gan avyse
> This litel spot of erthe that with the se
> Embraced is, and fully gan despise
> This wrecched world, and held al vanité
> To respect of the pleyn felicité
> That is in hevene above, and at the laste,
> Ther he was slayn his lokyng down he caste.
>
> And in hym self he lough right at the wo
> Of hem that wepten for his deth so faste,
> And dampned al oure werk that foloweth so
> The blynde lust, the which that may nat laste,
> And sholden al oure herte on heven caste;
> And forth he wente, shortly forto telle,
> Ther as Mercurye sorted hym to dwelle.　　(1807–27)

It is well known that there is nothing in the *Filostrato* corresponding
to this account of the journey of Troilus's soul after its release from
his body, but that Chaucer adapted the passage from three stanzas of

Boccaccio's *Teseida*, a poem which he was shortly to use as the chief source of his *Knight's Tale*. The inclusion of this passage in *Troilus and Criseyde*, then, was unmistakeably a deliberate act on Chaucer's part, and the fact that certain manuscripts of the poem lack these stanzas (along with some other philosophical passages not derived from the *Filostrato*) may indicate that their inclusion resulted from choices made in the process of composition.[35] They have no parallel in the concluding sections of other Middle English romances, which never follow their heroes beyond death, and at best risk no more than a vague assurance that they went to heaven:

> They lyved and dyed in gode entente,
> Her sowles I wote to hevenn wente,
>   Whenne they dede ware.   (*Sir Isumbras*)

The affinity of this Chaucerian passage is rather with works of a more learned kind, classical texts such as Lucan's *Pharsalia* and Cicero's *Somnium Scipionis* and modern Italian works by Dante and by Boccaccio himself which drew on classical sources.[36]

The first effect these stanzas convey is perhaps one of liberation (comparable to the book's liberation from its maker). At last Troilus's soul is released from the misery of its earthly existence, a misery that in Book v especially has been evoked as imprisonment: an unbearable constriction of time and space, as the ten days of Criseyde's arranged absence crawl past and finally run out, while Troilus remains confined within the walls of Troy, from which he looks out first in vain hope and then in despair of her return. We can only feel a sense of relief as his soul rises weightlessly through the concentric spheres of the medieval cosmos, until it reaches the eighth and from there looks down on the elements below. There has been much controversy as to what Chaucer meant by 'the eighthe spere', if indeed that was what he wrote: most of the manuscripts read *seventhe*, but Boccaccio has *cielo ottava*, and it is generally taken that *seventhe* is one of those scribal 'miswritings' that Chaucer rightly feared. Arguments can be found for thinking that Chaucer was counting either outwards from, or inwards towards, the lowest sphere, that of the moon; but since in the proem to Book iii he counted outwards to identify Venus's sphere as 'the thridde heven' (iii 2), it is probably safe to assume that he is doing the same here (especially since outwards is the direction in which Troilus's spirit is moving). If this is so, then the eighth sphere is that of the fixed stars – a place where some medieval thinkers, at least, might have expected the souls of dead pagans to be found.[37] The planetary spheres are imagined as the dwellings of the gods whom Troilus, as a pagan, has worshipped; now, from above, he can hear how their separate motions make up a single harmony. And below them, in turn, he sees 'This litel spot of erthe', now small and distant, and he regards it with contempt by contrast with the felicity of heaven.

An imagined view of the smallness of the earth when seen from the heavens is recurrent in Chaucer's work: salient examples are found in his dream-journey through the skies in the claws of an eagle in *The House of Fame*, when 'al the world, as to myn yë, / No more semed than a prikke' (906–7); in Scipio's vision of 'the lytel erthe that here is, / At regard of the hevenes quantité' (57–8) in the *Somnium Scipionis* section of *The Parliament of Fowls*; and in Philosophy's reminder in Chaucer's translation of Boethius's *De consolatione philosophiae* of

. . . the demonstracioun of astronomye, that al the envyrounynge of the erthe aboute ne halt but the resoun of a prykke at regard of the gretnesse of hevene.

(*Boece* II pr. 7, 23–8)

Throughout his work Chaucer shows an unusual gift for imagining what things would look like from a great variety of points of view, and these astronomical thought-experiments are but an extreme case of his relativizing habit of mind – a habit which inevitably has a strong tendency to undermine the claim to absolute validity of any viewpoint, whether of Knight or of Pardoner, of heavenly felicity or of earthly wretchedness. In *Troilus and Criseyde*, the effect is startling, even perhaps shocking: we rise in imagination with extraordinary speed, and then look down vertiginously with Troilus at the very spot where he was killed. He laughs at the grief of those who mourn his death, and condemns all human actions that derive from blind earthly desire; yet the ascent and shift in viewpoint have been too rapid for us to adjust to them, and we are still attached, as the possessive pronouns imply, to '*oure* werk' and '*oure* herte'. Indeed, as one of the poem's finest critics has pointed out, the very subject of the stanza's verbs changes imperceptibly, so that in line 1825 the verb *sholden* requires not Troilus as its subject but *we*.[38] Perspectives clash, and the text clings to what it condemns. A similar doubleness of effect will continue in the stanzas that follow.

Finally, and almost perfunctorily, we are told that Troilus goes wherever Mercury allotted as his dwelling-place. Troilus himself had earlier referred to Mercury as the guide of souls in the other world (v 321–2), and the continuing use of pagan mythology even after his death is striking. Until Mercury leads him away, Troilus has got no further than the sphere of the fixed stars: there is no mention even of the Primum Mobile, which lies beyond that, still less of the empyrean heaven, the dwelling of God and the elect, which surrounds everything else in the medieval Christian cosmos. As it has been throughout Chaucer's evocation of the Trojan world, the frame of reference is still that of Boethius's *De consolatione* – a philosophical paganism, which overlaps to a considerable extent with Christianity, and indeed is never incompatible with it, but does not extend to revealed truth. Thus when Troilus looks down, he sees what a pagan might be imagined to see at the moment of his death. (It is what the pagan Scipio had seen in a vision during his life.) He can recognize how trivial earthly concerns are, and that men should turn their hearts to heaven rather than earth, but his laughter is harsh and callous, and his vision is, 'in a theological sense, graceless', a cold vision of an earth unredeemed by God's love.[39] We are not told what the final destination of Troilus's soul is, because the question whether a virtuous pagan could achieve salvation was highly controversial in Chaucer's time. We are left free to believe, if we wish, that Troilus's dedication to *trouthe* has earned him a place in heaven despite his ignorance of the Christian revelation; but Chaucer does not commit himself to this or any other view of the matter.

With this uncertainty the *histoire* is concluded, but the *discours* still continues, and in the next stanza Chaucer makes a fresh attempt at ending, returning to the *Filostrato* as his source and repeating again and again the word *fyn* (end):

> Swich fyn hath, lo, this Troilus for love,
> Swich fyn hath al his grete worthynesse;
> Swich fyn hath his estat real above,
> Swich fyn his lust, swich fyn hath his noblesse;
> Swich fyn hath false worldes brotelnesse:
> And thus bigan his lovyng of Criseyde,
> As I have told, and in this wise he deyde.   (1828–34)

Taken out of context this stanza would be readily recognizable as corresponding to closural gestures common in romances, summing up events from the standpoint of the hero's death –

> Thus ended syr Isumbras,
> That an hardy knyghte was,
>   In sorowe allthowgh he wore

Narrative closure: the end of *Troilus and Criseyde*

– and perhaps using that death to point a moral lesson:

> Forthy schulde men and women als
> Them bethynke or they be false,
>   Hyt makyth so fowle an ende.   (*Le Bone Florence*)

Chaucer's stanza (with the help of Boccaccio's fourfold repetition of 'cotal fine ebbe') would appear only to give a more elevated rhetorical scaffolding to such familiar devices. In context, however, the effect is more complicated. We cannot help recognizing a continuity in thought and feeling between the previous stanza and this. It is as though the poet has been provoked into the uncompromising moral sternness of his comments by the example of Troilus as he looks down from above: hence the mere rejection of 'false worldes brotelnesse', harshly denunciatory in those clanging repetitions of 'Swich fyn . . .'. But Chaucer is not really 'above' human life as Troilus is after his death, and his abandonment of the 'Swich fyn . . .' pattern in the closing couplet of this stanza prepares the way for two more stanzas in which there is a complete change of tone, from rejection to pleading and from harshness to tenderness:

> O yonge, fresshe folkes, he or she,
> In which that love up groweth with youre age,
> Repeyreth hom fro worldly vanyté,
> And of youre herte up casteth the visage
> To thilke God that after his ymage
> Yow made, and thynketh al nys but a faire
> This world that passeth soone as floures faire.
>
> And loveth hym the which that right for love
> Upon a crois oure soules forto beye,
> First starf and roos and sit in hevene above;
> For he nyl falsen no wight, dar I seye,
> That wol his herte al holly on hym leye.
> And syn he best to love is and most meke,
> What nedeth feynede loves forto seke?   (1835–48)

Where Boccaccio had followed the antifeminist tradition by addressing young men and warning them against the fickleness of women, Chaucer addresses 'yonge, fresshe folkes, *he or she*'; he warns against all worldly vanity, and does not now reject love (as he seemed to in line 1828), but argues that it should find a proper object – God, who made men and women in his own image, took on human flesh and died for love of them, and will betray no one who loves him. Chaucer, then, supplies what Troilus, who died a pagan, could not: the idea of a loving God who redeems 'This wrecched

131

world'. The language used by Chaucer emphasizes, as it so often has done throughout the poem, the *naturalness* of earth's beauty and of human love: he refers to 'fresh' young people, in whom love 'grows' as they reach maturity, and he sees the world not just as a *faire*, a market-place, but as something beautiful that fades like flowers. (The *rime riche* on *faire* in its two senses is strikingly effective in linking the two ideas together.) The flowers fade, and so do men and women, but they *are* beautiful, and they were made so by the God who created them. And now, in the light of this emergent tenderness, we can look back and recognize touches of tenderness alongside and within the harshness of what precedes – 'This litel spot of erthe' (*litel* suggesting affection as well as contempt) that is *embraced* by the sea like a lover; or the modulation in the 'Swich fyn . . .' stanza from grand homiletic denunciation to the sad simplicity of

> And thus bigan his lovyng of Criseyde,
> As I have told, and in this wise he deyde.[40]

The attitude conveyed by the end of the poem is not single or simple: a variety of different attitudes are interwoven, some implying utter rejection of the story of pagan love, but others forming a continuation or development of the warm sympathy for both the lovers that characterized the earlier parts of the poem.

Thus the next stanza too begins with denunciation and with rhetorical repetition, offering the story as a demonstration of the folly of paganism:

> Lo here, of payens corsed olde rites,
> Lo here, what alle hire goddes may availle;
> Lo here, thise wrecched worldes appetites;
> Lo here, the fyn and guerdoun for travaille
> Of Jove, Appollo, of Mars, of swich rascaille;
> Lo here, the forme of olde clerkis speche
> In poetrie, if ye hire bokes seche.   (1849–55)

Yet by the time the last 'Lo here . . .' is reached, the effect has subtly shifted once again. Those 'olde clerkis' are not rejected like the 'olde rites'. (The word *olde* is itself the site of violent conflict within medieval culture between reverence and contempt.) They are revered, and their antique mythology has become not cursed error but *poetrie* – a term of high praise, like *poyesye* in line 1790, implying literature of classical dignity and beauty.

The poem's penultimate stanza defines it once more as a book relinquished by its maker, and at the same time looks outwards again towards its audience, but with a specificity unknown in other English romances. It dedicates the book not to ladies or to lovers but to a scholarly poet and to a scholar whose interest in its philosophical theme of predestination and free-will is recorded. The book is modestly offered for correction; but this implies at least that it merits a level of scholarly attention to which no Thomas Chestre or *Havelok*-poet would have dreamed of laying claim. Not for nothing was the author of *Troilus and Criseyde* referred to by Thomas Usk, within a year or two of its completion, as 'the noble philosophical poet in English'.

> O moral Gower, this book I directe
> To the, and to the, philosophical Strode,
> To vouchen-sauf, ther nede is, to correcte,
> Of youre benignités and zeles goode;
> And to that sothfast Crist that starf on rode,
> With al myn herte of mercy evere I preye,
> And to the Lord right thus I speke and seye: (1856–62)

But from these ideal human readers Chaucer turns to God, and the poem ends after all, like any other romance, with a prayer that links poet and audience in a single *us*:

> Thow oon, and two, and thre, eterne on lyve,
> That regnest ay in thre, and two, and oon,
> Uncircumscript, and al maist circumscrive,
> Us from visible and in-visible foon
> Defende, and to thy mercye, everichon,
> So make us, Ihesus, for thi mercy digne,
> For love of mayde and moder thyn benigne.   Amen. (1863–9)

'Like any other romance'; yet, as it passes through the familiar Christian formulas and paradoxes, this prayer confers on them a Latinate grandeur of style borrowed from Dante[41] and unknown to any earlier English romance-writer; on the other hand, it concludes simply and appropriately with a love that is both human and divine – Jesus's love for his mother. It is a superb ending for a poem of human love; yet it would not be possible to give an adequate reading of the whole sequence of the poem in the single perspective of its final stanza. Chaucer, as Usk knew, was a philosophical poet, and *Troilus and Criseyde* is a philosophical poem, but we certainly distort and impoverish it if we attempt to reduce it to a philosophical system or to extract a philosophy from it. It works as poetry, and poetry has the advantage over philosophy of being able to say different things, and even contradictory things, at the same time. Or at least the advantage of being able to admit that that is what it does.

6 · Alliterative poetry

The remainder of this book is concerned with alliterative poetry. Chapters 7, 8 and 9 will consider aspects of the work of the two major poets, William Langland and the anonymous *Gawain*-poet, who are the authors of the only Middle English alliterative verse at all likely to be known to modern readers other than academic specialists. Yet in their time these two were by no means isolated figures; there is a large body of alliterative poetry, over 40,000 lines in all, from the fourteenth and early fifteenth centuries, much of it of impressive merit. It includes works of many different kinds, but romances (ranging over the whole spectrum from fantastic to historical) and allegorical visions are especially prominent. The history of English alliterative poetry remains a subject of scholarly controversy;[1] but, superficially at least, it appears that about 1340, for unknown reasons, there was a revival of writing in a verse-form which can be traced back to nearly a thousand years earlier and which had flourished at a high level of artistry in the Anglo-Saxon period; by the early sixteenth century, however, the writing of unrhymed alliterative verse came to a complete halt, never to start again. It is misleading, though, to project back into the later Middle Ages the perspective of subsequent literary history, and to assume that, around 1400, it must have been obvious that alliterative verse belonged to the past and that the future would be dominated by the tradition newly established by Chaucer. If there was an 'Alliterative Revival' in the second half of the fourteenth century, it was only part of a revival of English poetry in general, and though it may have involved the transmission into the present of a style and attitudes that had their roots in a distant heroic past, there is no reason to suppose that it was seen as having no future. By the second half of the fourteenth century, for reasons too complex to analyse here, there existed both the ambition to produce major literature in English and the possibility of fulfilling it – to create writing that would transcend the traditional use of the vernacular to provide instruction and entertainment, and would aim to go down to posterity and even, as Chaucer hopes for his *Troilus*, to 'kis the steppes where as thow seest space/ Virgile, Ovide, Omer, Lucan and Stace' (v 1791–2).

To consider for the moment only the question of technique, what poetic form might have seemed suitable for the fulfilment of this ambition? The form best established for English narrative was borrowed from French – the octosyllabic couplet, as we have seen it in *Havelok* and *Sir Orfeo* and in Chaucer's earliest works, *The Book of the Duchess* and *The House of Fame*. This had a major disadvantage (one shared equally by the most common new narrative form of Chaucer's time, the tailrhyme stanza): its lines were too short and they required too frequent rhyme. Because by the fourteenth century the language had lost nearly all its inflections, rhymes in English were far harder to find than in French or Italian; indeed, Chaucer himself comments on this in the envoy of a poem adopted from three ballades by his French contemporary Oton de Graunson. He apologizes for his incompetent writing; old age, he says, has dulled his skill,

> And eke to me it ys a gret penaunce,
> Syth rym in Englissh hath such skarseté,
> To folowe word by word the curiosité
> Of Graunson, flour of hem that make in Fraunce.
>
> (*Complaint of Venus* 79–82)

The modesty is conventional, but there is no reason to suppose the excuse groundless. Chaucer's solution was to introduce into English a longer line, with five stresses instead of four, so that rhyme would be required less frequently and there would be less need of the constant resort to tags and fillers that we find in octosyllabic couplets and tailrhyme stanzas. But this did not happen until the 1380s; about the mid-century, the only English poetic form which overcame the difficulties about line length and frequency of rhyme was alliterative verse. Relying on alliteration rather than end-rhyme, it avoided the problem of scarcity of rhymes, and its lines could be long enough to provide room for stylistic manoeuvre. It was a medieval equivalent to the blank verse of the Elizabethans. Moreover, the English language was full of ready-made alliterative phrases, and the basic unit of alliterative verse – the two-stress phrase – was probably a basic unit of the language itself. To compose alliterative verse in English, at a level of mere competence, was (and indeed still is) comparatively easy; at the same time, it was a form capable of extreme stylistic intricacy and elevation. We do not know which poet or poets had the idea in the 1340s of reviving alliterative verse as the vehicle for vernacular writing of a relatively learned and sophisticated kind; but once the first step had been taken it must quickly have come to possess a strong appeal for ambitious and serious writers. The process was probably aided by William Langland's choice of alliterative verse for *Piers Plowman*, one of the most widely circulated English poems of the fourteenth century. Around, say, 1370 – after the A-text of *Piers Plowman* had begun to circulate, but long before the Chaucerian revolution that has changed our whole conception of English poetic history – alliterative verse may well have seemed the natural choice for an English writer who hoped to do something more serious than produce yet more popular romances, especially if he was not, like Chaucer's Parson, 'a Southren man' (*Parson's Prologue* x 42). After all, outside the works of Chaucer and Gower, virtually all major poems of any length in later Middle English are alliterative – *Piers Plowman* itself, the poems of the *Gawain*-manuscript, *Saint Erkenwald*, the *Morte Arthure*, *Winner and Waster*, *The Wars of Alexander*, *The Destruction of Troy*, *The Siege of Jerusalem*, and many others. This group of poems represents the first attempt since the Anglo-Saxon period to create for the English language an authentic literary style and dignity. Except for *Piers Plowman*, they do not seem to have been widely read; most of the others survive in only a single manuscript. Their difficulty of language and style may have made them caviare to the general in their own time; and certainly, since then, as their language has become still more dauntingly unfamiliar, they have found few readers.

My aim in the present chapter is to consider what can profitably be looked for in a reading of Middle English alliterative poetry, and that for two main reasons. I should like to regain attention for some poems that seem to me to be of real value and interest, and to that end, after some account of the general nature of alliterative poetry, I shall focus on two specific poems. These are the *Morte Arthure*, which has been the subject of a fair amount of scholarly discussion, including two books, but which seems to me to have been often misunderstood; and *The Siege of Jerusalem*, a poem surviving in eight manuscripts, and therefore presumably read comparatively widely in the Middle Ages, but one which has scarcely been discussed at all by modern scholars. My claim is not that these poems are masterpieces comparable with *Piers Plowman* or *Sir Gawain and the Green Knight*, but that they are interesting enough to deserve attention of a higher quality than they have often received. My second reason is that the poems of the 'Alliterative Revival' form a body of writing with much in common, and it will therefore be useful in our reading of Langland and the *Gawain*-poet to be able to see their work in the context of the more general capacities and achievements of alliterative poetry. This is not to imply that *Piers Plowman* or the *Gawain*-poet's works will be or ought to be considered solely as alliterative poems; but they are poems written by poets, and presumably for audiences, who knew other alliterative poetry and were capable of judging it by the appropriate criteria.

I want first to say something about the general nature of Middle English alliterative style. Individual poets may introduce their own modifications, but the whole body of alliterative poetry is strongly homogeneous in style, and it is against this homogeneity that individual modifications must have been designed to have their effect. First then it must be said that alliterative poetry is highly formulaic. In a loose sense, as we have seen, this is true of earlier medieval poetry in general, in works as different as the *Chanson de Roland* and *Sir Orfeo*. Medieval poets do not generally aim at stylistic originality, but are content to draw on a large body of existing ready-made phrases, which they aim to deploy as effectively as possible. In alliterative verse this formulaic quality is more prominent, because the half-line phrase which is the basic metrical unit is often itself a complete formula or member of a formulaic system. Thus in the *Morte Arthure* we find the following phrase repeated with trivial variation as the first half of several lines:[2]

And with his burlyche brande	(1111)
With a burlyche brannde	(2239)
With his burlyche brande	(2252)

And the following second half-lines clearly belong to a system in which a fixed syntactical frame (conjunction/preposition + possessive pronoun + adjective + noun) has a certain semantic stability (adjective = *bryghte*, noun = item[s] of military equipment) but otherwise allows for considerable variation:

and his bryghte wapen	(1193)
for hys bryghte wedes	(1349)
with theire bryghte swerdez	(1414)

The precise definition of the poetic formula remains a matter of difficulty: if its semantic element is over-emphasized, it becomes indistinguishable from 'loose collocational word groups' which may be spread over several lines, while if its 'grammetrical' (i.e. syntactical + metrical) element is over-emphasized it tends to dissolve into the formulaic quality of language itself.[3] But for our purposes exact definition is unnecessary; what is important is the constant repetition or near-repetition of phraseology, often in identical metrical positions, which marks Middle English alliterative poetry, and which does not in itself indicate either carelessness or common authorship.

This body of poetry is also marked by a distinctive vocabulary, some of which survived for many centuries, and which must have originated as an aid to the composition of alliterative verse in a period when its makers were unlettered, so that not only delivery but also composition was oral. Many of the commonest ideas (man/warrior, sword, horse, go, noble, quickly, violently, and many others) can be represented by several different words, which differ only negligibly in meaning but which begin with different sounds so that they can be used in various alliterative contexts. Many such words are found only, or most commonly, in alliterative verse, and, in verse, are nearly always used in the stressed, alliterating positions. Again, alliterative verse even has distinctive syntactical features: it tends to omit conjunctions and other connectives and also the pronoun–subjects of verbs, thus creating a terse, paratactic effect; its syntax is fluid in the sense that a noun or pronoun which is the object of one verb may then be the subject of the next; it frequently allows adjectives to stand by themselves and function as nouns.

The overall effect of these features of language is somewhat paradoxical. On the one hand, the syntax of alliterative verse is likely to have been close to that of everyday speech, with its omissions and ellipses; and this colloquial quality would be reinforced by the fact that the half-line metrical unit is a phrase with no fixed number of syllables, so that there would not normally be any tension between verse metre and speech rhythm. It may well be that one reason why alliterative verse survived for so long, even through centuries (such as the period c. 1240 to c. 1340) in which there is little evidence of its having been written down, was that it was so closely related to English speech. On the other hand, its traditional poetic diction and some of its other stylistic features may have distanced it from everyday life and language, and given it a heightened and even archaic air. Certainly it was capable of extra-ordinary elaboration and elevation, and it is difficult to believe that most of the poems of the fourteenth-century revival (with the exception of *Piers Plowman*, which lacks some of the traditional stylistic features) can have appealed to any but specialized audiences of connoisseurs.

I turn now to some other effects of style that late-medieval alliterative poems have in common; their flavour is so strong, yet so difficult to define exactly, that I would be tempted to call them qualities of imagination if that term did not imply that they were the product of individual poets rather than of a body of workers within a single tradition. First, then, one consequence of the very nature of alliterative verse, which calls for the repetition of the same initial sound three or more times within each line, is that sound–effects are more important than they are in metrical verse. This 'auditory foregrounding' most readily comes to the reader's awareness as onomatopoeia. Alliterative poems are full of battle scenes in which violent action and the accompanying noise appear to be conveyed directly through sound:

> Schaftes schedred wer sone and scheldes ythrelled,
> And many schalke thurghe schotte with the scharpe ende,
> Brunyes and bright wede blody by-runne,
> And many segge at that saute soughte to the grounde.
> Hacchen upon hard steel with an herty wylle,
> That fur out flowe as of flynt stonys;
> Of the helme and the hed hewen at-tonys,
> The stompe under stede feet in the steel leveth.
>
> (*Siege of Jerusalem* 1117–24)[4]

But equally the noise in which alliterative poets delight may be of many other kinds, whether that of female lamentation –

> Than cho yermys and yeyes at Yorke in hir chambire,
> Gronys full grysely with gretand teres   (*Morte Arthure* 3911–12)

– or that of whistling and chattering birds:

> Fore thare galede the gowke one grevez full lowde:
> Wyth alkyn gladchipe thay gladden them selven;
> Of the nyghtgale notez the noisez was swette –
> They threpide wyth the throstills, thre hundreth at ones.
>
> (*Morte Arthure* 927–30)

In almost every such case it would be unwise to claim more than that the sound supports the sense; a listener who did not understand the words would be most unlikely to guess what the subject matter was from the sound alone. What is undeniable, I think, is the prominence of the sound, which prevents the effect from being that of verbal transparency such as we found in *King Horn*. In alliterative verse we are almost always kept aware of the verbal texture and of the skill of the poet who is producing it.

And in general the alliterative poets are proud to display their skill, whether through sound effects or by other means. A straightforward example is this passage from *The Siege of Jerusalem* in which Nathan gives a list of Jesus's twelve apostles for the benefit of Titus:

> . . . this wer her names:
> Peter, James and Jon, and Jacob the ferthe,
> And the fifthe of his felawys Phelip was hoten,
> The sixte Symond was caled, and the seveth eke
> Bertholomewe, that his bone never breke nolde;
> The eyght man was Mathu, that is myche yloved,
> Taddé and Tomas; her ben ten even,
> And Andreu the elleveth, that auntred hym myche
> Byfor princes to preche, was Petrus brother.
> The laste man was unlele and luther of his dedis,
> Judas, that Jesu Crist to the Jewes solde. (140–50)

We saw how in *Havelok* catalogues were transformed into art by means of simple verbal patterns, but here the ingenuity involved is considerably greater. It is not a richly ornamented passage, but a long list of names is turned into technically perfect alliterative verse, in which no single line exactly repeats the alliterative sound or the rhythmic or syntactical pattern of any other, still less its precise words; and the entire list has a dramatic structure, holding back the one traitor till last and then further holding back the mention of his actual name with a complete line of description – the only instance of this in the whole list. This is at least craftsmanship of a high order, not ostentatious but on the other hand not ignorable or intending to be ignored. It can also happen, however, that an alliterative poet will go to excess in his display of verbal skill. One habit of the *Morte Arthure* poet is to continue alliteration on a single sound for several lines at a stretch, especially at moments of excitement in his narrative. In such cases the auditory foregrounding can become so insistent as to seem grotesque and even vulgar, especially if the alliteration is based not on a single consonant but on a pair of consonants. Thus:

> Swyftly with swerdes they swappen thereaftyre,
> Swappez doun full sweperlye swelltande knyghtez,
> That all swelltes one swarthe that they overswyngen;
> So many sweys in swoghe, swounande att ones.   (1464-7)

In context this is only the first of four such alliterative 'quatrains'. No doubt such ostentatious virtuosity appealed to late-medieval taste, but neither Langland nor the *Gawain*-poet ever indulges in comparable displays.

Another general quality of the alliterative style is its tendency towards specificity and concreteness. This may have its origins in the very need to provide alliteration: a large vocabulary is required, and this is partly provided by systems of synonyms, but it also leads to the mention of many specific things and specifying epithets. The poets drew on the technical terminology of areas of medieval life such as hunting, seamanship, armour, and so on, in their search for a wider lexical range; sometimes they used such terms in their precise technical senses, sometimes they employed them (as they would presumably not have done in speech) in substitution for more general terms. The *Morte Arthure* poet, at one point, embarking on a splendid description of a sea battle, explicitly alludes to the former phenomenon:

> Thane the marynerse mellys and maysters of chippis;
> Merily iche a mate menys till other:
> Of theire termys they talke, how thay ware tydd,
> Towyn trussell one trete, trussen upe sailes,
> Bet bonettez one brede, bettrede hatches,
> Brawndeste brown stele, braggede in trompes,
> Standis styffe one the stamyn, steris one aftyre,
> Strekyn over the streme thare stryvynge begynnes.   (3652-9)

The *termys* attributed to the mariners, masters and mates (the last itself virtually a technical term) include words such as *trussell* (furled sail), *bonettez* (small extra sails) and *stamyn* (prow), all belonging to the professional language of seamanship and all used in these lines to carry alliteration. Their use, though, is not only a matter of convenience; we have a sense of the poet's delight in the riches of the vocabulary at his command, that may remind us of the phrase used by the *Beowulf* poet some six centuries earlier to describe an eloquent speaker beginning his delivery – *wordhord onleac*, 'he unlocked his treasury of words'.[5] Among many cases of the use of specific for general terms might be mentioned the common substitution of *linde* (literally lime-tree) for 'tree', or of *mere* or *fole* (literally mare or foal) for 'horse', or the application of specific titles of rank (prince, princess, duke, and so on) to any nobleman or noblewoman.

An important concomitant of this pervasive specificity of the alliterative style is the effect of concreteness. The poet's 'treasury of words' may be pleasing in itself, especially for its auditory qualities, but the words also refer outwards to a world of things and their effects on the human senses. The alliterative poet often possesses what I referred to in discussing *Havelok* as a 'firm grasp on the material world', but he goes further than to devise lists which 'simply name a series of objects'.[6] He imagines the components of his fictional world in relation to human sensory experience. Thus, to take an example from the *Morte Arthure*, when the Roman ambassadors, having angered Arthur by their demand for tribute, are hurrying through England to get to the port before their safeconducts expire, they finally approach the coast, and we are told that

> Of all the glee undire Gode so glade ware they nevere,
> As of the sounde of the see and Sandwyche belles.   (489–90)

The details specifying what the ambassadors hear, given significance by their fear and longing to escape, admirably evoke the whole scene as experience (and of course without the aid of onomatopoeia). Or again, when Arthur with difficulty clambers up Mont-Saint-Michel in search of the lair of a giant, the same poet writes (in some lines from the passage discussed in Chapter 1),

> The Kyng coveris the cragge wyth cloughes full hye,
> To the creste of the clyffe he clymbez on lofte;
> Keste upe hys umbrer and kenly he lukes,
> Caughte of the colde wynde to comforthe hym selven.
> Two fyrez he fyndez, flawmande full hye . . .   (941–5)

The labouring rhythm of the first two lines effectively supports the sense of muscular effort, while the comfort the king takes from the cool breeze further evokes the strain involved in doing such a climb in full armour; and then the cold wind contrasts with the fires, and at the same time explains why their flames are so visible. Passages like these demonstrate how in alliterative poems the sensory world may be evoked not as a flat list or tapestry, but as a three-dimensional solid, experienced from a specific point of view. At its best, alliterative poetry leads us into fictive space, enabling us to move through it with a particular character or group of characters and thus realize for ourselves its depth and its appeal to all the senses.

This poetic style is strongly evaluative as well as concrete. Again, this quality may well be a by-product of the demands of alliteration itself: nouns are often accompanied by alliterating adjectives, verbs by alliterating adverbs, and these qualifying terms tend to demand our participation as we respond to them. Another passage from the *Morte Arthure* will illustrate this aspect of the style. It describes a single combat between Sir Gawain and the stranger knight Sir Priamus:

> Than theire launces they lachen, thes lordlyche byernez,
> Laggen with longe speres one lyarde stedes,
> Cowpen at awntere be kraftes of armes,
> Till bothe the crowell speres brousten att ones.
> Thorowe scheldys they schotte and scherde thorowe mayles,
> Bothe shere thorowe schoulders a schaftmonde large.
> Thus worthylye thes wyes wondede ere bothen –
> Or they wreke them of wrethe awaye will they never.
> Than they raughte in the reyne and agayne rydes,
> Redely theis rathe mene rusches owtte swerdez,
> Hittes one hellmes full hertelyche dynttys,
> Hewes appon hawberkes with full harde wapyns;
> Full stowttly they stryke, thire steryn knyghttes,
> Stokes at the stomake with stelyn poyntes,
> Feghtten and floresche withe flawmande swerdez,
> Till the flawes of fyre flawmes one theire helmes.   (2541–56)

Here adjectives and adverbs frequently bear the alliteration and at the same time go beyond description to demand assent to and emotional participation in judgments of worth and intensity: *lordlyche, longe, crowell, large, worthylye, redely, rathe, full hertelyche, full harde, full stowttly*. The poet's own participation is conveyed especially in line 2548, where he pushes the normal use of the historic present a little further, and enters into the scene so fully as to forecast what will (or rather will not) happen in the future. If we respond at all, we must do so with commitment, and be morally and emotionally engaged in the fictive events. The most sophisticated of alliterative poets – the *Gawain*-poet – can turn this style against itself, by making us wonder occasionally about the appropriateness of the terms of approval or disapproval, making us suspect that they may be merely automatic, not relevant to the specific context in which they are used: are Arthur's courtiers as they celebrate Christmas and New Year really 'so hardy a here on hille' (59), and does Gawain really have the right to call himself 'gode Gawayn' (2214) as he tremulously calls out his challenge at the Green Chapel? But most alliterative poets manifestly share, and demand that we should share, this commitment to the sensations and emotions of their characters.

No more than the transparency of *King Horn* should the concreteness of alliterative poetry be confused with realism. The 'density of specification' characteristic of alliterative style may certainly be used to create an illusory reality existing in all dimensions and appealing to all the senses; but if so, this is a reflection of the imaginative power and skill of the individual poet. In an account of landscape description in alliterative poetry, Derek Pearsall and Elizabeth Salter note its 'arbitrary concreteness of reference' and its technique 'of piling up detail, not of articulation'. For example, there is a passage in a dream-allegory, *The Parliament of the Three Ages*, where the poet, stalking a deer, says that he 'crepite to a crabtre and coverede me ther-undere', and on this they comment:

There is no reason in the nature of things why it should be a "crabtre", and no rhetorical advantage, nothing in fact beyond the exigencies of alliteration.[7]

A similar point might be made about many passages in the *Morte Arthure*, including the one quoted above to illustrate the alliterative poet's pleasure in bird-noises: cuckoos, nightingales and thrushes (and earlier falcons and pheasants) are likely to have been specified not because of the poet's sensitivity to the natural world but because they provide alliteration. On the other hand, in this case the specific details do fit together to create a scene possible in reality; and this is not infrequently so in the *Morte*.

I now pass from the style of alliterative poetry to its characteristic tone and scope. No generalization about the whole of such a large body of verse would be likely to be true, but it can at least be said, I think, that much alliterative poetry is serious, historical and heroic in quality. A heavy-handed humour is not uncommon, and Langland and the *Gawain*-poet possess respectively a biting and a sly and delicate wit; but the characteristic tone of alliterative poetry, in keeping with the commitment mentioned above, is serious and even solemn. The *Morte Arthure* begins with a prayer in which the poet begs that God will make his words 'nothyre voyde . . . ne vayne, bot wyrchip till Him selvyn,/ Plesande and profitabill to the popule

that them heres' (10–11). He goes on to insist on the historical worth
of his story:

> Ye that liste has to lyth or luffes for to here
> Off elders of alde tym and of theire awke dedys,
> How they were lele in theire lawe and lovede God Almyghty,
> Herkynes me heyndly and holdys yow styll,
> And I sall tell yow a tale that trewe es and nobyll,
> Off the ryeall renkys of the Rownnde Table . . .   (12–17)

The tale is true as well as noble; and there is every reason to believe
that most fourteenth-century writers (Chaucer is a notable excep-
tion) thought of the Arthurian legend as belonging to history. This
is especially likely to have been the case with the story told in the
Morte Arthure, of Arthur's struggle against the Roman Emperor to
reclaim control of continental Europe, and of the end of the Round
Table through Mordred's treachery. But the tale's 'truth' is not
simply a matter of its supposed correspondence to recorded fact, to
the written documents, the *rollez* and *cronicles* (112, 274) mentioned
in the poem itself as the basis for territorial claims. Judged by the
standards of modern historiography, the subject matter of nearly all
the supposedly historical alliterative poems is mere fiction. Yet they
retain a historical truth which is a matter of their serious interest in
the real concerns of history as it has traditionally been conceived and
recorded – public affairs, statecraft, political power and responsi-
bility, the whole realm of life which in most medieval courtly
romances is secondary to personal relationships, feelings and values.
For all the elements of fantasy in some poems – green knights or
child-devouring giants – it may be said that the typical alliterative
'romance' bears a closer resemblance in subject matter and attitude
to the *Chanson de Roland* than to *Troilus and Criseyde*.[8]

This means that the alliterative romance is essentially a masculine
work: its chief characters are men, women when they appear are
rarely regarded empathetically, and its concerns are those tradi-
tionally regarded as masculine – power, violence, justice, law. As in
most medieval literature (Chaucer is again an exception) these
things are set in a fictive past which is imagined in terms of the
present; and this serves only to intensify the profitableness 'to the
popule that them heres'. Siege warfare, the real focus of the struggle
for power in medieval Europe from the period after the First
Crusade until gunpowder gave the offensive the upper hand over
the defensive, is a central theme of both the *Morte Arthure* and

(naturally enough) *The Siege of Jerusalem*. Both poems are much interested in the military technology of the age in which they were written: *Morte Arthure* also shows detailed knowledge of diplomacy and of the law and logistics of international warfare, so much so that it has been suggested that its author might have been an official actually concerned with the organization of the Hundred Years' War, a man from 'the higher echelons of the royal administration'.[9] And the issues raised belong to this highly practical field – the proper balance between ruthlessness and mercy, between rashness and caution, between pride and cunning. Above all, these two poems and most other alliterative poetry are heroic in ethos, driven forward by an admiration for physical courage and prowess whether displayed in single combat or in massed battle, and showing men as motivated by concern for their reputation among other men. The 'ryeall renkys of the Rownnde Table', the *Morte Arthure* poet goes on,

> . . . chefe ware of chevalrye and cheftans nobyll,
> Bath ware in thire werkes and wyse men of armes,
> Doughty in theire doyngs and dredde ay schame,
> Kynde men and courtays and couthe of courte thewes;
> How they whanne wyth were wyrchippis many . . .   (18–22)

These knights, it is true, are courtiers as well as fighters; so are the 'Romans' of *The Siege of Jerusalem*, who, after a hard day's fighting, avoid all outward show of *wo* or *deil* and give themselves up to that joy that is a key value in medieval courtliness:

> Suth evereche a segge to the soper yede;
> Thogh they wounded wer, was no wo nempned
> Bot daunsyng and no deil, with dynnyng of pipis
> And the nakerer noyse alle the nyght-tyme.   (849–52)

(And, characteristically for an alliterative poet, the joy is imagined in auditory terms.) But the pursuit of honour (*wyrchippis*) and above all the fear of shame, which holds together the band of warriors even under extreme odds, and which we saw taken for granted in the *Chanson de Roland*, is the ultimate sanction that overcomes fear and commands heroic conduct. It has its roots deep in the past, but it is still operative, even in our own century, in the subculture of the military unit. A modern military historian has written:

Whenever one surveys the forces of the battlefield, it is to see that fear is general among men, but to observe further that men are commonly loath that their fear will be expressed in specific acts which their comrades will recognize as cowardice . . . When a soldier is . . . known to the men who are around him, he . . . has reason to fear losing the one thing that he is likely to value more highly than life – his reputation as a man among other men.[10]

This is an American general writing about the conscript army of a democratic state; what he says was doubtless even truer of the consciously solidary caste of warrior-aristocrats celebrated in the *Morte Arthure* and *The Siege of Jerusalem*.

One of the most acute critics of medieval English literature, John Burrow, has seen its period of greatest flourishing, the second half of the fourteenth century, as characterized by an 'unheroic temper'. '"Heroes" in the old manner are absent' from the poetry of this age, he claims, to such an extent that in the end the reader 'hungers for grandeur of thought, unguarded intensity of feeling, and sublimity of expression. He wants "earnest", for once, *without* "game".'[11] What Burrow writes is perhaps true of Chaucer and Gower, and, among alliterative poets, of the *Gawain*-poet; but it is surely not true of alliterative poetry generally. The *Gawain*-poet persistently gives an ironic and, as it were, Chaucerian turn to the alliterative style, thus questioning and sometimes undermining the heroic temper that normally characterizes it; but *Piers Plowman*, which Burrow specifically includes within his generalization, would be a far lesser achievement than it is had it not drawn on the heroic courage even in apparent defeat that belongs to the alliterative tradition and translated it from the physical to the spiritual sphere. To the poetic sphere too; for the lifetime spent writing and rewriting the poem in its several versions also shows a heroic determination and an equally heroic willingness to risk all in the hope of gaining the one thing that matters:

> Ac yut, I hope, as he that ofte hath ychaffared
> And ay loste and loste, and at the laste hym happed
> A bouhte suche a bargayn he was the bet evere,
> And sette al his los at a leef at the laste ende,
> Suche a wynnyng hym warth thorw wordes of grace, . . .
> So hope y to have of Hym that is almyghty
> A gobet of his grace, and bigynne a tyme
> That alle tymes of my tyme to profit shal turne.   (C v 94–101)[12]

It is within the alliterative tradition that this heroism, this earnest commitment entirely free from game, survives with greatest poetic strength amidst the subtle ironies and ambiguities of the sophisticated Plantagenet age.

Morte Arthure

Having generalized as much as seems profitable, I now propose to comment in more detail on my two specific examples, beginning with the *Morte Arthure*. This is a poem of some 4300 lines, telling the 'history' of Arthur from his conflict with the Roman Emperor Lucius, through his successful wars in Europe to regain territory that belonged to his ancestors, to the revolt of his deputy Mordred and the final battle in Britain that leads to the king's death and the end of the Round Table. It survives in a single manuscript, written in the fifteenth century by Robert Thornton; its original date and dialect have been obscured in the course of scribal transmission, but it may have originated in the East or North Midlands in the second half of the fourteenth century.[13] Its precise sources are also uncertain, but it goes back by some means to the Arthurian chronicle of Geoffrey of Monmouth, with the insertion of material from Alexander romances and from the French epic *Fierabras*. One such insertion is of a kind more closely related to courtly romance than to the poem's dominant mode of historical epic: in it Gawain rides out alone 'wondyrs to seke' (2514) and engages in single combat, unmotivated save by the conventions of literary chivalry, with the pagan knight Sir Priamus. The poem as a whole appears to have been shaped by the poet's knowledge of Edward III's continental campaigns in the Hundred Years' War, but scholars differ as to its degree of topicality. Most agree, however, in seeing it as 'one of the great achievements of alliterative poetry', a poem which 'deserves to be reckoned with *Pearl*, *Piers Plowman*, and *Sir Gawain and the Green Knight*'. One describes it as ranking 'just after the works of the *Gawain*-poet', while another goes further: 'If the *Morte Arthure* suffers by comparison to *Sir Gawain and the Green Knight*, the reverse is also true: *Sir Gawain* is a more perfect poem, but one of a lesser kind'. A third view, which seems to me more just, sees it as 'a most interesting and ambitious failure'.[14] At all events, the *Morte Arthure* is worth some discussion in its own right, quite apart from the interest it also possesses as one of Malory's only two identifiable English sources.

Examination of some specific passages will show how effectively (but also within what limits) the poet develops the heroic possibilities of alliterative verse. I begin with two extracts describing journeys. The first is that of the Roman ambassadors mentioned

events, motivated in the first case by fear of what lies behind, in the second by apprehension about what lies ahead. A separate action is often stated in each line, and the many synonyms or quasi-synonyms for 'go', 'hasten', or 'make for' available to the alliterative poet give variety to the pressure of events: in the first passage alone we find *Cayers* (480), *spede* (483), *reden* (485), *soghte* (487), *went* (492), *fleede* (494), *founde* (495), *Gosse* (497), *turne* (499), *sekes* (502), and *prekes* (503). In the second passage such synonyms are used even more thickly (*bownes*, *trynes*, *Turnys*, *Merkes*, *Ayres*, *Ferkes*, *Scherys*), along with negative forms corresponding to them (*taries bot litill*, *Lyghte noghte*, *schownes no lengere*), and the sense of urgency is heightened by the paratactic omission of conjunctions, which in turn enables five of the lines to have verbs of motion emphatically placed as the first word. In these passages, the variety of concrete detail encouraged by the alliterative style produces a realism that is by no means illusory, but that involves imaginative penetration of a real world as experienced by those travelling through it. The ambassadors leap on their horses, spur them so hard that they exhaust them and have to hire substitutes; their own horses are then presumably brought on with or after them, and are shipped for transport from Sandwich. Moving more slowly once they reach Italy, the Romans put on their ceremonial clothes in Pisa, in preparation for their audience with the emperor in Rome. Place names in both passages are rationally arranged, so that the journeys can easily be followed on a map; and as the travellers move from one district to another, they also pass through landscapes of different emotional quality, partly no doubt reflecting their own feelings. The sea is *wane* not only because the English Channel often is, but because the ambassadors are *Wery* from their journey (492); after the 'ful grevous wayes' of the St Gotthard pass, the plain of Lombardy is naturally 'lykande to shewe' (498); and I commented earlier on the evocative use of place name and sound when they reach the English sea coast. The *Morte Arthure* is a poem that displays an unusually strong geographical imagination: much of it represents the movements of great armies or smaller groups of men to and fro across countries and continents, and these are imagined as something more than the mainly empty fantasy-landscapes of most courtly romances. *Sir Gawain and the Green Knight* is of course the great exception, but even there, once Gawain has entered 'the wyldrenesse of Wyrale' (701), the landscapes, however richly evoked, lack geographical location. Certainly, in both passages from the *Morte*, the route travelled is more fully and systematically realized as a geographical panorama than, say, the journey of Chaucer's pilgrims from Southwark to Canterbury, or than the routes depicted in fourteenth-century English maps.[15] A particularly effective touch of concrete detail, found in both passages, is that the journeying groups are in such a hurry that they do not stop except when they lack daylight: 'whills them lyghte failede' (486) and 'bot when the lyghte failede' (3594) illustrate well the creative use of half-line phrases belonging to a formulaic system. A picture is called up of alternating day and night, light and dark, giving a sense of time as well as space traversed in these hasty journeys.

It is easy to believe that the poet himself had travelled as far as Italy, perhaps, like Chaucer, on diplomatic business; and it might be supposed that his geographical imagination would be accompanied by a sense of history such as Chaucer himself seems to have gained through his contact with the earliest stages of the Italian Renaissance. Certainly he possesses something of that sense of the change of language through space and time that Chaucer has in common with Dante: in the conversation between King Arthur and Sir Cradoke, who has come to Italy dressed as a pilgrim to bring news of Mordred's revolt, the language used is 'Latyn corrouppede all' (3478) (that is, presumably, late Latin on its way to becoming Italian), but Arthur recognizes that Cradoke is from Britain by his 'brode speche' (3508). The close parallel has been noted with Chaucer's use of the phrase 'A maner Latyn corrupt' in *The Man of Law's Tale* (II 519) to refer to the language spoken in post-Roman Britain:[16] and it has been suggested, too, that the *Morte* possesses a historical sense of the fragmentation of Christendom implied by the decay of what Dante calls 'latino . . . perpetuo e non corruttibile' into 'Latyn corrouppede all'.[17] But in general the *Morte Arthure* poet lacks the historical relativism that Chaucer reveals in his treatment of pagan antiquity in *Troilus and Criseyde* and *The Knight's Tale* or in such details as his imagining of an imperial Rome where the Pope himself 'woneth in halkes alwey to and fro,/ And dar nat ones putte forth his heed' (*Second Nun's Tale* VIII 311–12).

He lacks too the human relativism that characterizes nearly all of Chaucer's work. The alliterative poet enters his work as a partisan, for whom, in spite of historical and racial distance, the British are 'oure men' (1428), 'our bolde men' (1434), 'oure folke' (1441), 'oure chevalrous men' (2989), 'oure lele knyghttez' (2998), even 'our syde' (2802). When things go badly for 'our syde' he does not conceal his regret, remarking 'that noyes me sore' (1816) or 'my sorowe es the more' (3729). At times he purports to give a Roman view of Arthur, but really he has neither the wish nor the ability to enter into the alternative perspective, and employs it only to smuggle in adulatory praise of his hero. When the Roman ambassadors arrive, Arthur's mere glance is so fierce that they kneel to him – 'Cowchide as kenetez before the Kyng selvyn' (122) – and

> "Sir", sais the Senatour, "so Crist mott me helpe,
> The voute of thi vesage has woundyde us all!
> Thow arte the lordlyeste lede that ever I one lukyde;
> By lukyng, withowttyn lesse, a lyon the semys!" (136–9)

Arthur lays on a splendid feast for the Romans, while apologizing for the lack of luxuries, and the same spokesman makes a cringing response to the king's heavy irony:

> "Sir", sais the Senatour, "soo Criste motte me helpe,
> There ryngnede never syche realtee within Rome walles!
> There ne es prelatte, ne pape, ne prynce in this erthe,
> That he ne myghte be wele payede of thees pryce metes." (227–30)

And when they return to Rome, their account of Arthur to the Emperor is a totally uncritical eulogy:

> He may be chosyn cheftayne, cheefe of all other,
> Bathe be chauncez of armes and chevallrye noble,
> For whyeseste and worthyeste and wyghteste of hanndez;
> Of all the wyes thate I watte in this werlde ryche,
> The knyghtlyeste creatoure in Cristyndome halden,
> Of kyng or of conquerour crownede in erthe;
> Of countenaunce, of corage, of crewelle lates,
> The comlyeste of knyghtehode that undyre Cryste lyffes . . . (530–7)

And so on, interminably. The pretence of seeing the hero objectively goes just far enough for us to recognize that it is no more than a pretence.

This is an unpleasing side of the poet's achievement; another aspect of his heroic treatment of his subject, perhaps equally unattractive to modern sensibilities, is his preoccupation with bodily mutilation. The heroes of medieval epic and romance prove themselves by bodily encounters with opponents, in which blood is shed copiously and the body itself is often shattered.[18] An analogy may be found in representations of Christ's Passion in religious writing and art: the human body is the fundamental image of wholeness and holiness, but the power that inheres in it can be released only if its boundaries are pierced and its wholeness is violated. In the religious sphere it is Christ's own body, the perfect human body taken on by God himself, that must suffer in this way if mankind is to be redeemed; in the secular world of chivalry, the hero and his opponent must both suffer grievous damage in the name of knightly prowess. In the *Morte Arthure* this expected violence is taken to obsessive extremes. At an early stage in his continental expedition Arthur fights against the giant of Mont-Saint-Michel, which has been eating children and raping women in great numbers. There is a violent hand-to-hand battle, and the king pierces the monster deeply with his sword, so that

> The hott blode of the hulke unto the hilte rynnez;
> Ewyn into inmette the gyaunt he hyttez,
> Just to the genitales and jaggede tham in sondre. (1121–3)

Then he strikes it again, breaking open its groin, and

> Bothe the guttez and the gorr guschez owte at ones,
> That all englaymez the gresse one grounde ther he standez. (1130–1)

Not only giants disintegrate with such interesting results. In Arthur's major battle against the Emperor, Sir Kayous pierces a French knight with his lance 'That the lyver and the lunggez on the launce lengez' (2168), but is then in turn speared by an opponent

> That the boustous launce the bewells attamede,
> That braste at the brawlyng and brake in the myddys. (2175–6)

Sir Gawain in his single combat against Sir Priamus so damages him that

> Who lukes to the lefte syde when his horse launches
> With the lyghte of the sonne men myghte see his lyvere. (2560–1)

To give one other example, the enemy knight Feraunt challenges Sir Florent, but the latter pierces him through the forehead:

> Thurghe his bryghte bacennette his brayne has he towchede,
> And brusten his neke-bone, that all his breste stoppede. (2770–1)

Then, however, Feraunt's cousin attempts to avenge him, only to be attacked by Sir Floridas as he rides past:

> All the flesche of the flanke he flappes in sondyre,
> That all the filthe of the freke and fele of the guttes
> Foloes his fole fotte, whene he furthe rydes. (2781–3)

The poet has the fascination with what happens to the human body when it is pierced, crushed or sliced that is commonly expressed by small boys; we may like to think that in our time adults have outgrown such morbid tastes, but the popularity of comparable violence in the cinema and on television indicates otherwise. In the *Morte Arthure* it is at least only part of a larger treatment of heroic conflict, rather than being the sole focus of interest; and I suppose that anyone who took part in or witnessed a fourteenth-century battle would actually have seen such sights.

I turn to other, less distasteful elements in this poet's work. One is the use of stylistic devices which produce enrichments of the poem's overall earnest commitment. Two of these are especially noticeable. One is a device found in heroic poetry of many different cultures, including the *Iliad* and (as we have seen) the *Chanson de Roland*. The destructive violence which is the epic poet's inescapable theme is placed in settings of natural beauty and peace, usually described in traditional formulas which have the effect of suggesting their permanence as well as, perhaps, their fragility; and this is done with no apparent attempt to make an explicit point, but for us to draw our own conclusions from the emotional effect of the contrast. A straightforward example in the *Morte* comes at the beginning of the Priamus episode, when the foraging expedition rides out

> Thorowe hopes and hymland, hillys and other,
> Holtis and hare woddes with heslyn schawes,
> Thorowe marasse and mosse and montes so heghe;
> And in the myste of mornyng one a mede falles,
> Mawen and unmade, maynoyrede bott lyttyll,
> In swathes sweppen down, full of swete floures . . .   (2503–8)

In this idyllic setting Gawain first catches sight of a solitary knight, 'Baytand on a wattire banke by the wodde eyvis' (2516), with whom he will engage in mortal combat. The scene is moving in an entirely traditional way, enhanced only by the concreteness of the alliterative poet's evocation of a landscape that mingles the peace of nature with that of the meadow mown by human hands but left empty in the early morning. But the poet sometimes creates such juxtapositions of the heroic and the idyllic more ingeniously. In one case, the idyllic setting is deliberately chosen by enemies as a form of concealment. A party of Arthur's knights is travelling through France escorting prisoners, when, as Sir Clegis explains to their commander, Sir Cador, they find themselves ambushed:

We hafe founden in yone firthe, floresched with leves,
The flour of the faireste folke that to thi foo langez:
Fifty thosandez of folke of ferse men of armez,
That faire are fewteride on frounte undyr yone fre bowes;
They are enbuschede on blonkkes, with baners displayede,
In yone bechen wode appon the waye sydes.
Thay hafe the furthe forsette all of the faire watyre,
That fayfully of force feghte us byhowys.   (1708–15)

Here the formulaic epithets that, from one point of view, serve only
to complete alliteration – '*fre* bowes', '*faire* watyre' – also heighten
the contrast between the apparent peacefulness of the scene and its
actual danger, while the use of *flour* to mean 'finest part', common
enough in this poem and in Middle English generally, has the special
effect in this context, particularly when supported by *faireste*, of
identifying the concealed danger with the concealing landscape:
'look like the innocent flower,/ But be the serpent under't'. In
another passage we find the poet using the conventional features of
the idyllic landscape as 'negative similes' applied directly to martial
activities; Beryn of Brittany urges Arthur to care nothing for the
threats delivered by the Roman ambassadors:

No more dowtte the dynte of theire derfe wapyns
Than the dewe that es dannke when it doun falles,
Ne no more schoune fore the swape of theire scharpe suerddes
Then fore the faireste flour thatt on the folde growes!   (312–15)

The effect of this rousing contempt is inevitably complicated by the
comparisons which evoke even as they banish a fragile world of
flowers and dew.

The other kind of complicating device is the poet's occasional use
of sustained metaphors for ironic purposes. Three passages relating
to the giant of Mont-Saint-Michel will illustrate this. In the first
Arthur has been undergoing a mysterious inner struggle in his tent;
'Thare was no wy of this werlde that wyste whatt he menede' (891),
says the poet, evidently intending us to guess that the king is about
to seek spiritual aid at this famous shrine before facing his mon-
strous opponent:

He calles Sir Cayous, that of the cowpe serfede,
And Sir Bedvere the bolde, that bare hys brande ryche:
"Luke ye afytre evensang be armyde at ryghttez,
On blonkez by yone buscayle, by yone blythe stremez,
Fore I will passe in pilgremage prevely hereaftyre,
In the tyme of suppere, whene lordez are servede,
For to seken a saynte be yone salte stremes,
In Seynt Mighell Mount, there myraclez are schewede."   (892–9)

In the second passage, after arming himself and riding through landscape in which the sound of water and birds was so pleasant that 'It myghte salve hym of sore that sounde was nevere' (932) he asks his knights to leave him to ride forward alone,

> Fore I will seke this seynte by my selfe one,
> And mell with this mayster mane that this monte yemez;
> And seyn sall ye offyre, aythyre aftyre other,
> Menskfully at Saynt Mighell full myghtty with Criste.　　(937–40)

This still makes it appear that Arthur intends first to pray to the saint and then to deal with the giant; but what in fact happens is what we subsequently realize he must have intended all along – he immediately embarks alone on his struggle with the giant. His success is won only at great cost, and in the final struggle the king has three ribs broken and is found by Kayous and Bedvere lying unconscious. They think at first that he is dead, but when they realize that he is alive and has won, Bedvere takes up once more the cluster of ideas about saints, but now with jovial acknowledged irony:

> "Now certez," saise Sir Bedwere, "it semez, be my Lorde,
> He sekez seyntez bot selden, the sorer he grypes,
> That thus clekys this corsaunt owte of thir heghe clyffez,
> To carye forthe siche a carle at close hym in silver.
> Be Myghell, of syche a makk I hafe myche wondyre
> That ever owre soveraygne Lorde suffers hym in Heven;
> And all seyntez be syche that servez oure Lorde,
> I sall never no seynt bee, be my fadyre sawle!"
> Thane bourdez the bolde kyng at Bedvere wordez:
> "This seynt have I soghte, so helpe me owre Lorde!
> Forthy brayd owtte thi brande, and broche hym to the herte . . .".
> 　　　　　　　　　　　　　　　　　　　　　　　　　　(1162–72)[19]

The joking suggestions made by Bedvere – that Arthur cannot be much accustomed to visiting the shrines of saints if *this* is the action he takes to have the holy body enshrined in silver (we have seen how the king has mangled the giant's body) and that if *this* is what a saint looks like he is surprised that God allows them in heaven and is sure that he will never be one himself – are not subtle in their humour, but they have a rough power which is intensified by our memory of the earlier passages. And the unspoken implication of the whole sequence is that the religious devotion of a warrior-king is a matter of saving his territories from evil giants rather than of visiting saints' shrines.

The emotional focus of heroic poetry is the male loyalty and comradeship that ensure courageous action. The *Morte Arthure* is not narrow in its treatment of human relations, and it contains some touching passages concerning love between man and woman; but such passages derive from the unquestioned, if sad, necessity for the male concerns of politics and warfare to take priority over love between the sexes. The scene in which Arthur says farewell to Guenevere as he sets off for the continent and appoints Mordred as regent and her *dictour* (agent) (712) is full of feeling of a strong and direct kind; on the assumption that we already know the outcome of the story (the treachery of both Mordred and the queen), it is also charged with dramatic irony, but this does not interfere with the depiction of Guenevere's helpless grief, which wounds our hearts as Arthur says it does his (707):

And then cho swounes full swythe, when he hys swerde aschede,
Twys in a swounyng, swelte as cho walde.
He pressed to his palfray, in presance of lordes,
Prekys of the palez with his prys knyghtes;
Wyth a reall rowte of the Rounde Table
Soughte towarde Sandwyche – cho sees hym no more.   (715–20)

It is as if she is already widowed, and the ambiguity of tense of the final verb (there being no distinction in Middle English between present and future forms) is especially telling: Arthur disappears now from her sight as he rides off to the coast, but she will never see him again in this life. A comparable glimpse of tender feeling between the sexes occurs when Sir Kayous, knowing himself about to die, says to Arthur,

Grete wele my ladye the Qwene, yife the werlde happyne,
And all the burliche birdes that to hir boure lengez,
And my worthily weife, that wrethide me never,
Bid hire, for hir wyrchipe, wirke for my saulle.   (2189–92)

Here it may be that cultural distance has given Kayous's words a greater emotional power than they originally possessed. What now seems like manly reticence, subordinating his love for his wife to his courtly duty to the queen and her ladies and hiding it in the understatement of 'wrethide me never', may perhaps have been an accurate reflection of the values shared by the poet and his character. The wife's highest virtue is her obedience, and this makes her especially useful now, because she can be relied on to carry out devotions that will lessen his sufferings in purgatory. We may recall that when Arthur knows that Guenevere has been untrue to him, the 'derlyng dayntevous and full dere holden' (4196) whose loss he laments is not his queen but his sword Clarent, which she has allowed to fall into Mordred's hands.

In this world, women are at their most moving as widows, and it seems appropriate that on Mont-Saint-Michel Arthur should be greeted by

> A wery wafull wedowe, wryngande hire handez,
> And gretande on a grave grysely teres;
> Now merkyde on molde sen myddaye it semede. (950–2)

The occupant of the grave is not in fact her husband, as we are led to expect, but her foster-child the Duchess of Brittany, raped and murdered by the giant. The poem's most intense feeling, however, is reserved, as I indicated above, for the bond between male comrades or between lord and vassal. One scholar has noted that throughout the poem 'The action is presented in terms of corporate action and loyalty rather than individual prowess.'[20] We are promised from the beginning a tale of 'the ryeall renkes of the Rownnde Table' (17), and it is the loss of this male company, seen significantly as widowhood, that is the theme of Arthur's penultimate and most moving speech. The king has already knelt weeping to embrace and kiss the corpse of Gawain, pronounced over it a passionate elegy, swooned, recovered, and kissed it again 'Till his burliche berde was blody berown' (3971); now, on the verge of death himself, he bitterly laments the whole company slaughtered in the last battle:

> Kyng comly with crowne, in care am I levyde;
> All my lordchipe lawe in lande es layde undyre,
> That me has gyfen gwerdons, be grace of Hym selven,
> Mayntenyde my manhede be myghte of theire handes,
> Made me manly on molde and mayster in erthe,
> In a tenefull tym this torfere was reryde,
> That for a traytoure has tynte all my trewe lordys.
> Here rystys the riche blude of the Rownde Table,
> Rebukkede with a rebawde, and rewthe es the more!
> I may helples one hethe house be myn one,
> Alls a wafull wedowe that wanttes hir beryn;
> I may werye and wepe and wrynge myn handys,
> For my wytt and my wyrchipe awaye es for ever;
> Off all lordchips I take leve to myn ende.
> Here es the Bretons blode broughte owt of lyfe,
> And nowe in this journee all my joy endys. (4275–90)

This fine speech brings together many of the poem's most central concerns, not as abstractions but concretely embodied. Power (*lordchipe[s]*, *myghte*, *mayster*) is embodied in the *crowne*, and it is power over land (*molde*, *erthe*) which is now laid *lawe in lande*, in the form of corpses strewn over the battlefield. There is a fundamental dialectic of loyalty and treachery, the *trewe lordys* and the *traytoure*, and the earthly defeat of the loyalty that held the Round Table together produces a grief embodied in the image of the widow living alone in the wilderness (*on hethe* – another type of land, worthless to its possessor). Perhaps the most fundamental idea/ image of all is that of blood, the symbol of the kinship and the social rank that underlie feudalism and monarchy but also destroy them. (Mordred is Arthur's nephew, and he begets on Guenevere the heir that Arthur lacks; hence Arthur's final act is an order that Mordred's children should be 'sleyghely slayne and slongen in watyrs' [4321]). But blood is also the bodily fluid that flows so freely and clings so stickily in this poem of mutilations and manly embraces; and now 'the riche blude of the Rownde Table' is soaking into the earth that Arthur once possessed and to which he is himself about to return – for there is no suggestion in this version of the story of any journey to another world from which he will return when his people need him.

If we now stand back from the detail of such passages and try to assess the overall meaning of the *Morte Arthure*, we encounter serious difficulties. The alliterative poet has neither taken over his material wholesale from any single known source, nor does he appear to have heaped it up at random. The most obvious indication that he has imposed a shape on his narrative is the symmetry which frames Arthur's military triumphs between two terrifying dreams: one, dreamed on his outward voyage to the continent, of a battle between a dragon and a bear; the other, which comes to him just before he receives news of Mordred's rebellion, of the Nine Worthies (the greatest warriors of the world, three pagan, three Jewish, and three Christian, the last of whom is himself) in various positions on Fortune's wheel. Each dream is interpreted for Arthur by philosophers, and each prophesies what is to follow: the first foretells his victory over 'the tyrauntez that tourmentez thy pople' (824), while the second warns that 'thy fortune es passede' (3394) and that he will be dead within five years. The first of these dreams goes back to the poet's chronicle sources, but the second appears to be his own addition – it is the earliest known example of the combination of Fortune with the Nine Worthies. It is naturally tempting to suppose that this overarching narrative shape implies a single coherent programme of meaning for the poem; but there is little agreement as to what such meaning might be. The *Morte Arthure* has been widely regarded as a tragedy of Fortune, a medieval genre to which the narratives of Chaucer's *Monk's Tale* belong, illustrating, as the Monk explains, how

> Fortune alwey wole assaille
> With unwar strook the regnes that been proude;
> For whan men trusteth hire, thanne wol she faille,
> And covere hire brighte face with a clowde.   (VII 2763–6)

This, however, scarcely seems a sufficiently interesting programme to sustain a poem of over four thousand lines, and many scholars go further, arguing that the *Morte* shows Arthur's fall as a punishment for his sinful behaviour. William Matthews, for example, seeing Arthur as deliberately paralleled to both Alexander and Edward III, regards him as flawed from the beginning by pride, with the giant of Mont-Saint-Michel being a figure of what the king himself will eventually become; while John Finlayson interprets Arthur as a noble Christian ruler who fights a just war against the Emperor but then after his victory gives way to *desmesure*, love of conquest and recklessness.[21] Some more recent critics have gone still further, seeing the poem as an 'anti-romance' in which the apparent admiration for Arthur is really ironic or parodic, all war is shown as unjust, the vanity of conquest is displayed by means of 'stylistic bombast', heroic endeavour is 'meaningless', and Arthur 'has not learned his lesson' even when he dies.[22]

These latter views are open to the same objection as the readings of *Troilus and Criseyde* that distinguish a 'fallible narrator' completely from the poet, namely that they assure us that the poet means something different from what he apparently says, only in order that the poem can be unified on the basis of the critic's own ethical views, inserted into it behind the smokescreen of alleged irony. 'The irony, to be sure, is very subtle', remarks one such reader of the *Morte*'[23] but we have to ask ourselves which is more likely, that a fourteenth-century poet should happen to share the anti-heroic, anti-authoritarian and anti-war feelings of late-twentieth-century academics, or that his work should not in fact possess the consistent ethical position and purpose that modern readers would like to find in it. We have already seen how passages purporting to give a Roman view of Arthur are merely uncritical expressions of admiration; his behaviour towards the Roman ambassadors in the opening, evidently paradigmatic, scene may seem displeasingly arrogant to us, but both his anger at the demands they bring and his eventual self-control would probably have been seen as appropriately kingly in the Middle Ages. The poet clearly has no doubt that Arthur is right to reject the demand for tribute and to respond to it by seizing back from the Emperor lands that are justly his – for the poem never questions Arthur's assertion that

> I have title to take tribute of Rome;
> Myne ancestres ware emperours and aughte it them selven. (275–6)

And the notion that this initially just war subsequently turns into an unjust campaign of aggressive conquest is refuted by the fact that Arthur's reply to the Emperor, devised with the advice and consent of his council, already forecasts precisely the course of his campaigns to the end of the poem. Studies of the *Morte* in the light of the law of war in its own time show that Arthur's wars would have been likely to be regarded as just from beginning to end, and that his conduct as a military commander was more moderate and merciful than might have been expected of a medieval king.[24]

It is true that towards the end of the fourteenth century the apparently endless prolongation of the war between England and France had led some to long for peace between Christian nations and the diversion of their joint energies into a new crusade; it is also true that the traditional element of pacifism within Christianity had been given new prominence by Wyclif's followers. Above all, it is true that the poem itself does not conceal the destructive consequences of warfare, for civilians as well as soldiers. When Arthur takes by assault the besieged city of Metz, we are given a picture of the devastation of dwellings, hospitals and churches that seems almost to anticipate the consequences of mass bombing in the Second World War:

> Mynsteris and masondewes they malle to the erthe,
> Chirches and chapells chalke-whitte blawnchede.
> Stone stepells full styffe in the strete ligges,
> Chawmbyrs with chymnés and many cheefe inns:
> Paysede and pelid down playsterede walles –
> The pyne of the pople was peté for to here. (3038–43)

Here the usual alliterative method of focusing on concrete details – steeples lying in the street, fireplaces and plastered walls laid bare – is painfully evocative, and the final line reminds us of the human cost of this material destruction. Again, in the immediately following attack on Como, there is a brief glimpse of the citizens going about their normal work and play before the attackers spring out of ambush to bring normality to an end:

> Poverall and pastorelles passede on aftyre,
> With porkes to pasture at the price yates;
> Boyes in the subarbis bourden full heghe,
> At a bare synglere that to the bente rynnys.
> Thane brekes oure buschement and the brigge wynnes,
> Brayedez into the burghe with baners displayede;
> Stekes and stabbis thorowe that them ayayne-stondes;
> Fowre stretis or thay stynte they stroyen fore evere.   (3120-7)

Once more it is the concrete detail that makes the contrast so horrifying. But this does not mean that the poet believes that '*every war is unjust*' or that he is simply 'critical of war and all things pertaining to it'.[25] More than some of his contemporaries, he recognizes and imaginatively realizes the horrors of war; but equally he recognizes and realizes its grandeurs and what he perceives as its necessity. How can Arthur reclaim what is his by right (which, in medieval eyes, it is his duty to reclaim) except by assaulting cities that are fortified against him? And when a fortified city was taken by assault, widespread destruction was inevitable. What is striking indeed is that, immediately after the passage quoted above about the taking of Metz, the duchess and her ladies come to beg Arthur for mercy, and his chivalrous response, unhesitatingly given, is far more generous than could have been required or expected of a conquering prince at such a moment: he orders the assault to cease, promises that no citizens shall be harmed further, and swiftly makes provision for peace and public order in the city.

Just as, within passages such as I have quoted, the *Morte Arthure* poet juxtaposes contrasting concrete details, so in the poem as a whole he sets side by side opposing aspects of Arthur's war to regain his empire. So far as I can tell, he does so not polemically, in order to prove that war is always glorious or always wicked, but simply because these contrasts belonged to his experience of life and he wished to represent them as parts of historical truth – a truth that it was beyond his power to articulate as a whole. It might be expected that a medieval poet would take Christian doctrine as the principle of judgment that would enable him to set his historical world in order; and there can be no doubt of this poet's piety, his ultimate commitment to the ascetic faith that sees all earthly things as nugatory in relation to heaven. But the very asceticism of medieval Christianity, considered as articulable doctrine, greatly lessens its usefulness as a standard of judgment in a poem concerned with earthly affairs, with human history. One view of the *Morte Arthure* sees Arthur as condemned for his failure to live up to a religious truth stated by the philosophers who interpret his second dream and embodied in the figure of Sir Cradoke, who comes as a pilgrim to inform him of Mordred's treachery; just as one view of *Troilus and Criseyde* sees the poem as a systematic condemnation of 'The blynde lust, the which that may nat laste'. When we look more closely at both poems, however, we find that the situation is more complicated. In both there is a certain confusion of thought and attitude, a confusion which is actually necessary as a means of preventing the premature closure that religious truth would otherwise impose on them. This was one thing that emerged from the discussion of the end of *Troilus and Criseyde* in Chapter 5; in the later stages of the *Morte Arthure* we find confusion and even contradiction nearer the surface. The spokesman of the philosophers explains that Arthur is the ninth of the Nine Worthies (though the other two Christians, Charlemagne and Godfrey of Bouillon, have yet to be born); he too will be cast down by Fortune, to whom he has owed his success so far; and the philosopher begins and ends by urging him to confess and repent so that he may achieve salvation:[26]

> Thow has schedde myche blode and schalkes distroyede
> Sakeles, in cirquytrie, in sere kynges landis.
> Schryfe the of thy schame and schape for thyn ende . . .
>
> I rede thow rekkyn and reherse unresonable dedis,
> Ore the repenttes full rathe all thi rewthe werkes.
> Mane, amende thy mode, or thow myshappen,
> And mekely aske mercy for mede of thy saule. (3398–400, 3452–5)

Yet only a few lines earlier the same philosopher has spoken in a way that implies that Arthur will gain salvation as a result of the valiant deeds he has already performed, and that the verdict of the Last Judgment will be the same as that of human history

> Forethy Fortune the fetches to fulfill the nowmbyre,
> Alls nynne of the nobileste namede in erthe:
> This sall in romance be redde with ryall knyghttes,
> Rekkenede and renownde with ryotous kynges,
> And demyd on Domesdaye, for dedis of armes,

> For the doughtyeste that ever was duelland in erthe;
> So many clerkis and kynges sall karpe of youre dedis,
> And kepe youre conquestes in cronycle for ever. (3438–45)

Thus *romance* and *cronycle* – the categories to which the poem itself belongs – not only anticipate divine judgment, but obliquely appropriate its everlastingness in the poet's confident 'for ever'. This speech as a whole will not, in my view, sustain close intellectual analysis: it incorporates both religious and heroic perspectives in a rich confusion of greater value than anything this poet could have achieved on the basis of clear-cut doctrine.

Something similar is true of the Cradoke episode, which follows immediately. Having heard the philosopher's advice, Arthur dresses in his kingly robes and takes a solitary walk in the early morning; as the sun rises he meets a man dressed as a pilgrim travelling towards Rome. Arthur warns him of the danger of wandering about 'Qwhylls the werlde es o werre, . . . Bot yif thou hafe condethe of the Kynge selfen' (3480–3). The newcomer explains that, after he has made his pilgrimage to Rome,

> To purchese me pardone of the Pape selfen,
> And of the paynes of Purgatorie be plenerly assoyllede, (3497–8)

he wishes to find King Arthur. Once the two men have identified each other, Cradoke gives Arthur details of Mordred's treachery, and Arthur swears, 'By the Rode, . . . I sall it revenge!' (3559). The unhappy outcome, which fulfils the prophecy of Arthur's dream as interpreted by the philosopher, we already know. One interpretation of this episode sees it as confirming that the poem teaches the superiority of religious to heroic values:

The humble Cradoke is clearly a foil for the haughty Arthur, who is also just about to go to Rome, not as a repentant pilgrim but as a conqueror, full of pride and with rage in his heart, arrogantly claiming things to which he is not entitled. Cradoke thus embodies a clear alternative the king could have adopted.[27]

Yet when Arthur warned Cradoke of the danger he was in from hostile forces, his answer was:

> I sall forgyffe hym my dede, so me God helpe,
> Onye grome undire God that one this grownde walkes.
> Latte the keneste come that to the Kynge langes,
> I sall encountire hym as knyghte, so Criste hafe my sawle! (3488–91)

Pilgrim though he may be, Cradoke himself is far from having abandoned the 'pride' and 'rage' of knighthood; indeed, after reading the last two of these four lines, one may well want to read back into the first two an aggressive irony: 'Only by killing me – if anyone in this country is capable of doing so – can any assailant hope to gain my forgiveness!' Once again we face not a clear-cut opposition but a confused mixture of values. It is a mixture that can equally be found in some of the poem's commonest terms: analysis for which there is no room here would show, for example, that *ryot(ous)* and *crewell* are foci for conflict about the value of martial heroism (is it proud energy or destructive lawlessness?),[28] while *rente* focuses a deep-rooted uncertainty about the relation of conquest to profit (because from one point of view it is contemptible for a prince to be concerned with material gains, while from another his princely reputation and power depend on his material wealth and the generosity it makes possible).

In fundamental ways, then, the *Morte Arthure* poet seems to reflect conflicts within his culture. If Chaucer, with his far greater philosophical resource, was not able to settle the opposition within late-medieval culture between religious asceticism and the celebration of human love, but could only impose on it a closure that acknowledges its own arbitrariness, it is hardly surprising that this lesser poet, working within a style for which paratactic juxtaposition was a principle of operation, leaves us with unresolved doubt about the value of heroism. To attempt to resolve a doubt which is deeply embedded in the poetic text, as within the text of the culture that produced it, is to do the poet no service; it is to interpret as consistent but shallow writing which is actually deep and rich because inconsistent. The *Morte Arthure* poet is not supremely gifted, but he has a stronger grasp than most late-twentieth-century scholars of the splendour and the sadness of the heroic life. If he expresses this at the price of confusion, that is better than not expressing it at all.

The Siege of Jerusalem

The Siege of Jerusalem is less confused but also less rich. Surviving in eight manuscripts, 'which textually must be the remains of a considerably larger total',[29] it was presumably one of the most popular alliterative poems in its own time, though of course not necessarily eight times more popular than the *Morte Arthure*. At 1334 lines, it is less than a third as long as the *Morte*, and in style it is correspondingly more compressed, making greater use of absolute constructions, omission of pronoun-subjects, parataxis, and abrupt narrative transitions. Like much alliterative poetry, it probably originated in the North West Midlands in the late-fourteenth century, but the manuscripts come from a variety of dialect areas. It too is a 'historical' poem, derived from learned Latin sources – the *Vindicta Salvatoris*, Higden's *Polychronicon*, the *Legenda Aurea* – though with them it combines a French source, Roger d'Argenteuil's *Bible en françois*.[30] Its reception as a historical work is confirmed by the fact that in one manuscript (belonging to the Robert Thornton who copied the *Morte*) 'it takes a chronological place in a series of rhymed poems on sacred history'.[31] The *Siege* tells of how Titus and Vespasian were cured by miracle of supposedly incurable diseases, and were then sent by Nero to punish the Jews for their refusal to pay tribute. After being defeated in open battle, the Jews retreat into Jerusalem, the Romans invest it, and there follows a long and gruesome siege, with many scenes of bloodshed, torture and famine. Eventually the city falls and the Jews are sold into slavery. The learned sources have been reshaped into what is in many ways a typical medieval work of popular appeal; indeed, the modern reader's first response may be to see it as a perfect example of the weaknesses of medieval religious legend, and thus at best as 'of literary-historical rather than literary-critical value'.[32] The plot seems unnecessarily and irrelevantly elaborated, with the first three hundred lines or so full of confusing details about Nathan and Veronica (though in fact these are difficult to follow partly because the English poet greatly abbreviated them), and with an interlude in Rome (lines 893–948) which serves only to explain how Vespasian comes to be offered the imperial crown. For the poet and for his audience, the story would presumably have been sufficiently justified by its historical truth, but it is also full of utterly implausible elements – not only various miraculous cures, but such absurd statements as that Vespasian's illness was caused by the fact that ever since his youth a swarm of wasps had bred on his nose and lived on his head, which was why he was called 'Waspasian'! Then there is the poet's violent partisanship – far more intrusive than in the *Morte Arthure* – which makes him assert that in the battle of Jehoshaphat a hundred thousand Jews were slain, leaving only seven thousand to flee, while the Romans suffered not a single loss and not even their armour was damaged:

Unrevyn eche a renk, and noght a ryng brosten;
Was no poynt perschid of alle her pris armur,
So Crist his knyghtes gan kepe . . .   (606–8)

That last phrase points to another aspect of the poem's partisan-
ship that is likely to be particularly repellent to modern readers. It is
not only strongly and credulously prejudiced in favour of the
Christians, it is also permeated by the antisemitism that was so
common in the Middle Ages. The cruel destructiveness of the
Roman expedition is seen by the poet as a fitting vengeance against
the Jews for their execution of Christ;[33] it is assumed that the
appropriate response to Christ's sufferings is to inflict even worse
sufferings on the Jews, who, even when they are repeating the story
of God's preservation of his people against Pharaoh, are described as
faithles (481). The moral issue has been definitively settled by the
Jews' rejection of Christ, and we are left free to enjoy without
qualms the destruction of cities and the torturing of people. So,
when Caiaphas and his priests are captured, they are flayed, hung
upside down in full view of the people of Jerusalem, anointed with
honey, and attacked by dogs, cats and apes, 'That renten the rawe
flesche upon rede peces' (702). It is scarcely surprising that seven
hundred onlookers commit suicide, but we are not invited to feel
pity for them either. And this horrible delight in the suffering of the
Jews is only part of a morbid fascination with cruelty, pain and death
that runs right through the poem, and that goes far beyond the *Morte
Arthure* poet's interest in mutilation. Perhaps the most grotesque
expression of this is a description of the disembowelling of the
elephants that are killed in battle. Yet we ought perhaps to pause
before dismissing this side of *The Siege of Jerusalem* from the heights
of twentieth-century enlightenment. The implausibility, the
wanton cruelty, the violent racial feelings, and the naïve love of the
spectacular are all qualities that can be found in our popular art too –
in the cinema, for example, in the form of westerns and historical
'epics', not to mention the more specialized taste for which video
nasties provide. These are among the characteristics of popular art in
most periods.

The Siege of Jerusalem, too, is something more than an interest-
ingly deplorable example of debasement. We may not like what the
poet does, but it is done with skilful craftsmanship and sometimes
with brilliant virtuosity. Even in theme and structure, his poem is
not really so rambling as it may appear on a first reading. In these

respects as in style, it follows the alliterative method of tacit juxtaposition, involving contrast, parallel and variation. For example, it begins with a description of Christ's sufferings at the hands of the Jews – a typically detailed late-medieval account of that favourite topic of devotion. Within the poem's system of thought, one consequence of this Passion is to bring healing to true believers, such as Titus and Vespasian, who are cured by the impression of Christ's face on Veronica's veil; another consequence is the Roman campaign of vengeance against the Jews, which appropriately culminates in the destruction of Jerusalem, where Christ died; and the poem ends, symmetrically, with Pilate's description to Titus of Christ's death, which is followed by Pilate's own suicide. This thematically organized narrative is divided into four sections, the first two of about 450 lines each, the last two of about 220 (about half the length of the first two); and the end of each section is marked by a devotional exclamation – 'Now blesse us our Lorde!' (440), 'and Lord yyve us grace!' (892), 'and God yyve us joye!' (1108), and 'Now rede ous our Lord!' (1334).

I gave a taste of the poet's stylistic virtuosity earlier, in his versification of the list of the twelve apostles, but it can be seen at its simplest in the various set-pieces on topics common to the alliterative tradition as a whole. The *Siege* includes a fine example of the favourite theme of the sea-storm, full of verbs of action and noise – *clateren, blewe, bolned, dryveth, hurtled, scher, schot, rapis, to-bresteth* (54–66) – and conveying a heaving and jostling effect in crowded lines with varied and jagged rhythms. Another common theme (belonging of course not only to alliterative poetry but to heroic narrative in general) is the arming of the hero,[34] found also in the *Morte*; the *Siege* has a splendid passage on the arming of Vespasian before he goes out to battle. The poet not only shows a workmanlike knowledge of the various pieces of armour and the order in which they would really be put on, but also renders the scene fully into art, with an intertwining of grey steel and bright gold, metals symbolic respectively of warfare and of royal luxury:

> Waspasian bounys of bedde, busked hym fayr
> Fram the fote to the fourche in fyne gold clothes.
> Suth putteth the prince over his pallen wedes
> A brynye, browded thicke, with a brest-plate;
> The grate was of gray steel and of gold riche;
> Ther-over he casteth a cote, colourede of his armys;
> A grete girdel of gold with-out ger other

Layth umbe his lendis, with lacchetes ynow.
A bryght burnesched swerd he belteth alofte,
Of pur purged gold the pomel and the hulte;
A brod schynande scheld on scholdir he hongith,
Bocklyd myd bright gold aboute at the necke.
The gloves of gray steel, that wer with gold hemmyd,
Hauleth over harnays and his hors asketh;
The gold hewen helme haspeth he blyve,
With viser and with avental devysed for the nones.
A croune of clene gold was closed upon lofte,
Rybaunde umbe the rounde helm, ful of riche stones,
Pyght prudely with perles into the pur corners,
And so with saphyres sett the sydes aboute.
He strideth on a stif stede and striketh over the bente,
Light as a lyoun wer loused out of cheyne.
His segges seyen hym alle, and echon sayth to other,
"This is a comlich kyng knyghtes to lede!"   (741–64)

Passages comparable to this might be found in many alliterative
poems; what is more distinctive of the *Siege* is an extreme develop-
ment of the general tendency in alliterative poetry not to generalize
but to juxtapose directly contrasting sensory or emotional effects.
One aim of besieging a city was to starve out its inhabitants; the
effects of starvation on the Jews imprisoned in Jerusalem are realized
with sharp concreteness, and this is one area in which such juxta-
positions are put to work. First there is nothing to be bought in the
city, and money loses the value it had previously:

Sale in the cité was cesed with thanne:
Was noght for besauntes to bye that men bite myght.
For a ferthyng-worth of fode floryns an hundred
Princes profren in the toun to pay in the fuste;
Bot alle was boteles bale, for who so bred hadde
Nold a gobet have goven for goode upon erthe.   (1137–42)

Then the Jews really do begin to starve, and the poet suggests
painful before-and-after contrasts:

Was noght on ladies lafte bot the lene bones,
That wer fleschy byfor and fayr on to loke;
Burges with balies as barels or that tyme,
No gretter than a grehounde to grype on the medil.   (1245–8)

The bringing together of the barrel and the greyhound as concrete
images of fatness and thinness is a device characteristic of alliterative
poetry; and 'to grype on the medil' stimulates imaginary muscular
activity to test the thinness, just as in the previous passage 'that men
bite myght' calls up a ghostly sensation of ravenous chewing.

The most striking of such contrasts, however, occur earlier in the poem, in the very middle of its descriptions of warfare. They involve a subtle and, I think, undoubtedly deliberate clashing together of incongruous stylistic modes. On the one hand there is the brutal language used to describe the sufferings of the Jews, a kind of language that invites us to share in the Romans' pleasure in torturing them; on the other hand, immediately alongside this, is an exquisitely beautiful language used to mark the cycle of day and night in leisurely circumlocutions. Each kind of language is traditional and formulaic; bringing them together produces a clash of values, which implies, without ever stating, that the beauties of nature, and of the leisurely art that evokes nature, are quite unaffected by the hideous cruelty and suffering of human beings. I gave a couple of examples of such effects from the *Morte Arthure*, and they can be found in other alliterative poems too; but in *The Siege of Jerusalem* they seem to be used in a radical and systematic way. There are some interesting small-scale examples. When the Jews are driving back the Roman besiegers by hurling great rocks at them from the walls, the Romans go on attacking them through the whole day, 'Tille eche dale with dewe was donked aboute' (624). This is a measure of time, indicating how far into the evening the Romans kept up their assaults, but it also suggests an idyllic setting far different from the horrors of siege warfare yet no less real – the valleys are a nearby geographical fact. A little later, a line belonging to a similar stylistic register is used to indicate how early the Romans attacked next morning: their trumpets sounded 'Sone as the rede day ros on the schye' (633).

But to indicate the full power of such contrasts it will be necessary to discuss a longer passage. A suitable example comes immediately after the description of the torture of Caiaphas mentioned above – the passage concluding with the line 'That renten the rawe flesche upon rede peces' – and it begins with a further and more elaborate indication of time:

> So was he pyned fram prime, with persched sides,
> Tille the sonne doun sought in sommere tyme.   (703–4)

These lines convey the extreme length of his torture – sunset would be late in summertime, at least as imagined by an English poet – and at the same time they evoke the beauty of the natural background. Then come some lines describing the torture of the lesser priests, the

suicide of the onlooking Jews, the burning of the dead priests'
bodies, and the way the ashes were blown into the city, accom-
panied by insults:

> "Ther is doust to your drynke!" a duke to hem crieth,
> And bade hem bible of that broth for the bischopes soule.
> Thus ended coursed Cayphas and his clerkes alle,
> Al to-brused myd bestes, brent at the laste . . .   (719–22)

So much for Caiaphas and his clerks; and now comes a lovely
description of nightfall, referring with tender intimacy to the birds
perching so as to rest their wings, and evoking the picturesque
visual effect of campfires burning in the dusk. Sentries are
appointed, and the kings and knights take their rest; but Vespasian is
unable to sleep, and his restlessness of mind and body obviously
forms a further contrast with the quiet and peace of the natural
world. The passage is a variation on a familiar theme, having behind
it some alliterative lines from *The Destruction of Troy* translating a
Latin prose passage from the latter's source; and somewhere behind
all three is probably the famous scene in Book IV of the *Aeneid* in
which all nature sleeps while Dido is kept awake by the torments of
jealous love.[35] Yet in context it is highly effective; and so the poet
brings us to dawn, after the short summer night. It is imagined as
seen and heard by Vespasian, with more idyllic detail of larks
singing and bugles blowing among both besiegers and besieged –
for a brief moment, in this interlude of beauty, the enemies are at
one.

> By that was the day don, dymmed the skyes,
> Merked the montayns and mores aboute,
> Foules fallen to fote and her fethres rysten,
> The nyght-wacche to the walle and waytes to blowe;
> Bryght fures aboute betyn abrode in the oste,
> The kyng and his consail carpen togedr,
> Chosen chyventayns out and chiden no mor,
> Bot charged the chek-wecche and to chambr wenten,
> Kynges and knyghtes to cacchen hem reste.
> Waspasian lyth in his logge; litel he slepith,
> Bot walwyth and wyndith and waltreth aboute,
> Ofte tourneth for tene and on the toun thynketh.
> Whan schadewes and schir day scheden attwynne,
> Leverockes upon lofte lyften her stevenes,
> Burnes busken hem out of bedde with bemes loude,
> Bothe blowyng on bent and on the burwe walles.   (725–40)

And then follows the arming of Vespasian, quoted above. The
whole passage seems to me a most remarkable achievement, in its

combination of serene beauty and unbearable horror, both perfectly under the poet's control and brought together, so far as one can tell, with deliberate intention.

Alongside the contrast of horror and beauty the poem also includes contrasts of horror and comedy. These are perhaps equally common outside alliterative poetry, though rarely with such disturbing compression as here; I have in mind, for example, the savage farce of some treatments of the Massacre of the Innocents in the Mystery cycles, where the scene conveys at once pathos and a derisive, mock-heroic comedy. This contrast is present in *The Siege of Jerusalem* in an especially unsettling form in lines describing the starvation of the Jews. They have nothing to drink but their own tears, and (perhaps a famous scene in Charlie Chaplin's *Gold Rush* indicates part of the range of feeling here)

> Olde scheldes and schone scharply they eten;
> That liflode for ladies was luther to chewe. (1071–2)

One 'myld wyf' (1077) roasts and devours her own son, saying

> "Therfor yeld that I the yaf and ayen tourne,
> And entr ther thou cam out!" – and etyth a schoulder. (1083–4)

The smell of the cooking attracts her desperate fellow-citizens, and they break down the door to get at the food; but when she tells them what she has done, they go away weeping. It is a horrible passage, yet full of a daring typological wit, for the 'myld wyf' is called Mary, and there is surely an implied parallel between the victim of Jewish cannibalism and Christ, who said at the Last Supper, 'Take, eat; this is my body' (Matthew 26:26).

The Siege of Jerusalem is a brilliant and repellent work of art, and one that deserves to be more widely read, but it seems to me shallow compared with the *Morte Arthure*. Its clashes of feeling can be summed up with relative ease, and their neatness leaves no unresolved ambiguities in the reader's mind. The *Morte Arthure* by contrast is a loose and baggy monster of an alliterative poem, shambling along untidily not unlike the giant of Mont-Saint-Michel; but the richness that goes with its untidiness needs to be defended from scholars who are too ready to use against it the drastic method King Arthur applies to another giant, and cut it down to size:

> "Come down," quod the Kyng, "and karpe to thy ferys;
> Thowe arte to hye by the halfe, I hete the in trouthe:
> Thow sall be handsomere in hye, with the helpe of my Lorde!"
> With that stelen brande he strake ofe his hede. (2126–9)

7 · *Purity* and danger

The title of this chapter involves a play on words. *Purity and Danger* is a short but, for my purposes, very important book by the social anthropologist Mary Douglas, with the sub-title 'An analysis of the concepts of pollution and taboo'.[1] *Purity* is also the title sometimes given to one of the four poems in the *Gawain* manuscript, the poem known alternatively as *Cleanness*. (In the manuscript all four poems are untitled.) The poem, and the means by which we can make sense of it, are my main subject. Though one of Mary Douglas's many merits is the impressive breadth of reading her books reveal, I have no reason to suppose that she had read any of the *Gawain*-poet's work when she wrote the book in question; but I shall argue in this chapter that her book offers valuable assistance in understanding his work. I have certainly gained more help from *Purity and Danger* in understanding the way the *Gawain*-poet thinks, and especially in understanding *Purity*, than from any literary criticism or scholarship that I have so far encountered.

Of the four or possibly five poems attributable to the *Gawain*-poet (the authorship of *Saint Erkenwald*, a poem found in another manuscript, remains disputed), *Purity* is the only one that does not consist of a single narrative. It is made up of a group of linked narratives derived from Scripture, with various discursive passages connecting them, and it is precisely in the relationship of the component parts that the major difficulty of the poem is often felt to lie. Since this is the least well known of the four poems of the *Gawain* manuscript, I shall begin by summarizing the parts of which it is made up.

1–32 *Purity* begins with a passage declaring that the quality of *clannes* (1, 13) is an attribute of God himself, and is pleasing to him, and its opposite, *fylthe* or impurity (6, 14), is hateful to him. The Beatitudes promise to the 'clene of . . . hert' (27) the reward of the vision of God.

33–48 An earthly lord would be highly offended if some *ladde* (36) approached him in dirty old clothes while he was sitting in state at a feast.

49–176   Still more would such a thing be offensive to 'the hyghe Kyng . . . in heven' (50); and this is illustrated with a re-telling of the parable of the Great Feast and the guest without a wedding garment.

177–204   All sins may prevent men from seeing God, but none arouses his vengeful anger so strongly as 'fylthe of the flesch' (202).

205–34   The poet then proceeds to describe the first three occasions on which God punished his own creatures for their wickedness. The first was the punishment of Lucifer and his followers for their pride; God judged them severely, yet not in anger.

235–48   The second occasion was the punishment of Adam and Eve for their disobedience; yet this too was carried out in moderation, and was subsequently amended by a matchless virgin.

249–544   The third occasion was the Flood, which punished all living creatures except Noah and those he was permitted to preserve in the Ark. This punishment was more far-reaching than the first two, and was the expression of God's anger and disgust at the fleshly impurity of mankind, displayed in homosexuality and in mating with devils. The story of the Flood is told at much greater length than the first two examples of God's punishment, and forms the first of the poem's three large-scale exemplary narratives.

545–600   This should teach us that those who wish to see God and receive honour in his court must avoid 'the fylthe of the flesch' (547) and be as spotless and inviolate as pearls. God may have promised Noah never again to destroy all living creatures, but he subsequently took terrible vengeance on 'the vycios fylthe/ That bysulpez mannez saule' (574–5). He sees into the hearts of all men, rewarding the pure but spurning the wicked.

601–1048   This truth is then illustrated with the second main exemplary narrative. It is in fact a double narrative, telling first of God's visit to Abraham in the form of three angels, Abraham's hospitality, and God's declaration of his anger at the sexual perversions of Sodom and Gomorrah; and then of the visit of two angels to Lot in order to warn him of the coming destruction of these cities, Lot's hospitality, the gross impropriety shown to the angels by the Sodomites, the disobedience of Lot's wife to his command to put no salt into the angels' food, the destruction of the cities, the escape of Lot and his daughters, and the transformation of his wife into a pillar of salt. The traces of this expression of God's anger are yet to be seen in the barren and unnatural landscape of the Dead Sea.

1049–1148 God's anger with impurity shows how much he loves the pure. If we wish to see his face, we must, like Christ, be as *clene* as the pearl (1067–8). This is best shown in Christ's life on earth: he was born of a virgin, who was the *clener* (1072) for having conceived him; the birth itself occurred in *puryté* (1074) and without pain, and the very beasts recognized Christ 'by his clannes for Kyng of nature' (1087); Christ's touch was enough to heal the sick 'Wel clanner then any crafte cowthe devyse' (1100) and even to raise the dead; and he could break bread with his fingers as cleanly as if he had used a knife. We can gain such purity ourselves by being like the pearl; if it gets soiled, it can be restored by being washed, and so men, if they sin, can regain purity by confession and absolution. But once a soul has been purified in this way, God takes it as his own, and is doubly angry if it relapses into sin; he cannot abide the defilement of any vessel consecrated to his service.

1149–1332 This is shown by the story of Belshazzar. This is the third of the poet's chief exemplary narratives, and once more it has two episodes. In the first he relates how, because of Zedekiah's 'abominaciones of idolatrye' (1173), Nebuchadnezzar was permitted by God to defeat him and to take the sacred vessels from the temple. Nebuchadnezzar's general, Nebuzaradan, captures Jerusalem and slaughters its inhabitants, but Nebuchadnezzar himself treats the sacred vessels reverently and locks them in his treasury.

1333–1796 After his death, his idolatrous son Belshazzar treats them less well: he holds a great feast, and has the temple vessels brought out for himself and his concubines to drink from. At this a mysterious hand appears and writes on the wall of his palace 'Mane, Techal, Phares'. None can interpret the message except Daniel, who reminds Belshazzar of how his father was transformed into a beast for his pride but restored to his human shape when he acknowledged God's power, and then goes on to explain that the message means that Belshazzar's rule is over. That very night the Medes and Persians capture Babylon, and Belshazzar is gruesomely slaughtered.

1797–1812 In a brief conclusion, the poet explains that Belshazzar was punished for his *fylthe* (1798) in defiling the sacred vessels, and repeats that God punishes *unclannes* (1806) but will reward the pure.

Now clearly one way to approach this poem would be through the intricacies of its structure of narratives: the partially overlapping pairs and triads, the subtle proportions, the ways in which chronological sequence is made to convey semantic disjunction, and so on. This kind of formal analysis has not been much attempted, yet it would be appropriate to a poet who is keenly aware of the relationship of form and content: in *Purity* itself he begins by noting that the praise of *clannesse* would be readily conveyed by the 'Fayre formez' that match it, while in *Patience* (37–40) he comments on how the *forme* of the Beatitudes expresses their meaning.[2] Another approach which has been taken up by a few recent commentators is the analysis of recurrent themes which link together the different narratives.[3] An obvious and important theme is that of the feast, the shared meal in which hospitality is offered and received. This theme is already adumbrated in the brief sketch of the earthly lord, seated in state 'Abof dukez on dece, with dayntys served' (38), and offended by the breathless arrival of a ragged messenger or suppliant. It is developed more fully in the parable, in which the earthly becomes a heavenly feast, a figure of the heavenly reward from which the invited guests (the original chosen people, in the common allegorical interpretation) exclude themselves, and from which the unhappy conscript who lacks a 'festival frok' and comes in a garment 'fyled with werkkez' (136) (literally his work, allegorically his works) is hurled into outer darkness. There is a momentary dark inversion of the heavenly feast when the raven sent out by Noah fills its belly with the 'foule flesch' (462) of some carrion left over from the Flood. In the second major exemplum, man is host to God, as Abraham entertains the angels to a meal delightfully imagined as an English picnic, with a 'clene cloth' spread 'on the grene' (634); and then, when Lot similarly offers hospitality to angelic messengers, his wife disobeys his instructions to omit leaven and salt from their food. The aftermath of the destruction of the cities is a hideous parody of a feast: trees bearing Dead Sea fruit that look delicious but when bitten prove to be full of ashes. The theme reaches its culmination in the full-scale inversion of Belshazzar's feast, at which there is all the outward appearance of plenty and ceremonious order, but those seated at the high table with the king are his concubines, and the consecrated vessels are used to honour gluttony and lechery. This time it is the host who is cast into outer darkness, reduced from a king to 'a dogge . . . in a dych' (1792), and excluded for ever from the sight of God.

Another linking theme, and one that brings me nearer to my main subject, is that of washing, considered as a means of purification and renewal. This is connected with feasting, because washing is part of the etiquette of hospitality: Abraham hastens to wash the feet of his angelic guests (617–18), Lot offers to do the same (802), and his angels wash after supper (831). But washing also has larger significances. At the beginning we are warned not to approach heaven with 'handez unwaschen' (34); God speaks of the Flood as 'a water to wasch alle the worlde' (323); and just as the pearl may be cleaned if washed in wine, so a man who has sinned may be 'waschen wyth water of schryfte' (1133).

But for all these thematic parallels, there remains a large question about the real cohesiveness of the various narratives, with their apparently very different subject matter. The parallels may be no more than decorative, or barrenly ingenious. This is the view that has been taken by many commentators. One editor, in a note on the lines about Christ's breaking of bread (1105–8), wrote that 'The lines . . . have, of course, little to do with Christ's purity, and the passage is introduced only by means of a kind of play on words.'[4] Another scholar remarked about the structure of the whole poem that the 'ambitious scheme is not entirely successful, for, in order to include the story of Belshazzar's Feast, the poet has to juggle with his interpretation of "uncleanness" and make it cover the defiling of what belongs to God as well as unchastity'.[5] And the author of a more recent (and often very perceptive) book about the poet's work takes the same line:

The imprecise presentation of purity [in lines 17–20] (let alone the feebleness of the suggestion that we are to be impressed by the contents of God's linen-cupboards) reflects the poet's treatment for most of the poem . . . beneath the reasonable surface there is no actual reasoning, at least not a continuous reasoning, but rather an assembling of aspects of the idea of purity and its opposite . . . Logically Christ's clean breaking of bread and Belshazzar's unclean bibbing of wine have little, if anything, to do with one another . . .[6]

Such readers, who *know* what purity and uncleanness are ('of course'), and who *know* that, whatever the *Gawain*-poet may have thought or felt, Christ's clean breaking of bread and Belshazzar's unclean bibbing of wine have nothing to do with one another, are approaching the symbolic structure created by the medieval poet somewhat in the manner of missionaries contemplating the rites of a primitive tribe, or of rational Christians reading the precise statements of Judaic law in Leviticus. They *know* that, let us say, contact with a menstruating woman has no connection with sickness, or they *know* that holiness has nothing to do with not eating camels, rock-badgers, and hares.[7] A wiser approach, I believe, may be one comparable to that of the anthropologist, who tries to set aside the preconceptions that belong to his own culture, in order to enter into the whole world of thought and feeling of the culture he is studying, and to recognize its inner logic. It may not be the abstract logic that confidently denies that two concrete experiences can have anything to do with each other; it may depend on something more like the 'science of the concrete' that Claude Lévi-Strauss identifies as underlying totemic classifications.[8]

In one way the parallel with the anthropologist's approach to the primitive tribe is not a good one, because the *Gawain*-poet is no primitive, participating unquestioningly in the customs of his ancestors, but a highly sophisticated and self-conscious artist working within a complex international culture; he has a wide range of choices available to him, and is not at all afraid of innovation. But cultures such as his (including our own) also organize experience through symbolism and ritual, and that is where the anthropologist can help us. The method the *Gawain*-poet is using in *Purity* is fairly clear. The poem can be seen as offering a kind of definition of the opposing concepts of *clannes* and *fylthe*, and as doing so not in abstract terms but, as one might say, ideogrammatically. (Which is also to say, in the manner apt to alliterative poetry.) Ernest Fenollosa was evidently quite wrong about Chinese ideograms, but his conception of the ideogram, as transmitted by Ezra Pound, gives a useful clue to the *Gawain*-poet's method. Fenollosa distinguishes between what he calls 'the tyranny of mediaeval logic' on the one hand and science and poetry on the other. Logic moves further and further away from *things* and their powers and properties towards abstraction: thus it substitutes the concept 'redness' for things that are actually red – 'cherry, rose, sunset, iron-rust, flamingo'. Science, however, deals with things rather than classes, while

Poetic thought works by suggestion, crowding maximum meaning into the single phrase pregnant, charged, and luminous from within.

In Chinese character each work accumulated this sort of energy in itself.

And, in principle at least, the ideogram for 'red' would combine pictures of things such as those mentioned that are actually red. Hence

In reading Chinese we do not seem to be juggling mental counters, but to be watching *things* work out their own fate.[9]

In *Purity* the narrative exempla have a function analogous to Fenollosa's *things*, and, though the poet does not attempt to abandon completely the classifying abstractions of 'mediaeval logic', he never allows them to lose contact with the energy of narrative events. In effect, he does on the level of narrative what Chinese poetry, as imagined by Fenollosa, does on the level of language. In the poem's longest passage on *clannes* itself, that on Christ's earthly life, *clannes* 'is' whatever the various instances have in common – the clean birth from a clean virgin, the cleansing power of Christ's touch, the ability to break bread cleanly with his fingers. In the much longer passages exemplifying God's hatred and punishment of uncleanness, *fylthe* 'is' whatever the common property is of the guest in dirty clothes, the homosexuality and miscegenation of mankind in Noah's time, the perversion of the Sodomites, the leaven and salt that Lot's wife was forbidden to serve to the angels, Belshazzar's defilement of the sacred vessels. If we begin by simply denying, from a position of unassailable because unselfcritical commonsense, that these things and events have anything in common, we cannot hope to make any advance in understanding the poem. Mary Douglas can help us to understand what these apparently disparate items do have in common, and how they fit together into a meaningful pattern of thought.

Let us begin from the hypothesis that the *Gawain*-poet is thinking about *clannes* and *fylthe* in a way which is coherent and self-consistent, even if unfamiliar to us. A mere summary of the contents of his poem will imply that, if this is so, for him a single category encompasses both physical dirt and spiritual and moral pollution or defilement. This may indeed be an unfamiliar way of thinking, but Mary Douglas usefully reminds us that 'dirt' is not an absolute, for conceptions of dirt are relative: 'There is no such thing as absolute dirt: it exists in the eye of the beholder' (p. 2).[10] Because our feelings about dirt are so strong and so deeply embedded in our whole outlook on life, we are likely to resist recognizing this, appealing to universal custom or to the supposed objectivity of medical science to support our own assumptions; but any pair of people who live together, even if they belong to the same segment of the same culture, are likely to notice that their ideas as to whether crumbs, sawdust or mud count as dirt may differ, and may differ especially in accordance with where these things are found. The most general conception of dirt is provided by what Mary Douglas calls 'the old definition of dirt as matter out of place' (p. 35). She goes on: 'Where there is dirt there is system. Dirt is the by-product of a systematic ordering and classification of matter.' Thus we have the two complementary concepts of dirt and system, positive and negative aspects of the same whole. Elsewhere she makes the same point in other words: 'Dirt offends against order. Eliminating it is not a negative movement, but a positive effort to organize the environment' (p. 2).

The *Gawain*-poet's opening examples of *fylthe* clearly have this double aspect. Both the earthly and the heavenly feast are envisaged as manifestations of a hierarchical order, rather than as mere serve-yourself scrambles for food and drink. The earthly lord is 'sette solempnely in a sete ryche, / Abof dukez on dece, with dayntys served' (37–8), and the intruder is not literally in soiled clothes, but in old, torn ones.

> With rent cokrez at the kne and his clutte traschez,
> And his tabarde totorne, and his totez oute. (40–1)

It is because of this offence against etiquette that he is flung out, the ceremonial order being thereby strengthened. At the heavenly feast, even the strangers brought in from the highways and byways are seated in due order, according to the social status marked by their clothes:

> Ay the best byfore and bryghtest atyred,
> The derrest at the hyghe dese, that dubbed wer fayrest,
> And sythen on lenthe bilooghe ledez inogh.
> And ay as segges serly semed by her wedez,
> So with marschal at her mete mensked thay were.
> Clene men in compaynye forknowen wern lyte,
> And yet the symplest in that sale watz served to the fulle,
> Bothe with menske and with mete and mynstrasy noble,
> And alle the laykez that a lord aght in londe schewe. (114–22)

When the lord emerges from his private chamber to spread good cheer among his guests, he begins with 'the best on the bench' (130), and then moves down among the less noble guests. It is now that he catches sight of the wretch dressed in *fowle* (140), work-soiled clothes, angrily denounces him for daring to enter his presence in such insultingly improper dress, and orders him to be fettered and cast into his dungeon. From the point of view of a rational morality of intention, the guest is not blameworthy: he has come to the feast only because he has been press-ganged by the lord's officers, and it is hardly his fault if he is wearing working clothes – soiled, likely enough, by the relentless agricultural labour necessary to produce the food eaten at the feast. For all the officers knew, it might have been Piers the Plowman himself whom they forced to fill a place at the lord's table! The moral issue, however, is subtly blurred by the poet's use of a concealed level of meaning: a level of suggestion rather than the clear-cut allegorical exegesis found in most medieval interpretations of the parable, on which the clothes 'fyled with werkkez' (136) are soiled not only with the guest's work but with his works. The poet subsequently does allegorize his narrative in part, explaining that clothes generally – as often in medieval thought – represent the deeds or moral state of their wearer. The allegorical interpretation, though, by no means exhausts the narrative's full significance, and we are left chiefly with the sense that the wrongly clad guest is expelled for pollution rather than punished for sin. As with the earthly feast, the systematic order which has the lord as its centre is strengthened by this gesture which expels from it an element that threatens its inner boundaries.

If we now turn to the three main exempla of *fylthe* and its punishment, we shall see that they can be understood in similar terms, as involving the destruction of elements that threaten the 'systematic ordering and classification' of experience, an ordering and classification that are conceived as divinely ordained. God is represented as feeling towards acts defined as perversion or pollution the physical disgust, the nausea, that men feel towards the anomalous. He says himself of the perversions that are rife in Noah's time that 'With her unworthelych werk me wlatez withinne' (I am inwardly disgusted at their shameful behaviour) (305), and the same verb is used to describe his reaction to the misuse of the sacred vessels by Belshazzar: 'the worcher of this worlde wlates therwyth' (1501). Similarly, just before his visit to Abraham, we are told that his response to 'dedez of schame' is to be 'skoymos of that skathe' (revolted by that sin) (597–8). The offences of mankind that provoke the Flood are defined precisely as offences against the universal system of categories that depend on separation and appropriateness – the integrity of the human species as against other species, and the integrity of the basic binary classification that assigns appropriate roles to the two sexes. As Mary Douglas puts it, 'Holiness means keeping distinct the categories of creation' (p. 53). When sexual intercourse takes place within the same sex, or between one race and another (in this case between human females and the fallen angels), these categories begin to blur, and the whole system is threatened.

Neither here nor in the exemplum of Abraham and Lot is the offence, as the critic quoted above suggests, 'unchastity' in the normal sense of the word. On the contrary, far more than most medieval religious writers, this poet stresses (and imagines a God who stresses) the element of rightful pleasure in sexuality, without referring at all to the goal of reproduction which was usually seen as its only justification. So far as animals are concerned, God orders Noah to set males and females alongside each other, 'Uche payre by payre to plese ayther other' (338). And when it comes to human beings, God tells Abraham that, by contrast with the perversions practised by the Sodomites,

> I compast hem a kynde crafte and kende hit hem derne,
> And amed hit in myn ordenaunce oddely dere,
> And dyght drwry therinne, doole alther-swettest,
> And the play of paramorez I portrayed myselven,
> And made therto a maner myriest of other:
> When two true togeder had tyyed hemselven,
> Bytwene a male and his make such merthe schulde come,
> Welnyghe pure paradys moght preve no better.   (697–704)

In this remarkably outspoken passage, as one critic has put it,

God uses an idiom more acceptable to readers of romance than to students of theology, stressing not the utilitarian end of sex aimed at its procreative potential but the intrinsic aesthetic value of love made in accord with divine artifice . . . The "play of paramorez" is a peculiarly apt phrase for the poet's vision of sexuality at its best, for like feasting, love-play requires the artful – even gratuitous – refinement of natural functions.[11]

There is even apparently nothing wrong in Lot's offering his own daughters as a substitute for the angels to satisfy the lusts of the Sodomites: he urges them, unsuccessfully as it turns out, 'laykez wyth hem as yow lyst' (872). As this last episode suggests, the *Gawain*-poet is typical of medieval clerkly writers (and of alliterative poets) in presenting women as objects rather than subjects, but he is more unusual in seeing appropriate sexual relations as directed towards mutual pleasure 'Bytwene a male and his make'; and we do not find in him the connection, so common elsewhere in the Middle Ages, between denigration of women and denunciation of sexual pleasure as sinful.[12] In his treatment of *clannes* and *fylthe* in the sexual sphere, as in other spheres, he is concerned less with morality and sin than with system and the pollution that endangers it.

On the level of symbol, these ideas are perhaps developed more fully in the Lot episode than in that of Noah. For one thing, the Sodomites are shown as attempting to penetrate the boundary of an enclosure; and enclosed spaces are very often manifestations of orderly classification. The Sodomites attempt to break down the walls of Lot's house in order to seize the angels; when Lot goes out to parley with them, he naturally pushes the gate to, 'That a clyket hit cleght clos hym byhynde' (858); and, after the angels have pulled him back in again and barred the gate, the Sodomites seek in vain for a chink in the walls. The traditional theme of Lot's wife and the salt serves a parallel purpose. The idea that Lot's wife was turned into a pillar of salt not just because she looked back towards Sodom but as an appropriate punishment for disobeying her husband's orders not to put salt in the angels' food goes back to an ancient Jewish legend,[13] and the medieval poet, himself something of an anthropologist in his approach to Jewish material, makes the dietary restriction contribute to his grand theme. What Lot actually tells his wife is:

> Bot thenkkez on hit be threfte what thynk so ye make,
> For wyth no sour ne no salt servez hym never.   (819–20)

He does not explain why, but clearly *sour* and *salt* are thought of as impurities. *Threfte* means 'unleavened' (Abraham provides 'therve kakez' [635] for his angels), and *sour* thus means 'leaven' (as in sourdough bread); and leaven may be perceived as a threat to the boundaries which sustain the order of the world, because it makes things to which it is added rise up uncontrollably. An analogy might be drawn with the Mosaic exclusion of swarming creatures as food, as interpreted by Mary Douglas:

At the level of a general taxonomy of living beings the purity in question is the purity of the categories. Creeping, swarming, teeming creatures abominably destroy the taxonomic boundaries.[14]

The poet regards such effects as disgusting: elsewhere he refers to the Sodomites as uttering 'yestande sorwe' (frothing filth) (846) in what they say to the angels, and he actually uses the phrase 'frothande fylthe' (1721) to refer to Belshazzar's misuse of the sacred vessels to drink to his false gods. On the one hand, then, we have the ideal of the seamless and perfect enclosure; on the other, the nauseatingly uncontrollable expansion of a substance that resists and attacks enclosures, overwhelms and obscures boundaries.

In the exemplum of Belshazzar, the idea of *fylthe* as threatening the 'systematic ordering and classification' of reality is presented with the greatest subtlety. Belshazzar is placed at the centre of a system of enclosures and demarcations: Babylon is enclosed within 'a wonder wrogt walle wruxeled ful highe' (1381), and within that is a further enclosure which is 'ever ilych sware' (1386) and which has his abode 'in the myddes' (1388). At his feast, the different orders of guests are classified according to their places: knights on the hall-floor, barons at the side-tables, and Belshazzar himself on the dais. But with him he has 'his clere concubynes in clothes ful bryght' (1400), and we are forced to recognize that this is a mere travesty of order, as indeed the whole feast is a mere parody of the heavenly feast of the parable. Nebuchadnezzar, we notice, was *not* punished for breaching the integrity of Jerusalem and its temple, or for taking away the sacred vessels. This was permitted by God because of the 'abominaciones of idolatrye' (1173) that were being practised by the Jews under Zedekiah; and Nebuchadnezzar then proceeds to re-enclose the vessels reverently in his treasury. Punishment comes only when Belshazzar after him commands his marshal 'coferes to lauce' (1428); obediently 'he with keyes uncloses kystes ful mony' (1438), and the vessels are then used for the wrong purpose, for 'vanyté unclene' (1713). It is this overriding of categories, the use of sacred vessels for profane purposes, that is the real impurity, and that unleashes God's destructive anger.

There are certain passages in the poem that directly celebrate *clannes* rather than showing the rejection of *fylthe*. The chief of these, the bridge-passage between the second and third exempla, is a particularly clear illustration of how *clannes* is envisaged by the poet as a matter of order, classification, sharp boundaries, enclosures. Christ's conception caused no breach of the Blessed Virgin's bodily wholeness,

> When venkkyst watz no vergynyté, ne vyolence maked,
> Bot much clener watz hir corse, God kynned therinne.   (1071–2)

His birth did not involve the messiness of normal human births, but a sharp separation: 'And efte when he borne watz in Bethelen the

Purity and danger

ryche,/ In wych puryté thay departed . . .' (1073–4), 'For non so
clene of such a clos com never er thenne' (1088). In his earthly life
Jesus was intensely fastidious and 'nolde never towche/ Oght that
watz ungoderly other ordure watz inne' (1091–2), yet by his mere
touch he could cleanse the diseased and crippled. The list of evi-
dences of Christ's *clannes* reaches its culmination in what may seem
a trivial detail, even if we are willing to allow its relevance, his
ability to break bread with his fingers more delicately and exactly
than others could cut it with the sharpest blades:

> Forthy brek he the bred blades wythouten,
> For hit ferde freloker in fete in his fayre honde,
> Displayed more pryvyly when he hit part schulde
> Thenne alle the toles of Tolowse moght tyght hit to kerve.   (1105–8)

It was pointed out long ago that one point of this assertion is that
in the fourteenth century it was good manners to cut bread with a
knife; thus the poet, as elsewhere in his work, is defining God in
terms of a human conception of *cortaysye*.[15] That is a valid and
useful observation, but a more important point is that the passage
on Christ as exemplar of *clannes* should reach its climax in this act
of sharp separation. The poet did not invent it – it is found in
several of the Mystery cycles – but he did give it this key position.
The whole life of Christ is seen in terms of what Mary Douglas
calls 'gestures of separation, classifying and cleansing' (p. vii). And
what follows is the passage comparing the human soul to a pearl –
also of course a familiar idea elsewhere in the *Gawain*-poet's work.
The pearl is a supreme image of divine perfection and purity:
white, shining, incorruptible, round, seamless, altogether
'Wythouten faut other fylthe' (1122). The poem offers other
images, too, of the divine purity that is based on orderly classifi-
cation. A prominent one is the Ark, geometrically exact in shape,
'A cofer closed of tres clanlych planed' (310), every chink stopped
up, 'closed . . . with clay alle aboute' (346); and then internally
divided with precision into many separate compartments, 'wel
bounden penez' (322), which are used to keep apart the different
categories of beasts. (The division of animals into clean and
unclean at this point – *clene* and *horwed* [334–5] – derives, like so
much in the poem, from the Jewish conception of purity, trans-
mitted through the Old Testament.) The Ark is naturally opposed
in every way to the Flood, which rises up uncontrollably, destroy-
ing boundaries – 'Watz no brymme that abod unbrosten bylyve'

185

(365) – and mingling together the elements that were separated when God created the world.

Meaning itself depends on separation, as does the expression of meaning through the various symbolic systems, of which writing is the most complex and the most characteristically human. (Even the binary language of computers requires a clear separation between 0 and 1.) The *Gawain*-poet may well have been a cleric; he was certainly intensely clerkly, and his deep attachment to the apparatus of literacy reveals itself indirectly in some of his similes. A particularly splendid one is used to describe the destruction of the cities of the plain, when

> . . . alle the regioun torof in riftes ful grete,
> And cloven alle in lyttel cloutes the clyffez aywhere,
> As lauce levez of the boke that lepes in twynne. (964–6)

The ultimate destructive act is imagined as the tearing apart of a book (here with an allusion to the book of Creation, in which, in its wholeness, God's meanings are to be read); and later on, when the poet is discussing the purification of the soul, he says that the effect of shrift is to make it 'polysed als playn as parchmen schaven' (1134) – and thus presumably ready for the divine message to be written on it. Julia Kristeva, drawing out some implications of Mary Douglas's thought, points to the way in which defilement is a threat to the possibility of symbolism itself:

> . . . the danger of filth represents for the subject the risk to which the very symbolic order is permanently exposed, to the extent that it is a device of discriminations, of differences.

Later she speculates as follows:

> . . . the frequency of defilement rites in societies *without writing* leads one to think that such cathartic rites function like a "writing of the real." They parcel out, demarcate, delineate an order, a framework, a sociality, without having any other signification than the one inhering in that very parceling and the order thus concatenated. One might ask, proceeding in reverse, if all writing is not a second level rite, at the level of language, that is, which causes one to be reminded, through the linguistic signs themselves, of the demarcations that precondition them . . .[16]

Whether or not this is generally true, for the *Gawain*-poet writing appears to be the supreme form of demarcation, and thus the absolute antithesis of *fylthe*. And so it is peculiarly appropriate that, in his final exemplum, God's opposition to the *fylthe* of Belshazzar should be expressed in the form of writing – the writing on the wall of the palace of three words by a disembodied hand. (This is one of only two explicit references to writing in the whole poem, and by far the most elaborate: earlier references to the text of Scripture, except for *wryt* at line 657, mention it as spoken by Christ or by the Evangelists.)

The words on the palace wall are meaningless, not even distinguishable as words, to Belshazzar himself and his 'burnes . . . that were bok-lered' (1551). These interpreters of Belshazzar's are sinister pagan figures, men

> That wer wyse of wychecrafte, and warlawes other
> That con dele with demerlayk and devine lettres, . . .
>
> As the sage sathrapas that sorsory couthe,
> Wyches and walkyries wonnen to that sale,
> Devinores of demorlaykes that dremes cowthe rede,
> Sorsers of exorsismus and fele such clerkes;
> And alle that loked on that letter as lewed thay were
> As thay had loked in the lether of my lyft bote. (1560–1, 1576–81)

The poet's contemptuous pun on *letter* and *lether* disposes of the scholarly pretensions of these witch-doctors; and it is only Daniel, the prophet inspired by God, who is capable first of distinguishing 'the tyxte of the tede lettres' – that is, of recognizing them as language at all – then of interpreting 'the mater of the mode' (1634–5). And this intended meaning proves to concern separation, demarcation: God, Daniel tells Belshazzar, 'Hatz counted thy kyndam bi a clene noumbre' (1731) (number being, in the medieval view, the basis on which God produced the universe out of chaos), with the outcome that 'Departed is thy pryncipalté . . .' (1738). (Compare the use of the same verb of separation in the earlier reference to the cleanness of Christ's birth of the Virgin: 'In wych puryté thay departed . . .' [1074].)

A possible objection to my general line of argument might be that many of the items in the poem to which I have drawn attention are of little significance as symbols because they could scarcely be otherwise in reality. Medieval cities and gardens really were enclosed by walls and ditches, the Ark really had to have all chinks stopped up or it would not have been watertight, you really cannot get something out of a closed cupboard except by opening it, writing really is used to convey messages, and so on. But there is of course no necessary opposition between the functional and the symbolic, and in any case my argument is not that the poet creates symbolic oppositions out of nothing, but that he concentrates and focuses and develops symbolic oppositions that were part of the experience of his time, and that may indeed be part of universal human experience. He is speaking the language of his world, but in a clearer, subtler, more forceful idiom; or perhaps we should think of him as a Daniel, a writer-prophet inspired to understand the babble of his world as a text.

The point we have reached so far is that the poem's pervasive contrast of *fylthe* and *clannes* is equivalent to Mary Douglas's contrast between 'dirt' and 'order', and that the exemplary punishment of human *fylthe* by God can be seen, in her terms, as 'not a negative movement, but a positive effort to organize the environment', and thereby as a demonstration of God's own *clannes*, the holiness that depends on separation. But to leave it at that would be misleading, because it may well seem a paradox that this poem, explicitly dedicated to the commendation of *clannes*, should invest so much imaginative energy in boundary-wrecking violence and destruction. (It must be added that such paradoxes are familiar enough in our experience of major literature, *Paradise Lost* being only the most notorious case.) Many of the most powerful passages in *Purity* are evocations of the violent and vengeful destructiveness with which God punishes human transgression. For instance, the Flood and the suffering it causes to men and beasts are described with the extraordinary force that alliterative verse can confer on such subject matter, and with what can only be called relish:

> Then bolned the abyme, and bonkez con ryse,
> Waltes out uch walle-heved in ful wode stremez;
> Watz no brymme that abod unbrosten bylyve;
> The mukel lavande loghe to the lyfte rered.
> Mony clustered clowde clef alle in clowtez;
> Torent uch a rayn-ryfte and rusched to the urthe,
> Fon never in forty dayes, and then the flod ryses,
> Overwaltez uche a wod and the wyde feldez;
> For when the water of the welkyn with the worlde mette,
> Alle that deth moght dryghe drowned therinne.　　　(363–72)

Here and in the destruction of the cities of the plain, a sense is conveyed of the unleashing of dangerous energies that are inherent in the very substance of the world as God created it – 'the houndez of heven' (961) as they are called on that later occasion. Moreover, though the Flood comes as a punishment to human *fylthe*, its immediate effect is to create more *fylthe* of the most literal kind, by first obliterating distinctions, as between *wod* and *felde*, *welkyn* and *worlde*, and then turning the order of the living creation into mud and corruption:

> Thenne mourkne in the mudde most ful nede
> Alle that spyrakle inspranc – no sprawlyng awayled.   (407–8)

The carrion which attracts that unclean beast the raven would not be there if God had not commanded the deluge. From one point of view, the Flood is 'a water to wasche alle the world' (323), and its ultimate outcome is a re-establishment of the order of things on the firm basis of the rainbow covenant, after which times and seasons keep within their regular limits and the different species of animals return to their allotted habitats,

> Uche fowle to the flyght that fytherez myght serve,
> Uche fysch to the flod that fynne couthe nayte,
> Uche beste to the bent that bytes on erbez.   (530–2)

But from another point of view, very powerfully expressed in the poetry, the Flood is a manifestation of *fylthe*, not of *clannes*.

This is even more strikingly true of the divine vengeance taken on the cities of the plain. Sodom had been 'an erde of erthe the swettest,/ As aparaunt to paradis, that plantted the Dryghtyn' (1006–7), but when Abraham gazes at it after disaster has struck, it is obscured by a pall of smoke and ashes. The disaster itself is experienced as a tearing apart of the very elements, as we have seen in the simile of the book burst open. After the mushroom cloud has disappeared, the consequence is what we have come to know and fear in our own century: a dead landscape, and one rendered more hideous by elemental and genetic mutations – a sea

> That ay is drovy and dym, and ded in hit kynde,
> Blo, blubrande, and blak, unblythe to neghe;
> As a stynkande stanc that stryed synne,
> That ever of smelle and of smach smart is to fele,   (1016–19)

in which lead floats and feathers sink, a soil that eats away flesh and bones, and fruit that is outwardly 'the fayrest fryt that may on folde growe' (1043) but inwardly full of ashes. In one sense, it is appropriate that unnatural sin should be punished by the turning of a paradisal city into a place 'corsed of kynde' (1033); but, against that, the outcome seems to be not purification but a different kind of *fylthe*, produced by the destruction of elemental categories. And we find the same thing with the third main exemplum. In his punishment of Belshazzar, God works not through Nature but through man, and there is no deluge or nuclear explosion, but the taking of a city by assault. We saw, though, in the discussion of the *Morte Arthure* in Chapter 6, what destructive violence that event was likely to involve in medieval reality; it was intrinsically a matter of the breaking of boundaries, and in this case it culminates in a peculiarly sickening breach of a human body, and a mingling together of bodily substances that should be kept separate:

> Baltazar in his bed watz beten to dethe,
> That bothe his blod and his brayn blende on the clothes.   (1787–8)

I used to think it a flaw in the poem that its greatest strength should lie in these passages of violent destruction; they seem to suggest, after all, a God more notable for his vindictiveness than for his purity. But here too Mary Douglas's thought has helped me to recognize the poem's cohesiveness, though it now seems to me to cohere on a level which it cannot fully express in terms of its explicit doctrines. Douglas points out that there is a certain ambiguity in the general relation of disorder to pattern. She writes:

> Granted that disorder spoils pattern; it also provides the materials of pattern . . .
> This is why, though we seek to create order, we do not simply condemn disorder. We recognise that it is destructive to existing patterns; also that it has potentiality. It symbolises both danger and power.   (p. 94)

And she goes on to note that it is in margins, boundaries, transitional states, that both danger and power are to be perceived most strongly. To quote her again:

> The danger which is risked by boundary transgression is power. Those vulnerable margins and those attacking forces which threaten to destroy good order represent the powers inhering in the cosmos. Ritual which can harness these for good is harnessing power indeed.   (p. 161)

These 'powers inhering in the cosmos' are what the *Gawain*-poet meant by 'God', and in a real sense he celebrates God by meditating on the power and the danger which are inseparable from God's purity or holiness. On the one hand, his is a world in which everything is linked by a strenuous concrete logic, so that a touch of leaven in food or a misuse of the human body can unleash terrifying destructive forces; but on the other it is one in which the disorder thereby created is only the material for the creation of further order, including the order of his own poetic art. Out of the deluge comes the rainbow; and poetry such as his is the secular equivalent to a ritual which harnesses the forces of disorder for good.

I want to end this chapter by moving beyond *Purity* to look briefly at the *Gawain*-poet's work as a whole in the light of Mary Douglas's ideas. The *Gawain*-poet is notoriously one with a passion for pattern, a rage for order. Modern scholars have noted, for example, that the five fives of the pentangle Sir Gawain bears as his emblem are described in a stanza of five times five plus five lines in a poem consisting of twenty-five hundred and twenty-five plus five lines. Such numerological and metrical architecture may well underlie much of the poet's work; it is most obviously so in *Pearl* and *Sir Gawain and the Green Knight*, but it seems likely enough, for instance, that the many Scriptural numbers and measurements reproduced in *Purity* have further significances, even though attempts to interpret them now may not carry conviction. The poet's interest in number is only one aspect of his love for what is ordered, categorized, and demarcated – a castle or an ark minutely divided into different rooms, each with its own purpose, a hunt conducted precisely according to the accepted rules, a heavenly city built 'ful sware,/ As longe as brode as hyghe ful fayre' (*Pearl* 1023–4), a passage of Scripture in which the end exactly answers the beginning (such as the Beatitudes, as described in *Patience* 37–40), a poem built on the same cyclic model even though it includes the warning that 'The forme to the fynisment foldez ful selden' (*Gawain* 499), and so on. But the poet also possesses a willingness to confront, immerse himself in and express disorder and anomaly; and this is one of the things that make him a great poet, who can still speak to us today, and not merely a master craftsman of his own age.

Thus in *Patience*, very much as in *Purity*, God, the focus of cosmic order, displays his power centrally through dangerous violence, realized in the magnificent poetry of the great storm that first threatens shipwreck to the vessel in which Jonah has embarked, and then causes him to be swallowed up by the whale. The outbreak of violence is touched off by Jonah's refusal to fit into the category that God assigns to him, that of prophet to the Ninevites. Significantly for this chapter's argument, it takes place on the margins, when Jonah is fleeing from 'the termes of Judé' (61) and before he has arrived at Tarshish; and it takes place, of course, at sea, in that element that dissolves boundaries and forms, yet at the same time purifies and is the source of new life. The storm at sea, noted in

Chapter 6 as a repeated topic in alliterative poetry,[17] here engages with larger meanings and takes on a poetic resonance paralleled only in late Shakespeare. In being swallowed up by the whale, Jonah is plunged into *fylthe* itself, a hellish confusion of 'saym and . . . sorwe' (275), 'ramel ande myre' (279); and yet, at the very heart of this nauseating impurity, he prays to God, finds a single corner 'Ther no defoule of no fylthe watz fest hym abute' (290), and comes to a new understanding of God's power and his mercy. Here it cannot be said that purity and impurity are the poles of the poet's thought: he does not simply repeat himself from one poem to another. In *Patience* the point is rather that the dangerous power exists, but that God shows the full extent of his merciful control by drawing back at the last moment from using it and plunging Jonah or Nineveh into total disorder.

In *Sir Gawain and the Green Knight*, and still more in *Pearl*, the expression of violence is more muted. In *Gawain* it is controlled by the rules of a variety of games (hunting, 'the lel layk of luf' [1513], the Exchange of Winnings, the Beheading Game, and so on), and in *Pearl* it is merely potential. What is confronted in both poems is anomaly. The events of *Pearl* take place on the border between this world and the next: in a visionary state, in which his body is on earth but his spirit journeying elsewhere 'In aventure ther mervaylez meven' (64), the narrator comes to the precise border, the river barrier 'by schore that scherez' (107), between the earthly and heavenly realms. If we want an illustration of the truth that power and danger inhere in boundaries, we should note how the narrator's vision is brought abruptly to an end when he plunges recklessly into the river barrier itself. In this poem there is a pervasive contrast between the purity inhering in the Pearl Maiden herself and the heavenly world to which she now belongs, and the impurity of all that is fleshly or creaturely. The *clot* or *moul* (22–3) of the grave, that mars the brightness of the earthly pearl, is also thought of as the element inhabited by all those who live on earth, even before their deaths: as the dreamer says, 'I am bot mokke and mul among' (905). The contrast to which I am refer-ring is also one between the inorganic and the organic: heavenly purity is evoked in images of metal and mineral, gold and precious stones, earthly impurity in images of flowers, corn, blood. There is thus a tendency for the heavenly to be experienced as alien to man, and this can helpfully be seen in the light of what Mary Douglas calls the 'final paradox of the search for purity' (p. 162). She goes on:

Purity and danger

There is hardly any pollution which does not have some primary physiological reference. As life is in the body it cannot be rejected outright. And as life must be affirmed, the most complete philosophies . . . must find some ultimate way of affirming that which has been rejected.   (p. 164)

The same is true of the most complete works of art; and the way found by the *Gawain*-poet is the acknowledgment of paradox and anomaly. In *Pearl* the earthly rose mysteriously *becomes* a heavenly pearl –

> For that thou lestez watz bot a rose
> That flowred and fayled as kynde hyt gef;
> Now thurgh kynde of the kyste that hyt con close
> To a perle of prys hit is put in pref   (269–72)

– and the poem presents for painful acceptance a whole dimension of the anomalous: the lost child that is dead yet living, the small daughter who has become her father's superior and instructor, a heavenly order in which hierarchy coexists with equality. Experiencing the events of the vision through the mind and senses of the entirely human visionary, we are invited in the name of heavenly purity to immerse ourselves in eventually unbearable anomaly and contradiction.

Lastly, *Sir Gawain and the Green Knight* begins most emphatically as a poem of the marginal and the anomalous. It opens on the very border between one year and the next, at that vulnerable moment 'Wyle Nw Yer watz so yep that hit was nwe cummen' (60), and shows a hierarchical society temporarily disordered by festivity and confronted by a figure who is anomaly personified – the Green Knight, who refuses to fit into the categories of giant or man, game or earnest, human or supernatural, knight or churl, green or gold, nature or art. Yet at this opening, and throughout the poem, the sense of danger is resolved into nervously boisterous comedy (itself perhaps an anomalous category). Gawain rides out beyond the bounds of his civilization, into a wilderness where the normal demarcations are in abeyance, finally into a forest where the natural species are inextricably muddled:

> The hasel and the hawthorne were harled al samen,
> With roghe raged mosse rayled aywhere . . .   (744–5)

Here the alliterative pressure to specify, to mention crabtrees rather than trees, or cuckoos, nightingales and thrushes rather than birds, is turned against itself: botanical species are distinguished only to be shown as indistinguishable, so that the natural order seems on the verge of dissolving into primeval chaos. By the end of the poem, Gawain is forced to recognize anomaly at the heart of his own value-system, which was earlier set out with geometrical clarity in the allegorized emblem of the pentangle. He cannot achieve both *clannes* and *cortaysye*: the rigidity and unbrokenness of the pentangle prove to be ill-adapted to the human body with its instinctive love of life. Thus, as we shall see in the next chapter, the endless knot of the pentangle has to give way to the broken and knotted green girdle, which moulds itself so much more easily to the human shape. The poem ends with moral and spiritual enigma, but it is the richest and most relaxed of all the poet's explorations of pattern and anomaly, purity and danger.

8 · The *Gawain*-poet's sense of an ending

In Chapter 5 I considered some of the problems of narrative closure as they appear in *Troilus and Criseyde*, setting Chaucer's poem alongside a selection of Middle English romances in order to see what similarities and differences there were between Chaucer's handling of these problems and the methods of his anonymous fellow-makers. Among major medieval English poems, *Troilus and Criseyde* is by no means the only one where the ending is problematic, ambiguous, or even absent. To consider Chaucer's work alone, *The Parliament of Fowls* ends with the poet waking from his dream but still in search of the 'certeyn thing' (20) that he was lacking before he fell asleep; *The Canterbury Tales* ends with the Retractions, a statement purporting to come from outside the fiction, that simultaneously renounces nearly all of Chaucer's works and, by naming them, claims them as his own; while *The House of Fame*, *Anelida and Arcite*, *The Legend of Good Women*, several of the individual *Canterbury Tales* and the whole collection of tales, are all left unfinished. If we look outside Chaucer, there is the striking case of *Piers Plowman*, where Langland passes over what seems an obvious opportunity for satisfying closure at the end of Passus XVIII of the B-text. The dreamer wakes from his dream of Christ's Harrowing of Hell and is drawn from his solitude back into the life of his family and of the whole community as they go to mass at Easter; but instead of halting there, Langland prefers to go on and end with apocalyptic confusion and the further projection of the dreamer's quest outside the poem into an unimaginable future. By contrast with these difficult closures, the *Gawain*-poet seems to have a more confident and controlled sense of an ending.[1]

What might be expected of a late-twentieth-century critic is that he should place a strong emphasis on the word 'seems', and should then go on to expose the problematic and ambiguous effects that underlie a merely apparent decisiveness of closure; for in our time there is a marked preference among literary intellectuals for uncertainty, inconclusiveness and whatever does *not* satisfy and console. The point has been made by Richard Levin about the interpretation of Shakespeare's plays: you can find innumerable late-twentieth-century readings that purport to establish that Shakespeare's apparent happy endings are really sombre, problematic and inconclusive, but scarcely a single one claiming to show that his apparent unhappy or cynical endings really offer unnoticed grounds for satisfaction and consolation. As Levin remarks, in a chapter called 'Refuting the Ending', 'I have never seen a refutation which forecast a happier state of affairs than the one presented in the conclusion.'[2] On the whole, I must admit that I share the taste of our time; I have a fine nose for the pleasing doubts that undermine a superficially secure closure; but in the case of the *Gawain*-poet I am forced to concede that, so long as we do not make impossible demands (for total unity, or for endings that leave us feeling that 'we know all there is or all there is to know'), the confidence and control implied by his complete poetic structures, and especially by their endings, are just what they seem. His closural movements are not simple, but they are secure and genuine; and in this chapter I want to investigate the means by which he gains this security and authenticity of closure in the two best-known of the poems attributed to him, *Sir Gawain and the Green Knight* and *Pearl*.

These are both poems in which explicit symbolism is of central importance, and I shall argue that in both of them the ending is achieved by a final development or even transformation in meaning of the poem's central symbol or symbols. I begin with *Sir Gawain and the Green Knight*, and I want to take up the story very near the end, at the point where the Beheading Game is completed. Instead of being beheaded, as he had feared, Gawain has received from the Green Knight only a slight cut in his neck, and has learned from him that the real test he had to undergo was not the Beheading Game itself but the temptation by the seductive lady at the castle. The cut was his punishment for the slight fault of accepting from her and concealing from her husband (contrary to the Exchange of Winnings agreement) the green girdle which she had offered him when he would accept nothing more than kisses from her. She had claimed that if anyone wore it,

> Ther is no hathel under heven tohewe hym that myght,
> For he myght not be slayn for slyght upon erthe. (1853–4)

Perhaps Gawain really did benefit from this magical protection; but, if so, it was only at the expense of breaking his agreement and thus falling short of the perfection of Christian knighthood at which he had aimed. A striking revelation which, rather oddly, is only implied at this point, not quite explicitly stated, is that the Green Knight was himself, in a different form, Gawain's host at the castle and the husband of the lady who tempted him. As Green Knight he now shows the genial hospitality belonging to his other role as lord of the castle, and invites Gawain to come back there with him, to be reconciled with the lady. Gawain declines, though with his traditional courtesy; but in referring to the lady and her aged chaperone, he lapses, understandably perhaps, into discourteous bitterness, comparing himself to those Old Testament heroes who were brought low by women's wiles, and saying that if he has done no better than they he deserves forgiveness:

> And alle thay were biwyled,
> With wymmen that thay used.
> Thagh I be now bigyled,
> Me think me burde be excused.   (2425–8)

It is difficult at this moment to decide between two explanations of Gawain's regression into the deeprooted clerical antifeminism of the Middle Ages. Is it to be attributed to the poet himself? – he probably was a cleric, and we might suppose that in certain circumstances he would class all women, or all Old Testament temptresses from Eve to Bathsheba, with Lot's wife. Or is the regression to be understood as Gawain's own, an index of the inner distress caused by the revelation of his falling-short at the very moment when he seemed to have succeeded?

But the Green Knight also makes Gawain another offer: he invites him to keep the green girdle as a 'token/ Of the chaunce of the Grene Chapel' (2398–9) and a souvenir for the future of the contest that is now over. This Gawain accepts, but for him the girdle is not a kind of campaign medal but a humbling reminder of the weakness of the flesh. He refers to it as a *luf-lace* (2438), a love-token; he did not literally succumb to the lady's sexual advances, yet it has been shown convincingly that women's girdles in folklore and in medieval narrative have 'clear sexual connotations'. Thus in a sense 'the girdle represents an event which never occurred';[3] but the impression given is that Gawain feels as if it did occur. And he is surely right: the Green Knight told him that he knew that Gawain's motive in accepting the girdle was 'Bot for ye lufed your lyf' (2368); and the 'love of life' that caused him to accept it and break the Exchange of

Winnings agreement is undoubtedly connected, at a deep level, with the sexual instinct – the urge to survive and the urge to reproduce, both, in the eyes of medieval Christianity, almost inevitably tainted with sin, but both necessary for the continuance of the human race. It will be helpful to give a little more consideration to the nature of the girdle as a *token* or symbol. As a number of recent critics have pointed out,[4] it obviously stands in symbolic opposition to the pentangle, the symbol of Gawain's five-times-five virtues, inscribed on his 'schelde and cote' (637). Gawain began this adventure as the knight of the pentangle, that emblem of perfection in which the religious and courtly virtues were, as it seemed, indissolubly combined. But as his adventure proceeded, and he was subjected to unexpected temptations (not just the test of courage and *trawthe* he had envisaged when he accepted the Green Knight's challenge), the pentangle disappeared from view. It did so quite literally, because his shield and coat-armour were stripped from Gawain on his arrival at the castle and were not worn while he was indoors there – especially not when he was in bed and was being visited by the lady. The girdle that she offered him then emerged to take the pentangle's place. The final mention of the pentangle occurs when Gawain is rearming himself to set out for the Green Chapel, and now it has even lost its name and become merely the *conysaunce* (2026), the heraldic identification. Moreover, Gawain then puts on the girdle on top of it, winding it firmly 'double hym aboute,/ Swythe swethled umbe his swange' (2033–4), above his coat-armour.

It is not uncommon for medieval romances to incorporate in their narratives symbolic objects that in some way emblematize their central core of meaning. Such emblems act in part, perhaps, as mnemonic devices to make that core of meaning more accessible to memory, but they also sometimes form enigmas which, in Robert Hanning's words,

. . . demand for themselves and their contextual narratives . . . above all interpretation – without, however, offering the satisfaction of being susceptible of a single, consistent, unchanging interpretation.[5]

This is true of several of the *lais* of Marie de France, of whom one critic has written that 'Her great talent is to concentrate, to crystall-ize emotion in a single image or in a sequence of dramatic images', and another that 'Perhaps the most recognizable "signature" of her work is the symbolic creature or artifact around which a *lai* is organized for maximum intensity and suggestiveness within the least possible narrative duration'.[6] Obvious instances include the nightingale in *Laustic* and the great bird that flies through the lady's window in *Yonec*. An example from the greatest and most original of the creators of medieval romance is the coronation robe worn by the hero of Chrétien's *Erec*, a symbol of the knowledge and wisdom required for true kingship, which Erec has had to strive so hard to gain.[7]

Sometimes, too, romances have at their core a pair of antithetical symbols, that in their opposition focus the story's meaning. One example occurs in Chaucer's *Knight's Tale*, where the prison in which Palamon and Arcite are shut up and the garden in which they see Emelye walking as they look from the prison window – two enclosures bounded by the same wall – seem to symbolize opposite aspects of the civilized life. Another pair of symbols, open to a wide variety of interpretations, is found in *The Franklin's Tale*, in the form of the garden on the cliff, where Dorigen's friends try to distract her from her grief, and the sinister black rocks beneath it. The pentangle and the girdle form such a pair of opposed symbolic objects in *Sir Gawain and the Green Knight*. The pentangle, like the circle or the sphere, is a natural symbol of perfection because it is a complete enclosure: its boundary is unbroken and leaves no gaps for imperfection to enter.[8] This is a point the poet stresses more than any other in his expository stanza on the pentangle and its meaning:

> For hit is a figure that haldez fyve poyntez
> And uche lyne umbelappez and loukez in other
> And ayquere hit is endelez (and Englych hit callen
> Overal, as I here, "the endeles knot").   (627–30)

(For it is a figure that contains five points, and every line overlaps with and locks into the next, and everywhere it is endless, and, as I understand, the English everywhere call it the endless knot.)

He stresses the same point again in the following stanza:

> Now alle these fyve sythez forsothe were fetled on this knyght
> And uchone halched in other, that non ende hade,
> And fyched upon fyve poyntez that fayld never,
> Ne samned never in no syde, ne sundred nouther,
> Withouten ende at any noke I oquere fynde,
> Whereever the gomen bygan or glode to an ende.   (656–61)

(Now all these five multiples truly were fastened upon this knight, and each was joined to the next, so that there was no end, and they were fixed upon five points that never failed, and they neither began nor parted on any side, without an end at any angle that I can find anywhere, wherever the process began or came to an end.)

Hanning, in the article from which I quoted above, argues that the poetic emblem as he defines it may go beyond the crystallization of meaning or feeling within the poetic narrative: it 'transcends its role as an element of the fiction in which it appears and becomes a powerful comment on the artistic enterprise of its creator'.[9] Whether or not this is generally true, these passages about the pentangle certainly seem to point to the nature of the poem itself; for the poem too is a figure so intricately wrought that everything in it connects with everything else, and it is endless in the sense that its end leads straight back into its beginning, with the last long alliterative line being an almost verbatim repetition of the first. In introducing his story the poet described it as being 'With lel letteres loken' (35) (linked or locked together with true letters) – perhaps an allusion to its nature as alliterative verse. With this might be compared the line just quoted describing the pentangle: 'uche lyne vmbelappez and loukez in other' (628) – especially since *lyne* could mean a line of a poem as well as one of the lines forming the pentangle. And it is well known that the poem has built into its architecture the five fives of the pentangle, in the repeated five-line bob-and-wheels, and in the way that the line, five lines from the end, that repeats the first line is line 2525. But the pentangle also implies a higher kind of perfection, that of God or heaven. It is endless (the word is used twice [629, 630]), it has no end (658), it has no beginning (659), it is without end (660). Endlessness is the normal Middle English word for eternity. The mystic Julian of Norwich writes that God *is* endlessness:

. . . for his goodnes fulfillith all his creaturs and all his blessed workes, and over passith without end. For he is the endlesshead . . .[10]

And in the same period as Julian and the *Gawain*-poet, the first stanza of the York cycle of Mystery plays, spoken by God, begins by saying that he is without beginning and ends by saying (twice) that he is without ending:

> I am gracyus and grete, God withoutyn begynnyng,
> I am maker unmade, all mighte es in me;
> I am lyfe and way unto welth-wynnyng,
> I am formaste and fyrste, als I byd sall it be.
> My blyssing o ble sall be blendyng,
> And heldand, fro harme to be hydande,

My body in blys ay abydande,
Unendande, withoutyn any endyng.[11]

Moreover, on the one other occasion when the *Gawain*-poet himself uses the word 'endless', in *Pearl*, it is to describe the pearl at the Maiden's breast, which is 'endelez rounde' (738) and therefore appropriately, as in the parable of the Pearl of Great Price, symbolizes the kingdom of heaven.

But the pentangle is far from being a comfortable figure; it is rigidly geometric, shaped like a stiffly extended man, and it is certainly not easy for any man to live up to the standard of perfection it demands; perhaps indeed it is not possible. The girdle, by contrast, is more flexible. It will take any shape: it fits the Lady's waist, but it also fits Gawain's. It can easily be hidden, but equally it can be worn conspicuously as a baldric. Very comfortable and accommodating, then, but also very treacherous. And whereas the pentangle is described as an 'endeles knot', the girdle has ends and can easily be knotted and unknotted. It is thus surely a natural symbol of human imperfection.[12] And it too perhaps has a bearing on the poem as a whole, as well as on the poem's hero. I can best indicate in what way this is so by mentioning that in an earlier discussion of the poem, published in 1970, before I had recognized the emblematic force of the girdle, I described *Sir Gawain and the Green Knight* as an 'open-ended' poem.[13] I was thinking then of the way it apparently leaves us with ambiguity and uncertainty (as we have already seen in the difficulty of assessing Gawain's misogynistic outburst); but I now recognize that it is open-ended in the same way as the girdle, infinitely flexible and adaptable. The girdle eventually takes the place of the pentangle as Gawain's chosen emblem, the *bende* (2506) or blazon of his sin; and it then becomes the chosen emblem of the whole Arthurian court. It is a reminder of the necessary imperfection of all human structures, whether of virtue or of art, however high their aspirations. The poem, like its hero, has not achieved the fixity of absolute perfection; on the other hand, imperfection, as we saw in discussing *Purity*, is the ground for change and growth (it is a *green* girdle, after all), by contrast with the static perfection of a figure like the pentangle, where energy constantly travels round in a single circuit.

I now want to go back to the closing stanzas of the poem, where the loose ends of the *histoire* are tied up. In response to Gawain's questions, the Green Knight gives his real name – Bertilak de

Hautdesert – and that of the old lady at the castle, Morgan la Fay. This involves explaining that Morgan, the famous enchantress, was responsible for transforming him into a green knight and sending him to Camelot, to test its reputation and to frighten Guenevere to death. One purpose of these explanations is surely to give the effect of closure; though a little reflection discloses that the explanation is badly in need of being explained. It is capable of being explained, though, and in a way that does not simply rely on reference to other texts in the great intertextual field of Arthurian romance. The testing of Camelot's reputation makes good sense, because in this poem Gawain has been Camelot's chosen representative, and reputation has been a central theme: Gawain's concern for his own reputation has been both a strength (in urging him to persist in seeking out the Green Knight and completing the Beheading Game) and a weakness (because his reputation as the knight of courtesy prevented him from disentangling himself from the lady's wiles and was used by her as a weapon against him). The references to Morgan and Guenevere need further comment. First, the placing of the blame for the disruption of Camelot upon a woman, and indeed upon a woman's enmity for another woman, is in keeping with the antifeminism we have seen Gawain expressing. The aged chaperone and the beautiful young wife were initially described jointly, in such a way as to seem like two different aspects of the same being. They are, as it were, two manifestations of the female principle, the enchantress and the seductress – a principle which is dangerous to knightly integrity and chastity, to the interwoven virtues of the pentangle. It is more dangerous, perhaps, than the obvious perils of battle and Beheading Game, but it constitutes a test to which the knight must be subjected if he is to prove himself. (For a psychoanalytic interpretation of the poem, and of romance generally, the reason for that 'must', which appears as one of the conventions of romance, is that all female antagonists are versions of the mother, and the hero can achieve maturity only by escaping from her toils.[14]) Second, Morgan is not just any enchantress; as the Green Knight points out, she is Gawain's aunt. Gawain is Arthur's nephew, and has declared himself proud to have Arthur's blood flowing in his veins; now he has to face the fact that he is also Morgan's nephew, and that he inherits dangerous female blood as well as valiant male blood.[15] So perhaps it is not surprising that in this testing adventure he has done well but not perfectly. If only a man could be descended entirely from men! – that is the dream of medieval clerical culture, the product of celibate males. But it is not possible, and the fact that it is not makes life more dangerous but also more interesting. The poet does not attempt to realize in psychological terms Gawain's response to this revelation. But perhaps the revelation itself confirms that, when Gawain learned how he had fallen into a trap at Bertilak's castle, he was right not simply to displace his anger first on to the girdle – 'Lo! ther the falssyng – foule mot hit falle!' (2378) – and then on to women, but finally to direct it against himself, and to take the lady's girdle as his own emblem. Something in himself led him to accept the girdle; he was not just trapped by a deception external to his own nature.

In the course of Gawain's journey back to Camelot, the wound in his neck from the Green Knight's symbolic axe-blow heals, but he wears the girdle slantwise as a baldric, knotted under his left arm. He wears it on top of his coat-armour, on which the pentangle is inscribed; so the girdle is also like a diagonal stroke crossing out the pentangle. He wears it, we are told, 'In tokenyng he watz tane in tech of a faute' (2488) (to symbolize that he was detected as stained with a sin). Being found out was a crucial event for Gawain, for he showed no sign of feeling shame or guilt when he accepted and hid the girdle; it was only when he learned that his host *knew* what he had done that he blushed and winced with shame:

> Alle the blode of his brest blende in his face,
> That al he schrank for schome that the schalk talked.   (2370–1)

Reputation, as we have seen, is normally a central value in heroic narratives; they are products of what the anthropologists have taught us to call a shame-culture.[16] The general effect of later medieval Christianity was to press towards an internalization of the sense of sin, to move from shame to guilt, and that move is reflected in Gawain himself, as being shamed makes him recognize and feel his inner guilt. He wears the girdle openly, as a badge of shame, to mortify the reputation of which he has been so proud; and when he finally arrives at Camelot he voluntarily submits to the shame of telling the king and queen the story of his adventure. Once more he blushes:

> He tened quen he schulde telle,
> He groned for gref and grame;
> The blod in his face con melle,
> When he hit schulde schewe, for schame.   (2501–4)

But now, in the poem's final stanza, he can distinguish clearly between shame and guilt, as he could not before, and he says,

> . . . mon may hyden his harme bot unhap ne may hit,
> For ther hit onez is tachched twynne wil hit never.   (2511–12)

This is a very clear general statement that marks the transition from shame to guilt, for in a shame-culture a hidden fault would be as if it did not exist; but does it go too far? In *Purity*, as we have seen, and at several points in his other works, the *Gawain*-poet strongly emphasizes that by means of absolution the stain of sin *can* be wiped away; and this orthodox truth remains true whether or not the absolution that the Green Knight has purported to grant to Gawain at the Green Chapel is to be considered valid. Gawain, naturally enough in the circumstances, seems to have swung from one extreme to the other; but the court now redresses the balance.

They do so, apparently, without fully understanding what they are doing. They laugh loudly at Gawain's story, and their laughter suggests both resilience and a kind of foolishness. They have not undergone the chastening experiences that Gawain has suffered on their behalf, and they cannot fully understand them; but they can see that, as the Green Knight has pointed out, using the poet's favourite image of the pearl, Gawain is still the best of earthly knights:

> As perle bi the quite pese is of prys more,
> So is Gawayn, in god fayth, bi other gay knyghtez.   (2364–5)

He is only a man, subject to imperfection as all men are; so it is appropriate that, instead of being the sole wearer of the green girdle, he should be absorbed back into the court from which he emerged. They vow that they will all wear green girdles in just the same style,

> That lordes and ladis[17] that longed to the Table,
> Uche burne of the brotherhede, a bauderyk schulde have,
> A bende abelef hym aboute, of a bryght grene,
> And that, for sake of that segge, in swete to were.
> For that watz acorded the renoun of the Rounde Table
> And he honoured that hit hade, evermore after . . .   (2515–20)

For Gawain the girdle was a badge of shame marking his unique guilt; for the court it is a badge of honour in which the whole society can share. In one sense the effect of this, coming only a few lines from the end of the poem, is to leave it open-ended; whereas the pentangle had its meaning defined once and for all at the beginning, the girdle only acquires meanings as the poem proceeds, and it is left to us to complete the process of assigning a meaning to it.[18] But I would now say that openness and closure are not incompatible, and indeed that this poem achieves both in the same gesture.

Two medieval analogies can be offered to support this view. One is connected with the fact that the poem's final event is the establishment of a chivalric order, the Order of the Green Girdle. The fourteenth century, throughout Western Europe, is marked by a revival of chivalry as a conscious value-system through the establishment of many secular orders of chivalry. The first appears to have been the Order of the Band, founded by Alfonso XI of Castile about 1330, and having as its badge a sash or *banda* worn diagonally from the left shoulder to the waist (but vermilion, not green). This may possibly have become known in England through diplomatic contacts in the 1340s; in any case, it was followed in 1348 by Edward III's founding of one of the most famous and prestigious orders, the Order of the Garter.[19] (The king's original plan was for an Order of the Round Table; the Arthurian legend had already been absorbed into the political mythology of the English royal dynasties, and remained so down to the Tudors.) In many cases stories sprang up purporting to explain the origin of such orders; and in the case of the Garter, there is a fiction which can probably be traced at least to the 1430s, when the author of *Tirant lo Blanc* was in England. Edward III was dancing with a lady, when her garter fell to the ground; the onlookers laughed and, to cover her embarrassment, the King picked it up and fastened it round his own leg, saying 'Honi soit qui mal y pense' ('may he be shamed who thinks ill of it', or, in the better known version, 'evil be to him who evil thinks'). That saying became the motto of the order; and it is written in the *Gawain*-manuscript at the end of *Sir Gawain and the Green Knight*. Gollancz suggested that it might have been added 'by a later scribe', but this is by no means certain.[20] There is no reason, of course, to suppose that *Sir Gawain and the Green Knight* has any direct connection with the founding of the Order of the Garter, which took place nearly half a century before its probable date of composition; but the poem constitutes an aetiological myth or fiction of origin like the story of the Countess of Salisbury's garter, purporting to explain the foundation of the Order of the Green Girdle – also of course a fiction, at least so far as we know. It is of some interest that just as 'in early days there were lady associates of the Garter who received robes of the Order',[21] so the green girdle is to be worn by 'lordes *and ladis* that longed to the Table'. More important, the girdle, like the garter, is an article of ladies' apparel, with an unmistakeable sexual suggestiveness, adopted and worn by a man, and then turned into the badge of a chivalric order. More important still, what Edward III did in the story, by picking up the garter, was to convert a sign of shame into a sign of honour; and that is exactly what Arthur and his court do by adopting the girdle as a badge of *renoun*, 'And he honoured that hit hade, evermore after.'

The other analogy derives from the common practice in medieval religious writings of using wounds as an image for sins. In particular, Julian of Norwich, in Chapter 39 of the *Revelations of Divine Love*, explains (just as the *Gawain*-poet does in *Purity* and elsewhere) that the wounds of sin can be healed through shrift. Then 'contricion', 'compassion' and 'tru longyng to God' enable the sinner to be 'sodeynly delyverde of synne and of payne, and taken up to blysse'; and, once they have been healed, 'hys woundys be sene before God, nott as woundes but as wurshyppes'. And, she goes on, 'so shalle alle shame turne to worschyppe and to joy'.[22] Gawain's first badge of sin is the wound in his neck; he is certainly contrite, he receives a kind of absolution from the Green Knight, who tells him,

> I halde the polysed of that plyght and pured as clene
> As thou hadez never forfeted sythen thou watz fyrst borne,
>
> (2393–4)

and his wound heals on his homeward journey. It would be in accordance with Julian's thought for his other, voluntary badge of shame, the girdle, to be turned into a badge of honour. On the other hand, Julian is an unusually optimistic religious thinker; she finds it hard to imagine that God could be angry with man, and she insists on God's power to negate sin utterly, so that the wounds received from sin can themselves be honourable in God's sight, like the scars received by a knight in battle. The *Gawain*-poet is generally less optimistic, he believes most strongly in God's anger (as his accounts in *Purity* of God's punishments of sinners show), and we cannot necessarily impose Julian's solution on the poem's final paradox. However, like so many of the Middle English romances considered in Chapter 5, *Sir Gawain and the Green Knight* ends with a prayer, and one that in this case may be something more than a convention external to the substance of the work:

Mony aunterez herebiforne
Haf fallen suche er this.
Now that bere the croun of thorne,
He bryng uus to his blysse!
                    Amen   (2527–30)

Here a kenning substitutes for the name of Jesus the periphrasis
'[He] that bere the croun of thorne'. Christ was crowned with
thorns in mockery of his alleged claim to be King of the Jews; but
the crown of thorns has been transformed by his resurrection into a
badge of honour, a symbol of the triumph of the cross. It may be
worth bearing in mind that the crown of thorns is sometimes
described as green, and Langland indeed, in a phrase that turns it
into an emblem of triumph, calls it a 'garland of green thorn';[23]
moreover it is often depicted as looking not unlike a pentangle in its
spiky shape. Is this a glimpse of the mysterious way in which the
opposing symbols of pentangle and girdle could be reconciled? I
put that as a question rather than an answer. There may perhaps be
some transcendent level of royal power or divine grace on which
shame can be transformed into honour, and the poem does enough
to make us envisage that as a possibility. On the ordinary human
level we are left only with a prayer, which stands outside the formal
closure marked by the repetition of the poem's first line as line 2525,
and points towards a substantial closure elsewhere.

I now turn to *Pearl*, once more to focus on its ending; but first it
may be helpful to say something more generally about its patterned
quality. Even more than *Sir Gawain and the Green Knight*, *Pearl* as a
whole is an 'endless knot': each intricately rhymed stanza is linked to
the next by the repetition of words or phrases, and the last line
almost exactly repeats the first. Like *Sir Gawain and the Green Knight*
it has 101 stanzas; and the part played by fives in *Sir Gawain and the
Green Knight* is played even more prominently by twelves in *Pearl*,
where every stanza has twelve lines, and the line repeating the first is
line 1212. The numerical patterning of *Pearl* has been much dis-
cussed, and I shall not repeat the discussion: I think there would be
general agreement that, metrically and numerically, *Pearl* is 'prob-
ably the most complex poem written in English'.[24] Pattern-making
in any of the arts, though, can be relatively easy and trivial; what sets
the *Gawain*-poet above this level is that his work persistently
embraces that which resists pattern, whether the resistance is direct,
in the form of autonomous energies of growth and destruction, or

evasive, in the form of things like green girdles that are so flexible as to seem to escape categorization. In *Purity* especially, as we have observed, he writes of God's anger against *fylthe*, seeing it as a disruptive force comparable to human anger – 'Felle temptande tene towched his hert,/ As wyye wo hym withinne' (*Purity* 283–4) – and identifying it with the darker features of the natural world: floods, whirlwinds, storms at sea, flame descending from the heavens. He writes too about man's ineradicable desire to create structures that do not correspond to God's order. There is a constant dialectic in his work of pattern and resistance to pattern; while reading him one cannot fail to notice this, but it is evidently all too easy to forget it when discussing his work, and to reduce him to a mere maker of verbal and doctrinal patterns.

The pearl itself is manifestly the central symbol of the poem; and it does indeed symbolize the poem, just as I have argued the pentangle symbolizes *Sir Gawain and the Green Knight*. *Pearl* is a circular structure, ending where it begins, with the speaker returned to 'that erber wlonk' (1171) in which he originally fell asleep, and with a repetition of its first line as its last. The circle or sphere, a perfect two-dimensional or three-dimensional figure, is widely used as an emblem of divine perfection. In the medieval visual arts, from the thirteenth century on, God as creator is often depicted inscribing the great circle of the world with a compass, in accordance with Proverbs 8:27: 'When he prepared the heavens, I was there; when he set a compass upon the face of the depth'[25] – a text interpreted as the affirmation by Wisdom (that is, Christ) of his co-eternity with the Father. *Pearl* is full of pearls, earthly jewels which figure heavenly perfection, as in the parable of the Pearl of Great Price, which plays a crucial part in the poem; and the most prominent of them is the maiden called *Perle* whom the narrator meets, and recognizes as his dead daughter, in a vision of the other world. She is a human embodiment of heavenly perfection, in the form of an innocent who on her death has become one of the Brides of the Lamb in the heavenly Jerusalem. The poem's core of meaning is unquestionably focused in the pearl-symbol itself; in *Pearl* there is no antithetical central symbol, comparable to the girdle in *Sir Gawain and the Green Knight*, because the pearl and the Pearl Maiden are both heavenly *and* earthly. But two accompanying aspects of the poem's symbolism are worth comment.

One has been pointed out by Marie Borroff, namely that there *is* within the poem a symbolic opposite to the circular or spherical pearl, in the form of the line, even though this has no single objective embodiment.[26] As the pentangle is endless, so is the circle – 'endelez rounde' (738), as the poet puts it in the phrase I quoted earlier. This phrase comes from a passage comparable to the exposition of the pentangle symbolism in *Sir Gawain and the Green Knight*, where the Pearl Maiden is explaining why the pearl is an appropriate emblem for the kingdom of heaven, 'the reme of hevenesse clere' (735). And as the girdle has ends, so has the line. The line appears in *Pearl* in, for example, the retelling of the parable of the Labourers in the Vineyard, which the Pearl Maiden employs to explain to the dreamer the equality of heavenly rewards. In a detail that the poet has added to his Biblical source, the lord of the vineyard tells his steward to set the labourers 'upon a rawe' (545) (in a line) to receive their rewards at the end of the day.[27] The day of the parable (and this is strongly emphasized in the poem) has an end, a *date* or limit as the poet repeatedly calls it; and in the interpretation this symbolizes the end of the world, the end of time, which is stretched out as a line with a beginning and an end, by contrast with the unending circularity that symbolizes heaven and eternity. And the line in which the labourers are placed implies not only temporality but the secular position and rank that belong to the life lived in time. These are things with which the dreamer elsewhere shows himself to be preoccupied: he cannot believe that his daughter, who died so young, can have achieved the rank of queen in heaven –

> Of countes, damysel, par ma fay,
> Wer fayr in heven to halde asstate,
> Other ellez a lady of lasse aray;
> Bot a quene! – hit is to dere a date.   (489–92)

Yet the lord orders that each man in the line should be paid alike: each should receive a penny (another round, shining, valuable object), and this symbolizes that rewards in heaven are equal. The same wages are paid to those who have borne the burden and heat of the day of earthly life and to those who, like the child, have scarcely even begun to labour in the vineyard of the Lord. So the last shall be first, and the first last – the *logion* at the end of the parable (Matthew 20:16), which the Pearl Maiden also quotes:[28]

> The laste schal be the fyrst that strykez,
> And the fyrst the laste, be he never so swyft,
> For mony ben called, thagh fewe be mykez.   (570–2)

In the heavenly world, the linear sequences and hierarchies of earthly time will be dissolved, in a way that human beings in this life can conceive only as paradox.

Similarly (and this too is noted by Borroff), at the beginning of the 19th of the poem's 20 groups of stanzas the dreamer is able to peer into the heavenly city and see the Brides of the Lamb, all 'Depaynt in perlez and wedez qwyte' (1102) like his own transfigured daughter, in the form of a *prosessyoun* (1096). He sees them in this linear, sequential form, because the earthly imagination can only conceive of heaven in earthly terms; but he sees the procession filling the streets of the heavenly city in a single instant – it was 'sodanly ful, wythouten sommoun' (1098) – in a way that denies its very nature as a procession.

The other aspect of the symbolism of *Pearl* that deserves mention is that the poem is full of analogues to the pearl itself – objects that replicate its roundness, whiteness, brightness, and often its value. One of them is the moon, which appears at the beginning of the stanza just referred to. The appearance of the procession is compared to the rise of the moon before the sunlight has completely disappeared: it does not enter the sky at a specific moment, but one suddenly becomes aware that it has been there all along. Another analogue is the penny in the parable of the Vineyard; two more that we have yet to encounter are the 'garlande gay' (1186), the Pearl Maiden's crown, or possibly the circle of the blessed, and the mass-wafer of the poem's final stanza.[29] Everywhere in *Pearl*, as in the earthly world where the narrator begins and to which he is abruptly returned at the end, are found figures that give evidence of the eternal. The pearl itself has passed through a variety of identities in the course of the poem. Beginning as a lost jewel, apparently with merely earthly associations, it has become the Pearl Maiden of the heavenly world. We gradually come to understand that the lost jewel actually symbolizes a person, lost by death to the narrator (who is many times referred to as a jeweller), but surviving as the soul survives beyond death. Next the pearl has become the pearl of great price of the parable – that is, the heavenly kingdom itself, which the dead person, dying in innocence, has already gained. And in stanza-group XIX, the point at which I now take up the poem's ending, a final transformation of the symbol takes place, or rather is hinted at: the Lamb of God too begins to be associated with pearls. We have already been told that he is a source of light, brighter than the sun or moon, for the dwellers in the heavenly city: 'The self God watz her lombe-lyght' (1046), as the poet puts it in a daring pun on *lombe* and *lampe*. And he has been referred to as a jewel and as white and spotless. Now we are told that his garments are like 'praysed perlez' (1112) and that they are 'worthly whyt' (1133). It is important to realize that this hinted identification of the pearl with the Lamb, the object of value with the ground and source of all value, is never completed. The poem points towards a heavenly meaning that it never states; but that incompleteness is part of its earthly closure.[30] Only a genuine mystic would be able to *see* in a vision the identity of the pearl and the Lamb; the narrator of the poem is something less than that, and he lacks the patience and self-control to let his vision complete itself in such terms – which would in any case be beyond the scope of poetry. He is so overcome with longing to join his beloved Perle in the heavenly city that he attempts to cross the river that separates him from it; and the effort to do so wakes him up, and thus brings his vision to a premature end. He is left wishing that he could have endured longer and thus perhaps have been drawn into God's very presence and seen more of his *mysterys* (1194).

This is the culminating instance in *Pearl* of what was said above about the poet's willingness to embrace that which resists pattern. In Section XIX there are two ways in particular in which the dreamer expresses emotions that run counter to the mathematical perfection of his vision; and they are human emotions which demand our sympathy. (The situation is quite similar to that in *Sir Gawain and the Green Knight*: the pentangle is an emblem of geometric perfection, but we cannot help sympathizing with Gawain in his inability to live up to that perfection, and with the court in adopting not the pentangle but the green girdle as a badge of honour. In *Pearl* the balance is different. We are taken into the heavenly world itself, perfection is more strongly symbolized, given greater imaginative potency, and the imperfection of the dreamer is correspondingly felt to be more serious; but it claims our sympathy all the same, and I am sure it is meant to do so.) The emotions I have in mind are first his horror and incomprehension at the wound he notices in the Lamb's side when he sees him worshipped by the Brides in the heavenly city; and second his still-possessive desire for the Pearl Maiden. Although the New Jerusalem is the very heart of the heavenly world, in which the Lamb's blood has been transformed into the means of redemption (so that it is itself a badge of honour, not of shame), for the dreamer the wound still has the inexplicable horror of Christ's Passion about it:

> Bot a wounde ful wyde and weete con wyse
> Anende hys hert, thurgh hyde torente.
> Of his quyte syde his blod outsprent.
> Alas, thoght I, who did that spyt?
> Ani breste for bale aght haf forbrent
> Er he therto hade had delyt.   (1135–40)

A recent study has noted that representation of the Lamb as wounded is uncommon in medieval illuminated manuscripts of the Apocalypse (by which there are many signs that the poet was influenced), while in the scenes in which the Lamb appears in triumph, as *Agnus Victor*, there is a 'consistent absence of wounds'. The same scholar goes on to point out that the lines quoted above are 'the first and only occasion in the poem in which the Dreamer is sorry for anyone but himself'.[31] Compassion for Christ's Passion, the ground of most late-medieval devotion, may be unnecessary and discordant in heaven; but that the earthly dreamer should still feel it is not to his discredit. And who could fail to feel with him in seeing his own Perle not just as one of a multitude of indistinguishable Brides of the Lamb but still as 'my lyttel quene' (1147), *my* little queen? Nevertheless, it is that possessive love that leads to the end of the vision.

He wants to be where she is; and although he has been forbidden to cross the river, which is the barrier of death between earthly life and life everlasting, he cannot resist trying and cannot believe that he will be prevented. It often happens in medieval dream-poems that a physical action or sensation within the dream brings the dream and thus the poem to an end, and so it is here with the attempt to swim across the river. In *Pearl*, though, the device has a larger meaning than usual: this dreamer is disobeying God's will, and it is God's will that cuts the vision short and leaves him lying in the earthly garden where he originally lost his pearl. He is full of sorrow at his double loss, of the vision and of contact with the Pearl Maiden, and there is a delicate balance in what he says in the 20th and final group of stanzas between rejoicing and regret. If his dream is 'veray and soth sermoun', then he is glad to learn that she is 'in garlande gay' (1185–6) – a phrase which may allude, directly or indirectly, to the circle of the blessed, that image of perfection and eternity. He is glad that she is pleasing to 'that Prynse' (1188) (not the earthly princes to whom jewels are pleasing in the poem's opening line, but the Prince of heaven); but to him, now that he has finally lost contact with her, earth is 'thys doel-doungoun' (1187), this prison of sorrow. The phrase 'dongon of dole' is used in the York plays[32] and elsewhere to mean hell, and the implication is that, for the moment at least, continued life on earth is a hell to him. This is closure indeed, of the most terrible kind, the condition of the damned; but we are still two stanzas from the end of the poem.

In these last two stanzas the *Gawain*-poet works out a more subtle and consoling closure, with extraordinary compactness. In the 100th stanza the narrator regrets what he has lost, the Maiden herself and the possibility of seeing more of God's mysteries; but now he blames his own human greed and impatience for his loss, and ends by acknowledging that it is madness to strive against God's will. What has happened to him, he says, is the consequence of failings common to all men:

> Bot ay wolde man of happe more hente
> Then moghte by ryght upon hem clyven.   (1195–6)

We may perhaps remember Gawain at the Green Chapel bitterly regretting his failing and seeing himself as only one of many men who have been deceived by women. The narrator of *Pearl* is a far less glamorous figure than Gawain, but his contrition is more complete than Gawain's was at that moment. We first encountered Gawain as one member of a rejoicing court, before he went off on his solitary quest; the narrator of *Pearl* has been a solitary figure from the very beginning, but now, right at the end, like Gawain at the end of *Sir Gawain and the Green Knight*, he begins to become once more part of the human community.

That movement, from solitude to community, is completed in the final stanza. God, he recognizes, is a friend as well as a lord – 'A God, a Lorde, a frende ful fyin' (1204) – and now at last he is able to commit his pearl to God, instead of resenting that God has taken her away from him. The lines in which he does so resolve an uncertainty that has run right through the poem:

> And sythen to God I hit bytaghte
> In Krystez dere blessyng and myn.   (1207–8)

We have learned in the course of the poem that the earthly relationship between the dreamer and the Pearl Maiden had been a very close one. 'Ho watz me nerre then aunte or nece' (233), he remarked when he first recognized her in the form in which she appeared in his vision; but we have never been told explicitly what relationship it was, though there were strong suggestions that it was that of father and daughter. But, as Norman Davis has shown, the phrase 'in Christ's (or God's) blessing and mine', a common ending to medieval letters, was used only from parent to child;[33] so this line, besides being itself a closural or valedictory device, finally confirms that she was his daughter. Once more, there is a reminder of the end of *Sir Gawain and the Green Knight*, with the identification of the Green Knight as Sir Bertilak, and (more significant) of the old lady at his castle as Morgan la Fay, Gawain's aunt. In both cases, one means by which closure is effected is the replacement of the central character in his position in the web of family relationships.

In the same sentence the speaker of *Pearl* goes on,

> That in the forme of bred and wyn
> The preste uus schewez uch a daye. (1209–10)

(*That* here has the Christ of 'Krystez dere blessyng' as its antecedent.) The pearl had seemed to be the one link between the separate realms of heaven and earth; now the narrator is confined to his earthly prison, while the pearl remains for ever in heaven; but at this very last moment he recalls that there is still a link between the two worlds, in the daily miracle of the Eucharist. The consecrated bread and wine do not merely symbolize but *are* the body and blood of Christ. The bread is made from earthly grain, from the 'corne' that was being 'corven wyth crokez kene' (40) when the narrator fell asleep 'In Auguste in a hygh seysoun' (39); it becomes 'our daily bread', as requested in the Lord's Prayer (to which 'uch a daye' alludes); and then, in the form of the mass-wafer, it has the smallness, whiteness, roundness, purity, and supreme value attributed to the pearl. And it is given, the poet says, to *us*; in this last quatrain, instead of referring only to the singular *me*, as he has done all along, he associates himself with the plural *us* of the Christian community. The point would probably have been readily taken by a medieval audience, because widely read expositions of the Lord's Prayer, such as that in *The Book of Vices and Virtues*, explain that it says '"fadre oure" and not "fadre myn"', and asks '"yyve us" and not "yyve me"', precisely because

. . . whan we seyn "fadre oure" and "yyve us", we gaderen yn with us alle oure bretheren bi adopcioun, that ben children of holy chirche bi the bileve that thei

214

receyvede at here cristendome. Nowe scheweth us than this word "oure" the largenesse and the curtesye of God oure fadre . . . As seynt Jame seith, and it is gretliche oure profytt, for thou leist thi biddynge in comune, thou hast part of al the comunyté of Holy Chirche.[34]

Pearl ends, as *Sir Gawain and the Green Knight* ends, with a brief prayer:

> He gef uus to be his homly hyne
> Ande precious perlez unto his pay.
> Amen.   Amen.   (1211–12)

(May God may grant *us* [using the word again] to be his household servants, and precious pearls to please him.)

It is as though these last few lines effect a re-enactment of the whole poem on a higher level of meaning: now the penny a day paid equally to all the labourers in the vineyard reappears as the mass-wafer available daily to all the labourers in the vineyard of the world – the grapes from which supply the wine that is then transformed into Christ's blood.

This final stanza is extraordinarily close-packed in its symbolic implications; it seems to compress into a few words a new under-standing of the meaning of the whole poem.[35] As in *Sir Gawain and the Green Knight*, closure is brought about by homecoming but also by transformation: Camelot's transformation of the girdle from a badge of shame into a badge of honour, the priest's transformation of bread and wine into a means by which man's separation from God can become a reunion. In both cases there is a sudden acceleration in the production of meaning in the 100th and 101st stanzas, concluding in a prayer, and then a silence which leads us back to the poem's beginning. In neither case is there any pretence that all problems are solved, for the poem's central character or for us; but in no poem of any size and complexity is this likely to be so. Yet the effect of closure is unmistakeable: we have been shown a new way of looking at things, which leaves us exhilarated and satisfied by its aptness, its rapidity and its daring.

9 · *Piers Plowman*: allegory and verbal practice

Piers Plowman is, for me, the greatest poem of the English Middle Ages. It is not the most perfect artistic achievement: indeed, its greatness is partly a matter of the sense it gives of an unending struggle with material beyond the power of art to contain – a sense confirmed by its survival in three or possibly four successive versions, apparently the life's work of a single poet who was never satisfied with what he had done.[1] Its existence in over 50 manuscripts indicates that it was one of the most widely read English poems in the fourteenth and fifteenth centuries, but it is certainly not the medieval poem with the strongest immediate appeal for most modern readers. I have met scarcely anyone who read *Sir Gawain and the Green Knight* without enjoying it, whereas many who attempt *Piers Plowman* give up in boredom or despair long before reaching the end. I suppose I have read the B- and C-texts myself more often than any other large-scale literary work, except perhaps for some of Shakespeare's plays, but there are parts of them I find boring and irritating, parts I know I do not understand, parts I sometimes think I have understood only to change my mind at the next reading. A full understanding of *Piers Plowman* would require one somehow to get one's mind round *all* of the versions, and to grasp instantaneously their relationship as a sequence, rather as God is supposed to perceive history as an eternal present. I fear that that is not an attainable goal; and there is also the more mundane difficulty that what Langland actually wrote has been obscured to a marked extent by scribal corruption. Alliterative verse, with its formulaic style, variable rhythm and lack of rhyme, is less effective than, say, Chaucerian rhyme royal at perpetuating the poet's very words in written form, and there is almost certainly a considerable amount of scribal error in the texts of most alliterative poems. Moreover, Langland's particular version of the style of alliterative poetry, written in lines longer than usual, lacking in poetic diction, and somewhat lightly or unemphatically alliterated, may have been unusually close to the spoken English of his time; if so, that very fact, combined with the peculiar urgency of his poem's spiritual appeal to its early readers, seems to have encouraged copying that involved an unusual degree of scribal participation and rewriting.

In these circumstances, to read *Piers Plowman* closely is likely to be especially difficult; yet I think it is especially desirable. It is notoriously an allegorical poem, and much of what has been written about it has been concerned with interpreting the allegory; yet such attempts have all too often been unsupported by any understanding of the roots of the allegory in the poet's verbal practice. No amount of supplying of the historical and intellectual context of Langland's work is likely to be profitable in the absence of a concern with his habits as a poet. In Passus XII of the B-text, Ymaginatif – Langland's *vis imaginativa*, the faculty of his own mind that rules over memory and dreams – accuses him of having wasted his life on poetry:

> And thow medlest thee with makynges – and myghtest go seye thi Sauter,
> And bidde for hem that yyveth thee breed; for ther are bokes ynowe
> To telle men what Dowel is, Dobet and Dobest bothe,
> And prechours to preve what it is, of many a peire freres.   (XII 16–19)

From reading much published work on *Piers Plowman*, one would never guess that Langland saw himself as a man preoccupied with *makynges*, rather than as the mere versifier of a body of doctrine and an allegorical fiction that existed quite independently of the words in which they were expressed. In this chapter, therefore, I shall begin with some very detailed analyses of specimen passages from the B-text, before going on to explore two moments of crisis in the allegory. And in one respect at least the situation has become more favourable for close reading of *Piers Plowman* than it was until a dozen years ago. Our awareness of the nature and degree of scribal corruption in the manuscripts derives from editorial work that has also established the poem's texts on a sounder basis.[2] The words that Langland actually wrote may in many instances be lost beyond recall, but the devoted labours of textual scholars, even when account is taken of occasional eccentricities of conjecture, have undoubtedly brought us closer to them than anyone has been since the fourteenth century.

The first passage I examine is chosen for its ordinariness; passages illustrating the same methods and habits of composition might be found almost anywhere in *Piers Plowman*. It is the closing section of Passus I, in which Lady Holichirche comes to the end of the speech she has made in response to the dreamer's request that she should tell him not about worldly treasure but about the means to save his soul. The theme of her answer is that Treuthe is the highest treasure, and that Treuthe in man means love – love in action, shown above all in giving to others.

> For though ye be trewe of youre tonge and treweliche wynne,
> And as chaste as a child that in chirche wepeth, 180
> But if ye loven leelly and lene the povere,
> Of swich good as God sent goodliche parteth,[3]
> Ye have na moore merite in Masse ne in houres
> Than Malkyn of hire maydenhede, that no man desireth.
> For James the gentile jugged in hise bokes 185
> That feith withouten feet is feblere than nought,
> And as deed as a dorenail but if the dedes folwe:
> *Fides sine operibus mortua est &c.*
>   Forthi chastité withouten charité worth cheyned in helle;
> It is as lewed as a lampe that no light is inne.
> Manye chapeleyns arn chaste, ac charité is aweye; 190
> Are none hardere than hii whan hii ben avaunced:
> Unkynde to hire kyn and to alle Cristene,
> Chewen hire charité and chiden after moore –
> Swich chastité withouten charité worth cheyned in helle.
> Manye curatours kepen hem clene of hire bodies; 195
> Thei ben acombred with coveitise, thei konne noght out crepe,
> So harde hath avarice yhasped hem togideres.
> And that is no truthe of the Trinité, but trecherie of helle,
> And lernynge to lewed men the latter for to dele.
> For thise ben wordes writen in the Evaungelie: 200
> "*Date, et dabitur vobis* – for I deele yow alle,
> And that is the lok of love that leteth out my grace,
> To conforten the carefulle acombred with synne."
>   Love is leche of lif and nexte Oure Lord selve,
> And also the graithe gate that goth into heven. 205
> Forthi I seye as I seide er by sighte of the textes:
> Whan alle tresors ben tried, Treuthe is the beste.
>   Now have I tolde thee what truthe is – that no tresor is bettre –
> I may no lenger lenge thee with; now loke thee Oure Lord! (I 179–209)

These lines are to a large extent an amplification of the text quoted after line 187 from the Epistle of James, Chapter 2: Faith without works is dead. The whole of the second half of that chapter is concerned to drive home this simple yet hard doctrine, which it states three times over (verses 17, 20, 26) – faith without works *is dead* – and Langland's own method of writing here has much in common with that of the epistle, being simple, repetitive, and pressed home with concrete exempla. It is the method of much of *Piers Plowman*, as it has been admirably described by Elizabeth Salter: the absence of 'high rhetoric', the diction 'simpler, more

prosaic' than that of other alliterative poems, the 'almost unbeliev-
able naturalness in vocabulary and rhythm', the 'dramatic freedom
of phrasing', the reliance on *figurae verborum* involving different
kinds of verbal repetition, and the 'graphic directness . . . of the
popular preacher' in the choice of simile and metaphor.[4] One may
well be puzzled at first to see how Langland can possibly achieve
poetry by using such methods.

The language is that of everyday life, though not by any means
what Chaucer calls the 'cherles termes' (*Reeve's Prologue* I 3917) of
low life: there are many educated words such as *merite, chapeleyns,
avanced, curatours, acombred,* and so on. But there are no examples
here of the diction peculiar to alliterative verse: compared with any
extract from *Sir Gawain and the Green Knight* this passage is notably
plain and ordinary in its diction, not far distant, one may suppose,
from prose or educated speech. *Trewe of . . . tonge* (179) is a
commonplace collocation in Middle English; *as deed as a dorenail*
(187) is illustrated by *The Middle English Dictionary* only from
alliterative poems, including *William of Palerne* (which is earlier than
the earliest version of *Piers Plowman*), but its survival as a cliché in
modern colloquial English suggests that it may also have been a
common tag in fourteenth-century speech. In many lines, the words
that carry the alliteration are already linked in sense and etymology,
and must therefore have required little ingenuity or effort of
imagination to choose. Examples are: *trewe . . . treweliche* (179), *good
. . . goodliche* (182), *unkynde . . . kyn* (192), *gate . . . gooth* (205), *seye
. . . seide* (206), *lenger lenge* (209). The sequence *lernynge . . . lewed*
(199) offers only a slight grammatical variation on the familiar pair
of opposites, *lered/lewed.* Line 194 is an all but verbatim repetition of
line 188. The same sound is used for alliteration in many different
lines: six lines use *l-* (181, 189, 199, 202, 204, 209); five lines use *ch-*
(180, 188, 190, 193, 194); four lines use *t-* (179, 198, 207, 208); and
four use *c/k* (192, 195, 196, 203). Yet these repeated sounds do not
seem to be there for a particular expressive purpose, as for example
in *Sir Gawain* 1178–1207, a stanza recounting the first arrival of Sir
Bertilak's wife in Gawain's bedroom, in which nine lines (out of 30)
alliterating on *l-* clearly help to evoke the quiet atmosphere and
stealthy movement by contrast with the violent noise and activity of
the previous hunting scene. Nor are Langland's repeated sounds
there to display his virtuosity or to mark off specific sections of the
poem, as we saw was the case in the *Morte Arthure.* In this *Piers*

Plowman passage, it is worth noting how the continuation of *m*-alliteration over lines 183 and 184 gives a special cumulative emphasis or attack to the derisive sentiment being expressed (and perhaps something similar is true of lines 195–6); but apart from that the repetition of alliterative sounds seems to be merely the concomitant of an emphasis diffused throughout the passage on certain ideas and a certain message.

Specific words are repeated several times in the positions marked out by stress and alliteration: *charité*, *chast(ité)*, *trew(th)*, and so on. Repetition of this kind is a characteristic feature of the art of the medieval sermon, and its presence is no doubt one sign of Langland's debt to the theory and practice of preaching.[5] At first sight, it may seem a somewhat crude technique; but even on the level of sound it is worth noticing how often the manifest pattern of repeated alliterative sounds is only one part of a more complex auditory pattern.[6] Thus in line 197 the alliteration on *h*/vowel- is accompanied by a whole series of -*a*- sounds: 'So h*a*rde h*a*th *a*varice yh*a*sped hem togideres'. In line 203 both alliterating words in the first half have a second syllable beginning with *f*-, and all three alliterating words include an -*r*- sound: 'To con*f*o*r*ten the ca*r*e*f*ulle a*c*omb*r*ed with synne'. In line 205 all three alliterating words are monosyllables beginning with *g*- and ending with the similar sounds of -*t* or -*th*, so that these words differ significantly only in their vowels. This may be thought of as an example of verbal play of the kind also present in line 182 (*good/God*) and line 186 (*feith/feet*). The auditory patterning of Langland's verse, though rarely ostentatious, is often subtly pleasing.

Little progress, however, can be made in discussing the sound of a passage of verse without passing on to its content. In this passage the chief means by which Langland gives life to Holichirche's message is one characteristic, as we have seen, of alliterative poetry generally – the concrete realization of abstract ideas in terms of scenes and objects belonging to daily experience. The most noticeable here are the similes of the weeping child, of Malkyn and her virginity, and of the lamp without a light. None of those is in itself a learned comparison; though there may be Latin analogues, each belongs in its primary significance to common life and the common language; but each of them is strikingly and subtly related to the theological message that Holichirche wishes to convey. The weeping child is weeping in church, and therefore is presumably a baby howling as babies so often do when splashed with water at their christening:[7] what could be more chaste than a newly baptized infant, restored for an instant to man's original innocence? Malkyn is introduced suddenly and with pungent effect; the coarse saying rams home the argument unanswerably: what could be more unmeritorious than virginity retained only because no one desires to take it? But for any reader who recalls the passage from James's epistle that underlies this part of the poem, the allusion is subtle as well as coarse. James mentions as an exemplum of justification by works the harlot Rahab, whose story is told in the book of Joshua;[8] though a prostitute, she nevertheless showed courage and generosity in defying the king of Jericho to protect two spies sent by Joshua. Langland's Malkyn, claiming a merit in the very virginity she has been unable to lose, is precisely the opposite to Rahab, chastity without charity as opposed to charity without chastity. Finally, the lamp: anyone can immediately see the uselessness of a lamp that fails to serve the only purpose for which it is intended, to give light. But here too there is a Scriptural allusion intertwined with the everyday comparison, to the parable of the Wise and Foolish Virgins in Matthew 25:1–13. The foolish virgins who had no oil for their lamps were unable to light them to greet the bridegroom Christ and were refused entrance to his marriage; that is, they were denied salvation and were thus 'cheyned in helle'. An image taken from a parable about virgins is obviously an appropriate exemplum to illustrate the theme of *chastité*.

As the passage proceeds, we find more metaphors than similes, and these add even more forcibly to its concreteness. Some of them belong to trains of imagery that recur thematically throughout *Piers Plowman*. One such is that of treasure and keys, here developed unexpectedly out of the imprisoning and fettering power of an avaricious desire for earthly treasures, to become the 'lok of love' that sets free the spiritual treasure of divine grace.[9] Others are the images of love as a doctor and as a road in lines 204–5. There are also some startlingly concrete local metaphors, often in the form of verbs indicating powerful or violent activity. In line 193 the clergy who have gained advancement as chaplains or chantry priests, and who in Langland's view are selling spiritual services for material gain, 'Chewen hire charité': charity has now changed momentarily from what they ought to give to what they are greedy to receive; they gobble it up and swallow it down, and clamour for more.[10] Again, there is the group of verbs used to convey the oppressively cramping force of covetousness and avarice in lines 196–7: covetousness of others' goods is such a heavy burden to the parish priests that they cannot crawl out from underneath it, and avarice has clamped them up tightly, as if they were their own locked treasure-chests. Only God's grace can release them from their spiritual prison.

In the passage as a whole, then, simple and repetitious as it may seem, there is a genuine poetic creativeness in the solidity that Langland's imagination confers on his doctrine; but what is important to grasp is that it is, as it were, an unstable solidity. It is not a matter of the building up of a single image through the whole verse paragraph, but of a rapid movement from one forceful realization of the underlying doctrine to a second and then to a third. In general, Langland does not strike one as at all a Shakespearean poet, but in this particular respect there is real ground for comparison with the mature Shakespeare's manner of 'telescoping' one image into another. Given that Langland, in devoting all his energies to the creation of a single moral allegory, is doing something radically unShakespearean, this fact gives his allegory a most unusual and baffling nature: it feels solid yet it will not stay still; it is at once earthy and dreamlike. We cannot possibly understand the nature of Langland's allegory with fixing our attention with the greatest closeness on the way he uses words. What has been written of another visionary poet applies equally well to him:

His task is the exploration of the spiritual unknown. The poet works his way into this unknown, laboriously and self-doubtingly, and his words do not merely express the outcome of a search, but are essential instruments operating within the search.[11]

I hope this will emerge more clearly from my second example.

This is taken from the confessions of the Seven Deadly Sins in Passus v, and consists of the opening lines of Wrath's speech.

> "I am Wrathe", quod he, "I was som tyme a frere,   135
> And the coventes gardyner for to graffen impes.
> On lymitours and listres lesynges I ympted,
> Til thei beere leves of lowe speche, lordes to plese,
> And sithen thei blosmede abroad in boure to here shriftes.
> And now is fallen therof a fruyt – that folk han wel levere   140
> Shewen hire shriftes to hem than shryve hem to hir persons.
> And now persons han parceyved that freres parte with hem,
> Thise possessioners preche and deprave freres;
> And freres fyndeth hem in defaute, as folk bereth witnesse,
> That whan thei preche the peple in many places aboute,   145

I, Wrathe, walke with hem and wisse hem of my bokes.
Thus thei speken of spiritualté, that either despiseth oother,
Til thei be bothe beggers and by my spiritualté libben,
Or ellis al riche and ryden aboute; I, Wrathe, reste nevere
That I ne moste folwe this wikked folk, for swich is my grace.   150
     "I have an aunte to nonne and an abbesse:
Hir were levere swowe or swelte than suffre any peyne.
I have be cook in hir kichene and the covent served
Manye monthes with hem, and with monkes bothe.
I was the prioresse potager and other povere ladies,   155
And maad hem joutes of janglyng – that Dame Johane was a bastard,
And Dame Clarice a knyghtes doughter – ac a cokewold was hir sire,
And Dame Pernele a preestes fyle – Prioresse worth she nevere,
For she hadde child in chirie-tyme, al oure Chapitre it wiste!
Of wikkede wordes I Wrathe hire wortes made,   160
Til 'Thow lixt!' and 'Thow lixt!' lopen out at ones
And either hitte oother under the cheke;
Hadde thei had knyves, by Crist! hir either hadde kild oother."

                                                      (v 135–63)

It is often held that one of the great merits of Langland's presentation of the Seven Deadly Sins is the method of 'dramatic personification',[12] and at first sight that seems to be the case here. Wrath, unusually personified 'as the stirrer-up of anger in others, as a diabolical sower of discord, rather than as if he were the embodiment of anger',[13] describes his career in the last place that anger ought to be found – in the ecclesiastical world, ranging through friars, parish priests, monks, nuns – and he speaks of himself as having held three different positions in that world. First he was gardener to a house of friars; then, in lines 145–6, he appears momentarily in a grander role, as a teaching friar (like the Doctor of Divinity met by the dreamer in Passus XIII); and after that his role is as cook to a house of nuns. In principle I suppose it is possible that the same person could have held all three positions in the course of his life, though it is highly unlikely; but Langland's aim is clearly not to provide Wrath with a realistic and consistent life-history. Anger, like the other sins, is a failing found in men and women of all conditions – indeed in the C-text Wrath himself makes just this point when he says that 'Amonges alle manere men my dwellyng is som tyme' (C VI 115). Thus no particular manifestation of anger can be allowed to exclude all others. The ecclesiastical world is chosen as the setting here, but the only other link among Wrath's roles lies in the image of vegetables: what he grows for the friars as gardener, he then feeds to the nuns as cook.

The first section of the passage, lines 135–41, contains an ingeniously worked-out but tightly compressed allegory. As gardener, Wrath grafts shoots of lying on to the friars themselves (an idea acceptable, it is worth noting, only because it is *not* given any pictorial development). By means of this grafting process, the friars first bear leaves of humble speech, with which they flatter lords, and then 'blossom abroad' in the practice of hearing ladies' confessions privately in their 'bowers'. *Blosme* and *boure*, besides their alliterative link, are words which associate naturally together to suggest a courtly paradise or garden of the rose, but one which is seen here as the setting for distinctly furtive behaviour. This is partly a matter of confession made not to the parish priest but to the venal friar, who will impose an easier penance. But the following half-line – 'And now is fallen therof a fruyt . . .' – at least hints that what is going on in the bower is something more than shrift, and that its outcome is pregnancy. (*Fallen* combines two senses, abstract [ensued] and concrete [dropped from that which bears it]; and later, in line 159, an illegitimate child is associated with the fruit season.) In terms of the original allegory, the fruit is the widespread preference for confessing to a friar rather than to the parish priest. And so at last, by this indirect and paradoxical route, we get from flattery to anger, in the form of the general enmity between friars and beneficed clergy as they compete for the profitable right to hear confessions.

Then, in lines 142–4, Langland moves from allegory to literal social description: the mutual slanders of parsons and mendicants are part of the reality of his time, and the elaborate gardening-allegory, that in another poem might have occupied a whole book, has already dissolved after only five lines. The utter prodigality is typical of Langland, and we shall misunderstand the very structure of his poem if we fail to grasp that its segments of allegorical narrative do not form a continuous whole. Processes of growth and revision are constantly taking place, not just between the A-text and the B-text, or between B and C, but within each text. Langland may have hoped ultimately to arrive at a final and complete vision of life – a D-text, let us say, or an E-text – but in practice that is not what he offers in any of the texts we have. Every allegorical formulation is merely provisional; every text is already a palimpsest, with one formulation inscribed on top of another. It is not so much a matter, I think, of his 'deliberately frustrating the desire for allegorical tidiness',[14] as of the poem's very language having a flexibility, an unmechanical irregularity and changefulness, that lead the work as a whole towards something quite different, whatever Langland may have wished or planned. I think it likely enough that he hoped for 'allegorical tidiness', but he could only follow the bent of the life that his mind and body actually lived in language, and that was towards something other than the programmatic and the prescriptive.

In the second section, Anger as master and even perhaps prelate accompanies the friars as they wander about preaching, and teaches them from the books that mark his new status. The multiple meanings of *spiritualté* in these lines have been explored by editors,[15] but may perhaps still be clarified (or complicated) further. The friars and priests 'speken of spiritualté' (147); one would naturally take this to mean 'spiritual matters' (compare *Oxford English Dictionary*, sense 3: 'The quality or condition of being spiritual: attachment to or regard for things of the spirit as opposed to material or worldly interests'), but the context insists that its real meaning must be almost exactly opposite: 'ecclesiastical property or revenue held or received in return for spiritual services' (*Oxford English Dictionary*, sense 2). The two parties are quarrelling about the income to be obtained from confessions, and in this way their *spiritualté*, the endowment they live on (and also perhaps the spirit they live by) comes to be that of Wrath himself. Thus friar and parson reduce each other to the same condition – both beggars (with the priest reduced to the same contemptible state as the friar, begging for gifts from lords and ladies), or both rich men riding on horses (with the friar having totally abandoned the poverty claimed by his order); perhaps too beggars so far as spiritual qualities are concerned but rich in anger. There is a further play on *grace* (150): it is Wrath's chance or vocation (the lot assigned him by virtue of his very allegorical identity) but also the 'grace', such as it is, that he bestows on these ecclesiastics, to stick to them like a leech. The puns on *spiritualté* and *grace* both derive from the paradox, deeply troubling to Langland and to many of his contemporaries, of a Church which was founded to serve as the channel for spiritual truth and divine grace, but which has come to be a temporal institution of great wealth and power. In my laborious exposition, they lose their felicity; in Langland's text, they do not appear to be worked out systematically, but to be seized on the wing. This tendency to pun, in Langland as in Shakespeare, is one sign of the poet's reliance on the multidimensionality of language itself.[16]

In the third section (lines 151ff.) Wrath is cook to the nuns, though it is mentioned in passing that he has served in the same capacity with monks. After the satirical comment on his aunt the abbess, with her horror of any form of mortification of the flesh, the cook image looks as though it is going to be developed into another local allegory, like the earlier image of the grafted shoots. Wrath made the nuns 'joutes of janglyng' (156), stews or broths of gossip (with a glance at the other sense of *janglyng* as squabbling); but then the development takes a different direction, with no further unfolding of the suggested allegorical narrative, but a literal presentation of the malicious gossip that leads on to a further manifestation of anger. The parody of the sisters' spiteful whispers about each other is a little masterpiece of satirical comedy; and one notes how readily alliterative verse, with its closeness to the rhythms of spoken English and its 'dramatic freedom of phrasing', lends itself to mimicry of speech. Here the lines lengthen with additional, idiomatically slurred, unstressed syllables, to give a delightful imitation of the nuns' eager whispers. In line 160 yet another example of wordplay marks a brief revival of the allegory: the *wortes*, or vegetable soup, that Wrath makes for them naturally consists of malicious *wordes*. And then the allegory is fractured once more, and takes a sudden jump in yet another direction. The nuns' actual outbursts of angry words – 'You're a liar!' and 'You're another!' – are momentarily personified with sufficient energy to leap forth. That this is, at least potentially, a case of vigorous though very small-scale personification, is confirmed by the revised form of the lines in the C-text:

> Thus sytte they, tho sustres, sum tyme, and disputen
> Til "thow lixt" and "thou lixt" be lady over hem alle.   (C vi 137–8)

Here 'thow lixt' becomes 'lady' over all the sisters; that is, becomes mother superior of the convent. (The earlier gossip about who might be prioress prepares us to read the line in such terms.) There is of course no character in the poem called 'Thow lixt!', though there is one called Lyere, who at B II 216 leaps as 'Thow lixt!' does at B v 161. But even the dividing line between what does and what does not count as a character in *Piers Plowman* is blurred by the insistent tendency of Langland's poetic idiom towards momentary humanizations, and the coexistent rapidity and fluidity of movement that leaves them behind as soon as they are created. Almost every line has

a new charge of dramatizing energy; and the power to create
dramatic fictions is not focused on the level of overall design so
much as it is diffused throughout the poem on the level of the
sentence and even of the line.

The present passage ends with a line that soberly states the
outcome of gossip that began by sounding merely amusing: a
murderous anger that would lead even nuns to kill each other, if
they had the means. ('Even nuns' – but many of those who entered
the religious life in the Middle Ages, as Langland knew, had no
particular vocation for it, and the strains of communal living must
really have made religious houses fruitful sources of anger.) 'By
Crist!' (163) is surely not merely a formulaic expletive to fill out the
metre and the alliteration, but carries a significant reminder of the
supposed purpose of life in a religious order.

My third example can be treated more briefly. It is intended to
illustrate the characteristic juxtaposition of opposite extremes in
Langland's verse – the prosaic and the wildly imaginative, the satiric
and the sublime – and the way in which it proceeds by imaginative
association rather than by logic. This passage is extracted from a
long and apparently rambling discourse by Ymaginatif in which (as
he explains in the lines following the ones I quote) his purpose is to
correct the Dreamer's earlier assertion that the ignorant are more
likely to be saved than the learned. In these lines he distinguishes
between the natural philosophy of the ancients which, being based
merely on physical observation, can bring no man to salvation, and
the revelation of Christ's birth, which came equally to the shepherds
and to the wise men from the east – men whose learning rather than
their natural intelligence is emphasized, and who are described as
poetes (149) as well as *magi*.

> Olde lyveris toforn us useden to marke
> The selkouthes that thei seighen, hir sones to teche,
> And helden it an heigh science hir wittes to knowe.
> Ac thorugh hir science soothly was nevere no soule ysaved,
> Ne broght by hir bokes to blisse ne to joye;   135
> For alle hir kynde knowyng com but of diverse sightes.
>   Patriarkes and prophetes repreveden hir science,
> And seiden hir wordes ne hir wisdomes was but a folye;
> As to the clergie of Crist, counted it but a trufle:
> *Sapiencia huius mundi stultitia est apud Deum.*
> For the heighe Holy Goost hevene shal tocleve,   140
> And love shal lepe out after into this lowe erthe,
> And clennesse shal cacchen it and clerkes shullen it fynde:

Pastores loquebantur ad invicem.
He speketh there of riche men right noght, ne of right witty,
Ne of lordes that were lewed men, but of the hyeste lettred oute:
Ibant magi ab oriente.   145
(If any frere were founde there, I yyve thee fyve shillynges!)
Ne in none beggers cote was that barn born,
But in a burgeises place, of Bethlem the beste:
Set non erat ei locus in diversorio – et pauper non habet diversorium.
To pastours and to poetes appered the aungel,
And bad hem go to Bethlem Goddes burthe to honoure,   150
And songe a song of solas, *Gloria in excelsis Deo!*
Riche men rutte tho and in hir reste were,
Tho it shon to shepherdes, a shewer of blisse.   (B XII 131–53)

The progress of the thought here, as in the whole of Ymaginatif's
speech, is difficult to follow in detail, and it seems likely that it really
reflects the movements of Langland's ruminating mind as he puzzles
over the problem of the value of learning, to which he returns again
and again in this part of the poem. Once more it may be helpful to be
reminded of the mature Shakespeare's habitual movement of
thought, as described by Coleridge in a contrast between Shake-
speare's mode of composition and that of some of his contempo-
raries. 'Shakespeare's intellectual action', Coleridge is recorded to
have said,

is wholly unlike that of Ben Jonson or Beaumont and Fletcher. The latter see the
totality of a sentence or passage, and then project it entire. Shakespeare goes on
creating, and evolving B. out of A., and C. out of B., and so on, just as a serpent
moves, which makes a fulcrum of its own body, and seems forever twisting and
untwisting its own strength.[17]

Langland's method of procedure is often like Shakespeare's as
Coleridge describes it. On the intellectual level, his serpentine
motion seems sometimes to depend on mere sophistries, such as the
argument that Jesus was not born in a place of total poverty but in an
inn, 'and a poor man has no inn' (*et pauper non habet diversorium*).
(Langland is evidently taking sides in the controversy as to the
absolute poverty of Christ and the claim of one branch of the friars
that they alone achieved Christian perfection by imitating that
poverty.) But the real progress of the passage takes place not on the
level of propositions linked by logic but on that of images linked by
action. It begins with some lines of prosaic and somewhat grum-
bling argument asserting the ineffectiveness of the accumulated
knowledge of which the pagans were so proud; but then, with the
quotation from I Corinthians 3:19 ('the wisdom of this world is

foolishness with God'), the verse takes a quite unexpected leap into sublimity, a leap which enacts the suddenness of the Christian revelation itself. Its visionary quality is conveyed by the presentation as future of what has already happened (though there is also a sense in which, as an event in the individual soul, it can happen at any time); it is as if an angel prophesies to us as one did to the shepherds. The Holy Spirit splits open the heavens, love leaps from the height to the depth, and this personified and active love, which is also the incarnate Christ, is caught as it falls by *clennesse* and found by *clerkes*. In that characteristic pairing of abstract and concrete, *clennesse* is the Blessed Virgin, who 'catches' Christ in her womb, and the *clerkes* evidently include the shepherds (here figures of the priesthood, *pastores*, in Langland's fragmentary reminder of Luke's Nativity narrative), as well as the *magi*.

After this, the verse relapses once again to a more prosaic level, muttering unedifyingly of who was and was not present and of the material circumstances of the birth. The exalted vision of the very moment at which God became man does not exclude this, nor does it exclude satirical familiarity. Langland's sardonic 'If any frere were founde there, I yyve thee fyve shillynges!' (146), promising a larger tip than even the most optimistic friar could expect, has something of the effect of a grotesque misericord carving in a noble choir. Favourite themes for such carvings included antimendicant satire, such as the fox as friar preaching to a congregation of geese, and yet what Langland is depicting here – a conspicuous and derisible absence – is once more beyond the scope of pictorial or plastic art. As the attack on the claims of the friars continues in the next lines, Langland seems to have lost the sublime vision that he grasped briefly in lines 140–2; and then, equally unexpectedly, it returns in the closing lines of the extract, and especially in the last two. Everyday life is drenched in brilliant light, which discloses heaven in its very midst. In this extraordinarily compressed little scene, the grotesque becomes part of the sublime instead of being merely placed alongside it: the radiance of the star announcing the Nativity shows us not only the watchful shepherds as they glimpse the bliss of heaven, but the rich men manifesting their sloth and ignorance by their snores.

Having examined these short passages microscopically, with particular attention to the ways in which allegorical fiction grows out of the poetic resources of language, I now want to consider two episodes from the poem's allegorical narrative. These passages are somewhat larger than those examined above, but they are still comparatively short. They both constitute dramatic crises in the allegory, each containing a moment at which it is bafflingly fractured, to such an extent that we may seem to be faced with 'interpretative chaos'.[18] The first scene is perhaps the most discussed in the whole poem, that of Piers's Pardon from Truth. In the hope of approaching it with a certain freshness, I deliberately go round rather than over the formidable mound of existing commentary, but those who have read the earlier discussions will recognize how much I am indebted to them.[19]

In Passus V, the Seven Deadly Sins, as representatives of the whole Field Full of Folk, make their confessions and receive absolution from Repentance; the folk then set off on a pilgrimage to Treuthe under the guidance of Piers the Plowman. In Passus VI, still led by Piers, they aid him in ploughing his 'half acre . . . by the heighe weye' (4), and this ploughing, at first preliminary to their pilgrimage, then comes to seem to be the pilgrimage itself: the pilgrimage of life, acted out in the agricultural labour that was the lot of most medieval men and women. The scene on the half acre offers a model of the feudal community at work; but it fails in its attempt to establish a righteous life on earth on a communal basis. Under the attacks of Hunger, it becomes apparent that many of the folk work only 'for defaute of hire foode' (206), not for love of God and their neighbours; and the passus ends with a warning of flood and famine – 'But if God of his goodnesse graunte us a trewe' (330) – addressed to Langland's fellow-countrymen outside as well as inside the fiction. Passus VII begins with an intervention by Treuthe himself – that is, by God, perhaps offering the *trewe* (the play on words is of course deliberate) that the previous passus saw as a last resort. Treuthe sends a message to Piers and his followers to continue to 'tilien the erthe' (2), and at the same time promises pardon *a pena et a culpa* 'For hym and for hise heires for everemoore after' (4); this applies to all who help Piers in any occupation. Thus salvation may be gained by individual just men, if not by the community as a whole.

There is a profound ambiguity in the idea of pardon introduced here. A pardon in its commonest form, in the world in which Langland lived, was a document written on behalf of the Church, drawing on the 'Treasury of Grace' made available to it by the merits of Christ and the saints, to grant remission of the punishment for sin in return for good works, which might include material payment. But pardon *a pena et a culpa* implies God's pardon, granted normally through absolution after confession; and the pardon referred to in the opening lines of Passus VII comes from Treuthe himself. The former kind of pardon was questionable, and was already the cause of scandal in the fourteenth century, as is indicated by the pardoners of B Prologue 68–75 and V 639–40, not to mention Chaucer's Pardoner; the latter kind must be beyond question. This pardon is *purchaced* (3) by Treuthe, a term which could mean simply 'obtained from a constituted authority'[20] (but then what authority could be higher than Treuthe?). But it could also have its modern English sense of 'bought', thus suggesting the often disreputable practices of professional pardoners; yet, if it is *purchaced* by Treuthe, there might seem to be an allusion to the redemptive (i.e. 'buying back') sacrifice of Christ, which made possible salvation for mankind. Thus, even in a few lines, the associations of this key term have come to be complex and potentially contradictory. Nor is the ambiguity of pardon accidental; indeed, it is almost the necessary consequence of religious allegory, in which a material object stands for the spiritual meaning with which it must also be contrasted. If religion is more than magic, religious allegory is bound to give rise to opposing energies within its own textual field; and the question then is, whether the writer is the mere victim of these energies, or whether he can use their conflict to release further meanings.

After the brief but deeply ambiguous narrative of the first eight lines of Passus VII, there follow no fewer than 96 lines which apparently offer a gloss on the pardon Treuthe sends – an elaborate explanation, partly at least written 'in the margyne' (18) of the document, explaining exactly how its offer applies to different groups of people, from kings to beggars. What authority this gloss has, why it is presented before the text it glosses, and indeed who is to be imagined as the speaker of the lines expounding it, is never clear. The speaker has been variously identified as Piers, as Treuthe, and as the dreamer; but a situation in which it is uncertain who is speaking is by no means uncommon in *Piers Plowman*. Especially in the longer discursive passages one voice merges into another sufficiently often to lead one to suppose that the identification of an individual speaker may not be possible or even important. Langland probably did not think of every line of his poem as spoken by one distinct character rather than another, and here perhaps we should say that the gloss is delivered by the voice of the poem, though it is a voice subject, like the poem itself, to subsequent revision. Temporal and ecclesiastical rulers who carry out their duties righteously are promised salvation. The case of merchants is trickier, as it often is in *Piers Plowman*, for they were a class of dubious moral status according to traditional Christian standards, yet the thriving secular world of Langland's time could not manage without them.[21] The Pope would not pardon them *a culpa* as well as *a pena*, but Treuthe writes to them 'under his secret seel' (23) promising them salvation if they spend their profits on good causes. The lawyer who pleads without fees for the innocent poor will be saved, but those who accept payment will have little chance. Just labourers of all kinds share in what is offered to Piers; but the case of beggars is as troublesome as that of merchants (for the Gospels suggest that to be moneyless is virtuous, yet in terms of life on the half acre those who are idle without cause are a burden on their fellows).

If we look back over lines 9–104, we may see in them an apparent certainty about the detail of God's purposes towards different classes of men, and at the same time a rambling, obsessive quality somewhat at odds with the certainty. It is tempting to think of this passage as a direct expression of Langland's real state of mind, torn between the wish for certainty and the unavoidability of doubt, but also to guess that it includes some element of self-parody, or at least of parody of the wish to pin down God's mysterious purposes in legalistic documentary form – a wish embodied in the institutional Church, and one in which Langland himself must surely have shared. The longing for certainty is rebuked and shattered by what follows next, when the narrative resumes.

A priest speaks and offers to 'construe ech clause' (106) of the pardon and explain it to Piers in English. (Piers, hitherto a ploughman and overseer, might well be supposed unable to understand the Latin in which an ecclesiastical document would be couched.) Piers unfolds the pardon, and Langland, as dreamer and narrator of the poem, focuses our attention on it by introducing himself also peering at it from an unusual angle, as though, one critic has remarked, 'he were a ghost in his own dream':[22]

> And I bihynde hem bothe biheld al the bulle.
> In two lynes it lay, and noght a lettre moore,
> And was iwriten right thus in witnesse of truthe:

Et qui bona egerunt ibunt in vitam eternam;
Qui vero mala, in ignem eternum.
   "Peter!" quod the preest tho, "I kan no pardon fynde
But 'Do wel and have wel, and God shal have thi soule,'
And 'Do yvel and have yvel, and hope thow noon oother
That after thi deeth day the devel shal have thi soule!'"
   And Piers for pure tene pulled it atweyne
And seide, "*Si ambulavero in medio umbre mortis*
Non timebo mala, quoniam tu mecum es.
   "I shal cessen of my sowyng," quod Piers, "and swynke noght so harde,
Ne aboute my bely joye so bisy be na moore;
Of preieres and of penaunce my plough shal ben herafter,
And wepen whan I sholde slepe, though whete breed me faille."

(VII 108–21)

If, encouraged by the preceding elaborate gloss, we have been
expecting the pardon to offer mercy to sinners, the words that we
see over the shoulders of Piers and the priest are likely to come as a
shock. These two lines from the Athanasian Creed say only that
those who have done well shall go into eternal life, but those who
have done evil shall go into eternal fire. The priest translates it
correctly, saying at the same time – and we are likely to agree – that
he can find no pardon in it. Piers in sheer anger tears the document
apart, quoting a famous verse from Psalm 23 (Psalm 22 in the
Vulgate) which expresses total trust in God: 'though I should walk
in the midst of the shadow of death, I will fear no evils; for thou art
with me'. And he vows to change his way of life for one less
dominated by material considerations.

   What does this episode mean? On one level it represents a conflict
between layman and priest. The priest knows Latin, and is able to
translate the pardon, but his translation is strictly literal, paying no
attention to any inward meaning or further implications. Literally,
it is not a pardon of the sort to which the priest is accustomed, as a
representative of the institutional Church of Langland's time. A
pardon goes beyond strict justice, and freely offers mercy; this
pardon, read legalistically, does not appear to do that. Piers has
hitherto shown a strong tendency to see God as the dispenser of
exact justice (this indeed is what is implied by calling God Treuthe),
and, in accordance with this, the alleged pardon simply offers tit for
tat: do well, and you will be saved; do evil, and you will be damned.
Since the pardon comes from Treuthe, and its wording comes from
one of the Creeds, there can be no doubt that what it says is true; but
then how can it be a pardon?

But in another sense, deeper than the literal, it is a pardon. As a result of the Fall, no man *deserves* to be saved: all human beings have inherited sin, death and damnation from Adam and Eve, their first parents. In these circumstances for God to offer salvation to any man, on any conditions, is to offer him pardon, because it goes beyond the demands of strict justice. (Langland will come back to this vexed question of the relation between God's justice and his mercy in Passus XVIII, in his account of Christ's Harrowing of Hell and the Four Daughters of God.) It is possible that Langland had in mind here the mode of thought of one leading party in the intellectual controversies of the fourteenth century, the Ockhamists or *Moderni*, who argued that God had freely bound his own freedom of action by a covenant, according to which the man who does 'what is in him' – that is, the best he can – is guaranteed salvation.[23] Piers's quotation from the psalm would be in line with this, for there the Psalmist is speaking in the character of the just man, who has been led in the paths of righteousness by God, and now trusts to God to reward him at the hour of his death. Whether or not this is the passage's specific intellectual context, it enables us to recognize a sense in which the pardon *is* a pardon after all. But there still remains a problem: what is it to 'do well'? He who does well will be saved; but how can fallen man do well, and in what will his doing well consist? In a sense, the rest of the poem is concerned to answer this question: the pardon's contrast between those who do well and those who do evil rapidly leads to the dreamer's quest for 'Dowel', and that turns into a distinction between Dowel, Dobet and Dobest which is a major organizing principle in the remainder of *Piers Plowman*.

The most shocking part of this enigmatic episode is Piers's tearing of the pardon, which after all comes from Treuthe himself. He tears it 'for pure tene' (115), and, to judge from the text he quotes, he does so in rejection of the claim of any mere documents to spell out the relation of man to God: he will rely only on the faith that *tu mecum es*, not on written words. The tearing is an expression of a feeling not uncommon in late-fourteenth-century England. There was a widespread impulse to reject institutions and the documents by means of which they claim to imprison men in roles, ranks, and estates: parallels may be seen in two events with which *Piers Plowman* has much in common, the Peasants' Revolt, with its burnings of legal documents, and the Wycliffite movement, with its rejection of everything except the plain text of Scripture, directly accessible to the layman's understanding.[24] Langland, though, was neither a supporter of the Peasants' Revolt nor a Wycliffite, and the tearing of the pardon remains puzzling and disturbing. I do not think this is just because we have missed a point that would have been obvious to Langland's original readers. (In the C-text he simply omitted the tearing, perhaps because he found it too liable to misunderstanding.) Like some other memorable parts of *Piers Plowman*, this scene has a genuinely visionary quality: not that Langland literally dreamed it (though he might have done), but that it 'came to him', charged with felt significance, like a dream, but without his knowing precisely what it meant.[25] We have seen how, in short passages, Langland's allegory is fluid and unstable, growing out of and sinking back into the normal texture of his language. And medieval allegorical narrative is not necessarily an intellectual construct, devised as a means of expressing a fully preconceived meaning; it may be – and perhaps in *Piers Plowman* it quite often is – intuitive and creative, an attempt to point towards meanings that cannot be fully grasped with the intellectual instruments available.[26]

Such an attempt inevitably implies a critique of the very means by which meaning is habitually expressed. How can a pardon or even perhaps a creed, mere human documents, material objects, have any real equivalence to God's offer of eternal life to sinful man? The tearing of the pardon is an act that modern theory would call deconstructive, because it challenges the link between signifier and signified that constitutes the sign and thus makes possible what we habitually mean by meaning and understand by understanding. Roland Barthes, in an essay written late in his career, when he was moving on from structuralism and feeling his way towards what would now be called deconstruction, wrote of the necessity to go beyond revealing or even investigating the meaning of the text considered as a systematically structured object. What was necessary now, he wrote, was 'to fissure the very representation of meaning, . . . to challenge the symbolic itself'.[27] That is surely what Piers (and thus Langland) does in the scene we have been reading. The allegorical pardon, the document obtained for Piers by Treuthe, is a material signifier whose transcendent signified is God's pardon to mankind; and Piers then destroys it in an outbreak of anger at its inadequacy as a sign. It is literally fissured, torn apart, in an act that Barthes proposes to call 'semioclasm', the destruction of the sign. This is a deconstructive act, though not in the sense that deconstruction too often has in modern academic practice, the mechanical demonstration that any text, whatever it may be and whoever may be reading it, incorporates opposing systems of signification and thus contradicts or undoes itself. Here the act of 'undoing' is not a display of cleverness with a preordained outcome: it is an angry and impulsive assault on the limits of human thought and of the language which is its only means of expression. And the moment at which the sign itself is destroyed is the moment at which we glimpse a meaning beyond allegory and beyond language. Only that act of destruction makes possible the momentary release of a meaning that escapes structure.

Once the act is completed, it is bound to seem merely negative. Piers is not content to stop there, and he now resolves to go beyond the life of honest communal work attempted in the half acre scene. He will devote himself to 'preieres and . . . penaunce' (120), for God will provide. What that ideal would mean if put into earthly practice is unclear, and it is not made clear because now, after a further exchange of contentious words between Piers and the priest, the dreamer is wakened by the noise of their disputation. Piers disappears from the poem for a long time, entering into some mysterious realm in which he proceeds far beyond the dreamer in spiritual understanding and closeness to God. The long-term consequence is that

The prospect of grounding the narrative process of making sense of this world in the unsullied conscience of a lay workman becomes attenuated, a distant hope; Hawkyn and Actyf may be seen as a sad afterimage of a possibility from which sustained conviction has been drained.[28]

And the immediate consequence is that the dreamer is left to puzzle over the meaning and reliability of his dream. He ends his speculations by warning his audience not to rely on written pardons – 'indulgences ...,/ Biennals and triennals and bisshopes lettres' (170–1) – but only on God's pardon, gained by the aid of Dowel.

My second narrative example comes from Passus XVI. I shall not attempt to summarize what has happened between this and the pardon scene, but it can be said that the dreamer has continued to search for Dowel in a quest which has become more inward and has placed Wille's own life history and understanding more firmly at the centre of his visionary enterprise. In Passus XV, still seeking a 'kynde knowyng' (2) (that is, a personal, experiential knowledge) of

Dowel, he receives a long lecture from Anima on the nature of charity. This is one of the most confusing parts of the whole poem, and it demands great patience from the reader (and from Wille) to recognize in it the gradual condensation of a complex of recurrent themes into a more fully realized sense of what true charity – love in action – is. At the beginning of Passus XVI, the dreamer thanks Anima for his 'faire shewyng' (1), but confesses that 'yit am I in a weer what charité is to mene' (3). Anima therefore attempts a different method of explanation, through an allegorical image of a tree, which eventually becomes a *shewyng* in a different sense, a vision or revelation. (At this point I must assume that the reader will have available for consultation a text of B XVI 1–96, a passage uneconomically long to be quoted here in full. As with my account of the pardon scene, I shall not attempt to argue in detail through existing interpretations of the passage.[29])

This allegorical tree has many predecessors in earlier religious, and to a lesser extent secular, writings,[30] among them the trees of vices or virtues which often illustrate medieval didactic treatises to show the relationships of good or bad qualities. It is called Patience (8), which may seem surprising, but then St Paul, in his famous definition of charity in I Corinthians 13 says that 'Caritas patiens est' ('Charity suffereth long' in the Authorized Version). Its root is mercy, its trunk pity, its leaves the faithful words that conform to the Church's teachings, its blossoms are obedience, and its fruit is charity, which grows 'thorugh God and thorugh goode men' (9). That co-operation of God and man, which is necessary for charity to exist as action (its only true form of existence) is a major theme of the whole passus. Wille is excited by the description, and longs to see this tree and 'to have my fulle of that fruyt' (11). In Passus XV, charity has often been associated with images of feeding; but this, as it were, devouring curiosity of Wille's displays his characteristic longing for knowledge – not just the theoretical knowledge through definition that belongs to scholastic philosophy, but *kynde knowyng*. Moreover, the desire to eat fruit from a tree can scarcely fail to touch off reverberations of Eden and the Fall of Man. So Anima tells him where it grows: 'in a gardyn . . . that God made hymselve' (13) (and that again is bound to suggest Eden); but its root is in man's body, the arbour in which it grows is the human heart, and Liberum Arbitrium (that is, man's free will) has the tending of it 'Under Piers the Plowman' (17).

Again, the details are suggestive beyond the doctrine they convey. A tree rooted in a body might remind a medieval reader of the common image of the Jesse-tree, in which the human ancestry of Jesus is shown in the form of a tree whose trunk grows from the recumbent body of Jesse, the father of David, and which has at its top the Blessed Virgin holding the infant Christ. Equally, a tree of love set in the heart can be found in both religious and courtly allegories. The role of Piers is evidently that of overseer, as in the half acre scene, but now the agricultural, or horticultural, setting is not literal but is part of an explicitly allegorical account. For all its suggestive quality, this initial allegorical tree is static and somewhat diagrammatic: it explains something compactly, without apparently leading anywhere.

What follows sets it in motion. At the mention of Piers's name, Wille swoons and falls into a dream, variously described in the manuscripts as a *lone dreem* and a *love dreem* – readings between which it is difficult to decide. In it Piers himself at last appears and urges him to examine the tree more closely. At this point in fact Wille is already asleep, indeed has been asleep since the beginning of Passus xv, but there is no reason to suppose that Langland has overlooked that. He twice makes Wille fall into a kind of inner dream when he is already dreaming – once at xi 6-404, and once here, at xvi 20-167 – and in both cases the purpose is apparently to indicate a deeper level of vision. In Passus xi, Wille sees his own past life and as a result comes painfully to a new understanding of his imperfection and the need for his vision of the world to be grounded in self-knowledge. Here his swoon at the mention of Piers's name suggests something more like a mystical vision in which, somewhat as in *Pearl*, the soul is carried out of the body in order to see deeper into God's mysteries. What Wille sees here is Piers himself, who shows him 'al the place' (21) and bids him *look* at the tree which Anima has only described. And already the continuity of the allegory is fractured, and what is seen differs in significant respects from what was expounded.

Now Wille sees that the tree is supported by three props, which Piers explains serve to hold it up and to protect it and its flowers against winds. (Only in a dream could props offer protection to blossom!) The text Piers quotes to 'support' the allegory here is of great importance: *Cum ceciderit iustus non collidetur quia Dominus supponit manum suam* (Psalm 36:24). When the just man shall fall, 'he shall not be utterly cast down', as the Authorized Version puts it; but the Douai translation of the Vulgate translates, 'he shall not be bruised', and Langland may intend a pun on *collidetur*, which can very appropriately mean 'bruised' if it is applied to fruit. 'For the Lord upholdeth him with his hand'. Even the just man falls; he cannot avoid sin; but God's sustaining hand prevents him from being destroyed by his fall. Anima had described charity as originally planted by God but subsequently dependent on human free will, while in his vision Wille sees charity as constantly supported and protected by God against the dangers that would otherwise destroy it. Charity is possible only because God's upholding hand is always intervening in the world; indeed, it is for this very reason that the earlier, static allegory has had to give way to one in which action occurs.

Accordingly, then, the props are interpreted as the three persons of the Trinity, while the winds against which they act are the traditional 'three temptations', the soul's chief enemies: the world, the flesh, and the devil. The first wind is the world, from which covetousness comes and creeps among the leaves and eats the fruit, sin now being seen as a destructive grub. Against this, Piers says that he employs the first prop, *Potencia Dei Patris* – but not passively, as a prop, but actively, transforming it into a weapon. The second wind is the flesh; it blows 'Thorugh likynge and lustes' (32) and nourishes 'wormes of synne' (34), which eat away the tree's blossoms 'right to the bare leves' (35). In Anima's earlier allegorical exposition, the leaves were 'lele wordes, the lawe of Holy Chirche' (6); so perhaps we are to understand that when sin eats away the blossoms, what is left is mere words, mere outward conformity to 'the lawe of Holy Chirche'; possibly, too, 'bare leves' may suggest the pages of Scripture, read literally, without spiritual understanding. These are no more than possibilities, however; it is difficult to set limits to the meaning of such an exceptionally rich allegory, which works less by precise definition than by a kind of suggestive vibration of the complex, multidimensional web of medieval religious thought and language. Against the second wind, Piers's weapon is *Sapiencia Dei Patris*, 'That is the passion and the power of oure prince Jesu' (37). (The point here is that the Wisdom of the Father means the Son: the text in the background is Proverbs 8:22–31, in which Wisdom himself speaks and says that he has existed 'from the beginning, before ever the earth was'. Though the Incarnation occurred at a specific historical moment, the Son has existed eternally, like the Father.)

Thus the tree's fruit is protected until it is ripe. And then the allegory shifts, and instead of a third wind the devil himself attacks the tree, and with terrifying energy – shaking the root, throwing missiles of contention at the top, and setting against the tree a ladder of lies. (The devil is 'the father of lies', and it was of course by lying that he persuaded Eve to eat the fruit of the forbidden tree in Eden.) Sometimes, Piers explains, *Liberum Arbitrium* hinders the devil without calling on Piers himself for help. Two texts are quoted to justify this statement: Matthew 12:32 – 'He who sins against the Holy Ghost, it shall not be forgiven him' – and then, explaining that mysterious and threatening assertion, 'he who sins through his free will does not resist [sin]'. The question of the nature of the sin against the Holy Ghost was highly controversial, but what Langland has in mind may perhaps be that the second text implies the possibility of resisting even the greatest sin by one's free will, though men do not always do so. (Later Langland, taking further an analogy proposed by St Augustine, implies the identification of human free will with the Holy Spirit itself.) So sometimes *Liberum Arbitrium*, man's free will, manages to resist the devil alone; but when the devil 'and the flessh forth with the world' (48) attack unexpectedly from behind, then *Liberum Arbitrium* has to seize the third prop to knock down the devil 'pureliche thorugh grace/ And help of the Holy Goost' (51–2). Thus the third prop must be the third person of the Trinity, the Holy Spirit, whose aid can be summoned by human free will to defeat the devil – another example of the dependence of charity on divine intervention.

Wille thanks Piers for his explanation, but says that he is full of curiosity about the three props and their origins: they are so similar that he thinks they must have grown from a single root. Piers answers briefly that 'this tree' (61) means the Trinity; but he goes no further, and a mere look from him warns Wille to ask no more about this divine mystery, so instead he asks Piers to explain the fruit. Most commentators assume that Piers is still referring to the same tree, but it is at least possible that for the moment it is another; after all, it would be surprising if the props came from the same root as the tree itself. The tree of Charity and the tree of the Trinity are doubtless analogous – the Augustinian conception of a 'trinity' of faculties in man's soul, expressing the divine image in which man was created, was widely known – but that is not to say that they are identical. On the other hand, the very suggestiveness of Langland's allegory makes it unwise to insist on the distinction between analogy and identicality.

Now Piers names the fruit of the tree of Charity, and, in this particularly Trinitarian section of the poem, there are of course three of them – yet another traditional triad, representing the three states of human life, matrimony, widowhood, and virginity. Drawn once more into the poem's space, as we were when reading the pardon, we look up at the tree from below with Piers, and the first fruit we see is Matrimony 'Heer . . . bynethe' (67), 'a moiste fruyt withalle' (68): the way of life that is nearest to the earth, ripe and yet liable to go bad quickly. The second fruit, 'neer the crop' (69) (nearer to the top), is Continence, a 'kaylewey bastard' or grafted Cailloux pear, partly attached to the world and partly not. And the third, the purest fruit at the very top, is Maidenhood. It is 'swete withouten swellyng' (72) (implying without rottenness, but also without pregnancy), and is described as 'aungeles peeris' (71) (that is, the pears but also the peers of the angels). This brief section illustrates particularly well how Langland's allegory unfolds not simply in accordance with pre-existing conceptual systems – the three persons of the Trinity, three temptations, three states of life, and so on – but in response to the suggestive properties of language. The two forms of development sometimes coincide perfectly, sometimes they temporarily diverge, and sometimes it is as though the imagination working through language shifts or even fractures the existing system of concepts.

What happens next is startling indeed. Wille begs Piers to 'pulle adoun an appul, and he wolde,/ And suffre me to assaien what savour it hadde' (73–4); and Piers does so. What does this extra-ordinary act mean? The allegory passes through three stages before, at line 90, it completely disappears. First there was the static allegory as described by Anima; then Piers describes a series of actions – winds blowing, worms creeping and gnawing, the devil shaking the trunk and throwing allegorical stones, and *Liberum Arbitrium* and Piers seizing props and hitting out with them. Now, in the third stage, action is not just described but takes place, and the allegorical mould is shattered under the impact of new meanings. Wille shows yet again the curiosity, the unslakeable desire for *kynde knowyng*, that has impelled him all through the poem. He has been repeatedly rebuked for it, most recently by Anima in Passus xv, when he admitted that

> Alle the sciences under sonne and alle the sotile craftes
> I wolde I knewe and kouthe kyndely in myn herte, (xv 48–9)

and was sternly reminded, in lines that of course allude to the eating of fruit, that

> Coveitise to konne and to knowe science
> Putte out of Paradis Adam and Eve. (xv 62–3)

And as recently as xvi 64–5 Piers has deterred him with a sharp look from asking any more questions. The desire for knowledge is dangerous and potentially sinful; yet without it, the poem could not exist – or at least could exist only as a sermon, not as a dramatic fiction. And Piers now gives way without question to Wille's request to let him taste an apple, in effect abetting him in a re-enactment of the Fall of Adam, that primal attempt to achieve *kynde knowyng*, the forbidden knowledge of good and evil. Adam's eating of the apple was not only a sin; it was also a fortunate event, a *felix culpa*, because it was part of a divine plan leading to the Incarnation and thus to the redemption of man and the final defeat of the devil. As the well-known fifteenth-century lyric puts it,

> Adam lay ibowndyn, bowndyn in a bond;
> Fowre thowsand wynter thowt he not to long.
> And al was for an appil, an appil that he tok,
> As clerkis fyndyn wretyn in here bok.
>
> Ne hadde the appil take ben, the appil taken ben,
> Ne hadde never Our Lady a ben hevene qwen.
> Blyssid be the tyme that appil take was.
> Therefore we mown syngyn, "Deo gracias".[31]

Within Langland's allegory too, the consequence of the attempt to eat the apple is the birth of Christ. As the allegory enters into motion, it enters into the dimension of real, not fictive, time. Human history begins with original sin, and it begins again when God becomes man; and, in a mysterious sense, those two events are the same. In this 'inner vision', Langland is seeing things not as the theologians see them but as the mystics see them; and there is a striking parallel to this section of *Piers Plowman* in Julian of Norwich's *Revelations of Divine Love*:

When Adam felle, Godes Sonne fell; for the ryght onyng whych was made in hevyn, Goddys Sonne myght nott be separath from Adam, for by Adam I understond alle man. Adam fell fro lyfe to deth in to the slade of this wrechyd worlde and aftyr that in to hell. Goddys Son fell with Adam in to the slade of the meydens wombe, whych was the feyerest doughter of Adam, and that for to excuse Adam from blame in hevyn and in erth; and myghtely he fechyd hym out of hell.[32]

Wille's persistent desire for *kynde knowyng* seems to be justified by the outcome of the inner vision, for what immediately follows is Gabriel's announcement of the coming birth of Christ:

> And thanne spak *Spiritus Sanctus* in Gabrielis mouthe
> To a maide that highte Marie, a meke thyng withalle . . .   (XVI 90–1)

This can be connected with a fact emphasized elsewhere in the poem, that by means of the Incarnation God too satisfied a desire for experiential knowledge. God is omniscient, yet all the same Langland imagines him as unable truly to know what it is like to be a man, a created being, without actually becoming one. Thus further on in this passus Abraham tells Wille that 'creatour weex creature to knowe what was bothe' (215). In Passus XVIII are passages that make the same point more elaborately. Pees argues from the 'doctrine of contraries' that Adam and Eve and their descendents would not have known truly what happiness was if they had not endured the miseries that were consequences of the Fall, including death itself. She then proceeds, daringly, to apply the same argument to God:

> So God that bigan al of his goode wille
> Bicam man of a mayde mankynde to save,
> And suffrede to be sold, to se the sorwe of deying,
> The which unknytteth alle care, and comsynge is of reste.
> For til *modicum* mete with us, I may it wel avowe,
> Woot no wight, as I wene, what is ynogh to mene.   (XVIII 211–16)

Therefore God permitted Adam to sin; and therefore too he permitted himself to suffer the creaturely life on earth and in hell (when Christ harrowed it), in order to *know* the widest possible range of experience. This ultimate justification for the existence of a genuinely exploratory poem, one that ventures into the unknown that lies beyond the mapped ground of theology, is thus present, at least by implication, within *Piers Plowman* itself – though Langland was perhaps never able (or perhaps never willing) to formulate it quite explicitly.[33]

Piers begins to knock down apples from the tree. Those representing virginity cry out; widowhood weeps, and matrimony makes 'a foul noise' (XVI 77). All the fruit, representing all the human souls that have suffered death, from Adam to John the

Baptist, are gathered up by the devil and taken '*in Limbo Inferni/* There is derknesse and drede and the devel maister' (84–5). At this Piers, acting once more 'for pure tene', seizes 'that a pil' (86) (the one, single prop) and hits out at the devil with it in order to recapture the fruit. The three persons of the Trinity – '*Filius* by the Fadre wille and frenesse of *Spiritūs Sancti*' (88) – are conjoined in a single deed, the three props becoming a single prop, to bring about the Incarnation of God as man. With this violent and mysterious action, the allegory of the tree suddenly disappears, to give way to the literal truth of the Annunciation and Incarnation, except that we are told that the ripening of the fruit and the final struggle for its possession are now to take place when '*plenitudo temporis* tyme comen were' (93).

There is a clear parallel between Piers's two angry acts, at VII 115 and at XVI 86. The tearing of the pardon marks the breaking of the poem's action out of the historical present into the dreamer's inward, spiritual quest; the hitting out at the devil with the Trinity marks a break back into history again. From the Annunciation, which takes place now, human history proceeds until by the end of the poem we have been brought back to Langland's present and are once more on the field full of folk where it began – only now it can be seen to be a battlefield. The tearing of the pardon seemed to express exasperation with the limits of symbolism itself: the challenge to the symbolic order involved the physical destruction of the sign, an explicit gesture of semioclasm. That is not quite so in Passus XVI: Piers does not chop down the tree of Charity, it simply vanishes from the poem. But for all that, here too allegory is exploded by the impossibility of its containing a transcendent meaning. Human signs – allegories, symbols, words – are inadequate to convey divine meanings, and God, the transcendent signified, can be read only through the contradictions and the final exhaustion and evaporation of the human signifier.

Like the allegorical fictions it contains, *Piers Plowman* as a whole evades the pretension of monumentality by displacing and deconstructing itself as it is produced. Langland may perhaps have begun with the hope of creating a monument, a complete and objective vision of the field full of folk seen from outside time; but what he actually wrote was not a finished work but an unfinished text, which inhabits human time and exists as process. Its location within a history which is incomplete (and which is also the necessarily incomplete life-history of its poet) is of special importance in an age which believed, as we may not, in a reality outside history; Langland resists what was usually an irresistible temptation to take refuge in a total, providential system. His poem incorporates fragments of the monumental and the systematic, but they are experienced as floating freely within the processes of history and of language. John Lawlor long ago wrote of *Piers Plowman* as a work which 'succeeds by communicating the mind, not behind, but *in* the poem – a poem which is always, in a sense, unfinished';[34] but the overall effect of the article in which he does so, as indeed is suggested by its title, 'The Imaginative Unity of *Piers Plowman*', is to contain and defuse the poem's existence as process. 'Unity' is not a helpful concept, because it implies the possibility of standing outside the text and judging it as something complete. *Piers Plowman* may aim at completeness, but it never reaches it; it ends with the prospect of yet another journey, 'as wide as the world lasteth' (xx 382), towards the transcendence that has always evaded it, and that could only be gained by an escape from language itself.

Notes

1 Elaborated and restricted codes

1 Quoted, here and subsequently, from *La Chanson de Roland*, ed. F. Whitehead, 2nd edn (Oxford 1946)

2 *The Song of Roland*, trans. Frederick Goldin (New York 1978)

3 I quote from and give page references to the revised edition (London 1974).

4 See for example Ronald King, 'Bernstein's Sociology of the School – a Further Testing', *British Journal of Sociology* 32 (1981), 259–65: 'Bernstein's theories have been generated independently of original research, and so are explanations of a supposed social reality, which has been shown here to be, in part, empirically false' (p. 261).

5 Useful collections are *Selected Writings of Edward Sapir in Language, Culture and Personality*, ed. D. Mandelbaum (Berkeley 1956), and *Language, Thought, and Reality: Selected Writings of Benjamin Lee Whorf*, ed. John B. Carroll (n.p. 1956).

6 'Social Class, Speech Systems and Psycho-Therapy', *British Journal of Sociology* 15 (1964), 54–64; p. 60

7 R. W. Southern, *The Making of the Middle Ages* (London 1953), p. 221

8 Colin Morris, *The Discovery of the Individual* (London 1972) and 'Individualism in Twelfth-Century Religion. Some Further Reflections', *Journal of Ecclesiastical History* 31 (1980), 195–206; Caroline W. Bynum, *Jesus as Mother* (Berkeley 1982), chap. III; John F. Benton, 'Consciousness of Self and Perceptions of Individuality', in *Renaissance and Renewal in the Twelfth Century*, ed. Robert L. Benson and Giles Constable (Cambridge MA 1982), pp. 263–95.

9 Bynum, pp. 87–8

10 Cf. David Knowles, *The Historian and Character* (Cambridge 1962), chap. 2

11 *Mimesis*, trans. Willard Trask (Princeton 1953), pp. 105, 106, 101

12 *The Rise of Romance* (Oxford 1971), p. 6

13 Stephen Heath, *The Nouveau Roman* (London 1972), p. 189. In context the passage quoted has a quite different reference.

14 *The Making of the Middle Ages*, p. 242

15 On women as audience and patrons, see, e.g., Lee C. Ramsey, *Chivalric Romances* (Bloomington 1983), pp. 9–10.

16 'Social Class, Speech Systems and Psycho-Therapy', p. 56

17 On Ganelon's exploitation of the distinction in feudal law between the treacherous act of murder and the open and potentially redeemable act of vengeance, see R. Howard Bloch, *Medieval French Literature and Law* (Berkeley 1977), p. 39.

18 I am indebted here to Eugene Vance, *Reading the Song of Roland* (Englewood Cliffs 1970), pp. 84ff.

19 Quoted here and subsequently from *The Alliterative Morte Arthure*, ed. Valerie Krishna (New York 1976)
20 From *Six Middle English Romances*, ed. Maldwyn Mills (London 1973)
21 Susan Wittig, *Stylistic and Narrative Structures in the Middle English Romances* (Austin 1978), p. 13
22 *The Rise of Romance*, p. 15
23 Works of Chaucer other than *Troilus and Criseyde* are quoted here and subsequently from *The Works of Geoffrey Chaucer*, ed. F. N. Robinson, 2nd edn (London 1957).

2 Early medieval narrative style

1 Quoted by James Monaco, *How to Read a Film*, rev. edn (New York 1981), p. 128. I have found Monaco's book of great use as a beginner's guide to film technique and the language in which it can be analysed. I must also acknowledge a general debt in this chapter to Seymour Chatman, *Story and Discourse* (Ithaca 1978), for analogies between cinematic narrative and verbal narrative.
2 John Keats, *Hyperion* I 73–4. The same illustration is used in *Poetry of the Age of Chaucer*, ed. A. C. and J. E. Spearing (London 1974), p. 14.
3 *Troilus and Criseyde* is quoted here and subsequently from the edition of B. A. Windeatt (London 1984).
4 The works of the *Gawain*-poet are quoted here and subsequently from *The Poems of the Pearl Manuscript*, ed. Malcolm Andrew and Ronald Waldron (London 1978).
5 *Poetics*, chapter 22
6 'Studies in the Epic Technique of Oral Verse-Making: I. Homer and Homeric Style', *Harvard Studies in Classical Philology* 41 (1930), 73–147; p. 124
7 Cf. the remarks of N. H. Keeble, 'The Narrative Achievement of *Sir Orfeo*', *English Studies* 56 (1975), 193–206, p. 195, about another, somewhat later, pre-Chaucerian romance:

> The poet is reticent throughout his work: not only (as we should expect in a Medieval poem which antedates Langland and Chaucer) is he not present as a personality, but he so restrains all personal idiosyncracies as to give an exceptionally pure line to his narrative. We have no digressions, no indulgent description, no catalogues and few elaborate rhetorical effects . . . As a result, the action seems to unfold of its own volition . . . It seems transparent: we are barely aware that it has been 'made'.

8 For comment, see, for example, Edmund Leach, *Genesis as Myth* (London 1969), pp. 7–8, and *Lévi-Strauss* (London 1970), pp. 59–60; Anne Wilson, *Traditional Romance and Tale* (Ipswich 1976), pp. 59–62; Derek Brewer, *Symbolic Stories* (Cambridge 1980), pp. 64–6.
9 *King Horn* is quoted here and subsequently from the Cambridge text as given by the edition of Joseph Hall (Oxford 1901).
10 Mary Hynes-Berry, 'Cohesion in *King Horn* and *Sir Orfeo*', *Speculum* 50 (1975), 652–70; p. 654
11 According to Hynes-Berry (ibid., p. 652), the exact figure is 692.

12 As suggested, to take a single example, by the parallels between Orfeo's return from the land of fairy and resumption of his kingdom and the 'return' of the pseudo-Baldwin from supposed death and his acceptance as Count of Flanders in 1224–5 (see chronicle accounts summarized by Norman Cohn, *The Pursuit of the Millenium* [London 1957], pp. 77ff).

13 Roman Jakobson, 'Two Aspects of Language and Two Types of Aphasic Disturbances' in *Fundamentals of Language*, ed. Roman Jakobson and Morris Halle (The Hague 1956), pp. 69–96, and 'Closing Statement: Linguistics and Poetics', in *Style in Language*, ed. Thomas A. Sebeok (Cambridge MA 1960), pp. 350–77; David Lodge, *The Modes of Modern Writing* (London 1977), pp. 73ff.

14 John M. Ganim, *Style and Consciousness in Middle English Narrative* (Princeton 1983), p. 42

15 Cf. Marie Borroff, *Sir Gawain and the Green Knight: A Stylistic and Metrical Study* (New Haven 1962), pp. 70–2

16 Roland Barthes, *Mythologies*, trans. Annette Lavers (London 1972), p. 27

17 Ibid., p. 28. The phrase 'healthy state of the sign' is used, in interpretation of the thought of Barthes, by Stephen Heath, *The Nouveau Roman*, p. 193. For a clear exposition of Barthes' views in this respect, see also Stephen Heath, *Vertige du déplacement* (Paris 1974), pp. 48ff.

18 *Mythologies*, p. 8

19 *Havelok* is quoted here and subsequently from *The Lay of Havelok the Dane*, ed. W. W. Skeat, 2nd edn rev. K. Sisam (Oxford 1923).

20 For further examples of similar constructions, cf. note on line 1008 in Skeat-Sisam edition.

21 *Comus*, 671–3

22 *The Eve of Saint Agnes*, stanza xxx

3   Interpreting a medieval romance

1 Peter Dronke, 'The Return of Eurydice', *Classica et Mediaevalia* 23 (1962), 198–215

2 *Sir Orfeo* is quoted here and subsequently from the Auchinleck MS as edited by A. J. Bliss, 2nd edn (Oxford 1966). The Ovidian version to which I refer in this paragraph is in *Metamorphoses* x–xi.

3 I have repunctuated Bliss's text here, placing a full stop at the end of line 324 instead of the end of line 326. Note once again the use of the relative construction ('That had ben so riche and so heiye') to convey the identity of the king and the exile.

4 E. D. Hirsch, *Validity in Interpretation* (New Haven 1967), p. 8. In an appendix Hirsch relies on the same 'fundamental distinction' (p. 255) as a basis for his critique of the hermeneutic theories of Gadamer.

5 'Introduction to the Structural Analysis of Narratives', in Roland Barthes, *Image-Music-Text*, trans. Stephen Heath (London 1977), p. 89

6 I owe this analogy to a lecture by my friend and colleague Professor John Holloway, given longer ago than either of us would probably care to specify.

7 Sermon XL.1, trans. S. J. Eales, *Cantica Canticorum* (London 1895), p. 252

8 Odo Tusculanus, *Sermones*, ed. J. B. Pitra, *Analecta novissima Spicilegii*

Solesmensis (1885–8), II 227, quoted by D. W. Robertson, *A Preface to Chaucer* (Princeton 1963), pp. 89–90.

9 J. F. Knapp, 'The Meaning of *Sir Orfeo*,' *Modern Language Quarterly* 29 (1968), 263–73; p. 270

10 D. M. Hill, 'The Structure of *Sir Orfeo*', *Mediaeval Studies* 23 (1961), 136–53; p. 144

11 Doreena Allen, 'Orpheus and Orfeo: the Dead and the *Taken*', *Medium Aevum* 33 (1964), 102–11; pp. 104, 109, 110

12 'The Significance of Sir Orfeo's Self-Exile', *Review of English Studies* ns 18 (1967), 245–52; pp. 247–50

13 John Speirs, *Medieval English Poetry* (London 1957), p. 147

14 'The Exiled King: Sir Orfeo's Harp and the Second Death of Eurydice', *Mosaic* 9/2 (1976), 45–60; pp. 51–2

15 *Patience* 95–6

16 J. B. Friedman, *Orpheus in the Middle Ages* (Cambridge MA 1970), p. 90, citing Boethius, *De consolatione philosophiae* III metrum 12. I am much indebted to Friedman's comprehensive study of medieval interpretations of the Orpheus myth.

17 From *The Poems of Robert Henryson*, ed. Denton Fox (Oxford 1981)

18 (New Haven 1974), pp. 174, 176

19 *Orpheus in the Middle Ages*, pp. 184, 188, 189–90

20 William of Conches, commentary on *De consolatione philosophiae*, metrum 12, cited from MS Troyes 1331 by Friedman, ibid., p. 108; Pierre Bersuire, *Metamorphosis Ovidiana*, summarized ibid., pp. 127–31.

21 Cf. Bruce Harbert, 'Chaucer and the Latin Classics', in *Geoffrey Chaucer*, ed. Derek Brewer (London 1974), pp. 137–53, p. 145:

> He was interested in ancient stories for their own sake. In the case of the one moralization that he did certainly read – the *Ovide Moralisé* – we know that he used the parts of the work that translate direct from Ovid, but no parallels have been discovered between Chaucer and the allegorical sections.

22 *Anatomy of Criticism* (Princeton 1957), p. 89

23 The distinction is that made by Frank Kermode, *The Classic* (London 1975), p. 75. Cf. Peter Haidu, 'Romance: Idealistic Genre or Historical Text?', in *The Craft of Fiction*, ed. Leigh A. Arrathoon (Rochester, Michigan, 1984), pp. 1–46, p. 6:

> When it comes to the interpretation of ancient texts, the predominant medieval attitude was not at all "historical" but "modernist": it consisted of resolutely reading the classical texts such as Virgil and Ovid in terms of contemporary eleventh- or twelfth-century codes.

24 Hill, 'The Structure of *Sir Orfeo*', makes some suggestions to this effect.

25 It is striking that all three of the above references to madness occur only in the Auchinleck MS. This is unquestionably the most authoritative of the three manuscripts, and it might be hypothesized that later scribes failed to grasp one of the poet's crucial ideas.

26 See Friedman, *Orpheus in the Middle Ages*, pp. 147–55

27 For general information about the medieval use of music as medical therapy,

see Madeleine P. Cosman, 'Machaut's Medical Musical World', in *Machaut's World*, ed. Madeleine P. Cosman and Bruce Chandler (New York 1978), pp. 1–36. The quotation from *De proprietatibus rerum* is from the Middle English translation, *On the Properties of Things*, ed. M. C. Seymour (Oxford 1975), vol. I, p. 350.

28 *King Lear* IV 7 16; *The Tempest* V 1 58; *Macbeth* II 1 49–51

29 The two Woolf passages are quoted by Quentin Bell in his *Virginia Woolf: A Biography* (London 1972), vol. II, pp. 84, 226

30 R. D. Laing, *The Politics of Experience and the Bird of Paradise* (Harmondsworth 1967), p. 40

31 The last few paragraphs are an expanded and partly rewritten version of *Poetry of the Age of Chaucer*, ed. A. C. and J. E. Spearing, pp. 47–9.

4 Early Chaucer

1 This was suggested by L. H. Loomis, 'Chaucer and the Auchinleck MS', in *Essays and Studies in Honor of Carleton Brown* (New York 1940), pp. 111–28.

2 See D. S. Brewer, 'The Relationship of Chaucer to the English and European Traditions', in *Chaucer and Chaucerians*, ed. D. S. Brewer (London 1966), pp. 1–47, esp. pp. 22–5; P. M. Kean, *Chaucer and the Making of English Poetry* (London 1972), vol. I, pp. 1–30.

3 I have discussed this in more detail in *Medieval to Renaissance in English Poetry* (Cambridge 1985), chapters 2–3.

4 The pre-Chaucerian romances that come nearest to sustained courtliness in style and outlook are perhaps *Kyng Alysaunder* (c. 1300) and *William of Palerne* (c. 1360).

5 Thomas Usk in *The Testament of Love*, in *Chaucerian and Other Pieces*, ed. W. W. Skeat (Oxford 1897), p. 123

6 See *Medieval to Renaissance in English Poetry*, pp. 22–30

7 For further comment on 'yif I kan', see ibid., p. 22 and n. 18. Much of Erich Auerbach's brilliant discussion, in chapter 3 of his *Literary Language and its Public* (London 1965), of the stylistic relation of the Old French *Eneas* to Virgil's *Aeneid* applies equally well to this part of *The House of Fame*.

8 For Chaucerian urbanity, cf. P. M. Kean, *Chaucer and the Making of English Poetry*, vol. I, chapter 2

9 Noted by J. A. W. Bennett, *Chaucer's Book of Fame* (Oxford 1968), p. 29

10 *The Waning of the Middle Ages* (Harmondsworth 1955), pp. 285, 281

11 For the concept of intertextuality, cf. Julia Kristeva, *Semiotikè* (Paris 1969), p. 146, cited by Jonathan Culler, *Structuralist Poetics* (London 1975), p. 139: 'every text takes shape as a mosaic of citations, every text is the absorption and transformation of other texts'. I use the term here, however, in a simpler sense than is common among recent theorists; for them the 'citations' are of other cultural discourses rather than of specific sources and analogues. In this respect as in others, the concepts of recent theory seem to have an application of a simpler and more obvious kind to medieval than to modern writing.

12 Piero Boitani, in *Literature in Fourteenth-Century England*, ed. Piero Boitani and Anna Torti (Tübingen 1983), p. 13.

13 For a clear account of the occasion and the poem's relation to it, see Derek Brewer, *Chaucer and his World* (London 1978), pp. 111–13.

14 For the remainder of this paragraph, cf. my *Medieval Dream-Poetry* (Cam-

bridge 1976) and, more briefly, 'Dream-Poems' in *The New Pelican Guide to English Literature*, ed. Boris Ford, vol. 1, part 1 (Harmondsworth 1982), pp. 235–47.

15 For comparable definitions of 'literature', see Tzvetan Todorov, 'The Notion of Literature', *New Literary History* 5 (1973–4), 5–16.

16 Benjamin S. Harrison, 'Medieval Rhetoric in the *Book of the Duchesse*', *Publications of the Modern Language Association of America* 49 (1934), 428–42; p. 442. The Chaucer passages referred to are *Troilus* I 1065–9 (see p. 107 below), translated from *Poetria nova* 43–5, and *Canterbury Tales* VII 3347.

17 *Wreye* may mean 'reveal' or 'betray'; in this context, as is assumed by Stevens in the passage indicated in note 18, it seems more likely to mean 'conceal': cf. Troilus's anxiety 'Hym self to wrey' when he first falls in love with Criseyde (*Troilus* I 329). Perhaps significantly, the general sense of the *Franklin's Tale* passage and its relevance for my purpose are unaltered whichever meaning is assumed for *wreye*.

18 John Stevens, *Music and Poetry in the Early Tudor Court* (London 1961), p. 216

19 Harold Bloom, 'Freud's Concepts of Defense and the Poetic Will', in *The Literary Freud: Mechanisms of Defense and the Poetic Will*, ed. Joseph H. Smith (New Haven 1980), pp. 1–28; p. 1

20 Geoffroi de Vinsauf, *Poetria nova*, line 61, in *Les arts poétiques du XIIe et du XIIIe siècle*, ed. Edmond Faral (Paris 1924); trans. Margaret F. Nims (Toronto 1967)

21 Cf. Robert F. Jordan, 'The Compositional Structure of the *Book of the Duchess*', *Chaucer Review* 9 (1974–5), 99–117, p. 108:

> . . . in the disjunct, discontinuous narrative mode of the poem the dreamer's transitional function overrides his dramatic function and characterization. Serving primarily as the agent of movement from one element of the poem's matter to another, the dreamer takes on the traits requisite at a given stage of the poem's progress. This is not to deny that Chaucer has endowed the dreamer with certain consistently recognizable personality traits, but it is to question the basis for regarding the dreamer as a unified consciousness, developing consistently through experience.

22 *The Pursuit of Signs* (London 1981), p. 143

23 One closely similar earlier example (translated from a French source) occurs in the romance *Floris and Blancheflour* (ed. George H. McKnight, *King Horn, Floriz and Blauncheflur, The Assumption of our Lady*, EETS OS 14, re-ed. [London 1901]):

> "Deeth," he seide, "ful of envye,
> And of alle trechorye,
> Refte thou hast me my lemman." (281–3)

Chaucer's source at this point in *The Book of the Duchess*, Machaut's *Jugement dou Roy de Behaigne*, personifies death but does not apostrophize it. The personification of death in *Sir Orfeo* 332 (see p. 63 above) approaches apostrophe but does not quite reach it.

24 'Chaucer's *Book of the Duchess*: An Art to Consume Art', *Durham University Journal* 69 (1976–7), 201–5; p. 201

5 Narrative closure: the end of *Troilus and Criseyde*

1 The passage cited is from *Poetria nova*, lines 43–7; in the *Troilus* it represents Pandarus's thoughts about the planning of a love affair.

2 Peter Dronke, 'The Conclusion of *Troilus and Criseyde*', *Medium Aevum* 33 (1964), 47–52; p. 49. For general scepticism about ideas of 'organic unity' as applied to medieval literature and for drawing-out of the implications of the architectural metaphor, see Robert M. Jordan, *Chaucer and the Shape of Creation* (Cambridge MA 1967).

3 See, e.g. Arnold van Gennep, *The Rites of Passage*, trans. M. B. Vizedom and G. L. Caffee (London 1960); Mary Douglas, *Purity and Danger*, 2nd edn (London 1969); and my discussion of Mary Douglas's ideas in Chapter 8 below, passim.

4 A. C. Spearing, *Medieval Dream-Poetry*, p. 54

5 Seymour Chatman, *Story and Discourse*, p. 47; David Lodge, *Working with Structuralism* (London 1981), p. 150; Wolfgang Iser, 'Indeterminacy and the Reader's Response in Prose Fiction', in *Aspects of Narrative*, ed. J. Hillis Miller (New York 1971), 1–45, p. 11. The Conrad quotation is cited by Lodge, op. cit., p. 151, from Conrad's 'Henry James: An Appreciation'.

6 Barbara Herrnstein Smith, *Poetic Closure* (Chicago 1968), p. 120

7 Stephen Knight, 'Chaucer and the Sociology of Literature', *Studies in the Age of Chaucer* 2 (1980), 15–51; p. 27. I borrow Knight's formulation because it conveniently sums up a widespread modern expectation; but his point is precisely that closure in this sense is *not* characteristic of medieval art.

8 Gerald Morgan, 'The Ending of *Troilus and Criseyde*', *Modern Language Review* 77 (1982), 257–71, p. 257, referring to Aquinas, *Summa theologiae* 2a 2ae 145.2 *corp*. Morgan's assumption, that, having encountered this aesthetic theory through his reading of Dante, Chaucer would have found it entirely convincing, seems to me questionable. What Chaucer would actually have learned from reading the *Commedia* (the work of Dante's we can be sure he knew), in a passage attributed to Aquinas himself, was that the products of Nature were necessarily imperfect, because Nature always expresses the divine image 'defectively, working like the artist who has the skill of his art and a hand that trembles' (*Paradiso* 13: 86–8, trans. John D. Sinclair, [London 1939]). Cf. Bonnie Wheeler, 'Dante, Chaucer, and the Ending of *Troilus and Criseyde*', *Philological Quarterly* 61 (1982), 105–23. Chaucer was always aware of the trembling hand that accompanied the poet's skill, and never more so perhaps than at the end of the *Troilus*.

9 The translation is that of John Stevens, in his 'Dante and Music', *Italian Studies* 23 (1968), 1–18, p. 14, from *De vulgari eloquentia* II viii 5 (my italics). I am particularly indebted to Professor Stevens for discussing the matter with me and for calling attention to this passage.

10 Matthieu and Geoffroi are quoted from *Les arts poétiques*, ed. Faral, pp. 191–2 and 319–20. Translation of the former is from Matthew of Vendôme, *The Art of Versification*, trans. Aubrey E. Galyon (Ames 1980), p. 111. Jean is quoted from *The Parisiana Poetria of John of Garland*, ed. and trans. Traugott Lawler (New Haven 1974), pp. 88–91.

11 For categorizations, see Ramsey, *Chivalric Romances*, and Wittig, *Stylistic and Narrative Structures*, ch. 4

12 *The Tale of Gamelyn*, ed. W. W. Skeat, 2nd edn (Oxford 1893)

13 Ed. MacEdward Leach, EETS OS 203 (London 1937)
14 Ed. A. McI. Trounce (London 1933)
15 *Sir Isumbras*, ed. Mills, *Six Middle English Romances*
16 *Ywain and Gawain*, ed. Albert B. Friedman and Norman T. Harrington, EETS OS 254 (London 1964)
17 Ed. Mills, *Six Middle English Romances*
18 Ed. A. J. Bliss (London 1960)
19 Ed. Thomas C. Rumble, ed. *The Breton Lays in Middle English* (Detroit 1965)
20 Ed. Mills, *Six Middle English Romances*
21 Ibid.
22 Ibid.
23 Ed. M. Mills, EETS OS 261 (London 1969)
24 Ed. Carol Falvo Heffernan (Manchester 1976)
25 Ed. Rumble, *The Breton Lays in Middle English*
26 *The Testament of Cresseid*, line 61
27 For some of the many discussions of this subject, see E. Benveniste, *Problèmes de linguistique générale* (Paris 1966), pp. 238ff; T. Todorov, 'Les catégories du récit littéraire', *Communications* 8 (Paris 1966), pp. 133ff, and *The Poetics of Prose* (Oxford 1977), pp. 25ff; Chatman, *Story and Discourse*, passim; Jonathan Culler, *Structuralist Poetics*, pp. 197ff, and *The Pursuit of Signs*, ch. 9; G. Genette, *Figures of Literary Discourse* (Oxford 1982), pp. 138ff.
28 *The Pursuit of Signs*, p. 171
29 I mention this example because the view has been expressed that what Pandarus is forgiven for is committing incest with his niece in the immediately preceding scene: see, e.g., Beryl Rowland, 'Pandarus and the Fate of Tantalus', *Orbis Litterarum* 24 (1969), 3–15. I find this unconvincing, but I cannot see that Chaucer makes himself clear about the matter.
30 Cf. Ian Bishop, *Chaucer's Troilus and Criseyde: A Critical Study* (Bristol 1981), p. 30
31 This is the refrain line of Chaucer's *Balade de Bon Conseil*; cf. John 8:32.
32 Recent examples of this include two otherwise highly intelligent books, Monica McAlpine, *The Genre of Troilus and Criseyde* (Ithaca 1978), and Winthrop Wetherbee, *Chaucer and the Poets* (Ithaca 1984). For an admirably sane treatment of the narrator, to which I am much indebted, see Elizabeth Salter, '*Troilus and Criseyde*: Poet and Narrator', in *Acts of Interpretation*, ed. Mary J. Carruthers and Elizabeth D. Kirk (Norman 1982), pp. 281–91.
33 See my *Medieval to Renaissance in English Poetry*, pp. 32–4
34 Cf. Walter J. Ong, *Interfaces of the Word* (Ithaca 1977), p. 238, on the written text as monument.
35 The view that the poem originally existed in a distinct unrevised version lacking the 'philosophical' passages has been convincingly rejected by Windeatt: see his edition, pp. 36ff. For *Troilus and Criseyde* as a work bearing traces of the poet's changing responses to his source, see Elizabeth Salter, '*Troilus and Criseyde*: a Reconsideration', in *Patterns of Love and Courtesy*, ed. John Lawlor (London 1966), pp. 86–106.
36 For a wide-ranging survey of the Latin and Italian sources and analogues of these stanzas, see John M. Steadman, *Disembodied Laughter* (Berkeley 1972).
37 See Morton W. Bloomfield, 'The Eighth Sphere', *Modern Language Review* 53 (1958), 408–10

38 E. Talbot Donaldson, 'The Ending of *Troilus*', in his *Speaking of Chaucer* (London 1970), pp. 84–101; p. 97

39 The quoted phrase is from Edward Wilson, *The Gawain-Poet* (Leiden 1976), p. 6. (Wilson is comparing the Chaucer of the *Troilus* with the Maiden in *Pearl*, both of whom go beyond 'the pagan's philosophic condemnation of earthly affection'.) It was of course possible for a Christian too to be imagined as laughing at the worthlessness of earth when seen from the heavens, as Dante does in the *Paradiso*, also looking down from the eighth sphere, in a passage that influenced Boccaccio in the *Teseida* and may also have influenced Chaucer directly:

> Col viso ritornai per tutte quante
> le sette spere, e vidi questo globo
> tal, ch'io sorrisi del suo vil sembiante.　　(22:133–5)

(With my sight I returned through every one of the seven spheres, and I saw this globe such that I smiled at its paltry semblance [trans. Sinclair].)

But Chaucer strongly emphasizes the paganism of Troilus, and this changes the overall effect: it must be borne in mind that, when he borrows from Dante or any other source, he does not necessarily mean exactly what the source means: cf. Elizabeth Salter, *Fourteenth-Century English Poetry* (Oxford 1983), p. 129, in relation to recollections of Dante in *The Parliament of Fowls*. For an attempt to read the ending of the *Troilus* in Dantean terms, see Morgan, 'The Ending of *Troilus and Criseyde*'.

40 In this paragraph I am much indebted to the perceptive comments of Donaldson, 'The Ending of *Troilus*'. I would differ from his reading of the end of *Troilus and Criseyde* only in doubting, for the reasons given on p. 122 above, the validity of his absolute distinction between the poet and the simple-minded narrator. I am encouraged to find that in his most recent discussion of the poem he has written that 'I think many of us, myself included, have been too anxious to separate the narrator from the poet Chaucer' (*The Swan at the Well* [New Haven 1985], p. 128). Since this chapter was written I have read James Dean's interesting article, 'Chaucer's *Troilus*, Boccaccio's *Filostrato*, and the Poetics of Closure', *Philological Quarterly* 64 (1985), 175–84, in which the ambivalence of *litel* is noted.

41 Lines 1863–5 translate *Paradiso* 14:28–30, elevating the style still further by turning statement into apostrophe.

6　Alliterative poetry

1 The best accounts of this history, to which I am much indebted at various points in this chapter, are Thorlac Turville-Petre, *The Alliterative Revival* (Cambridge 1977), and two articles by Derek Pearsall: 'The Origins of the Alliterative Revival', in *The Alliterative Tradition in the Fourteenth Century*, ed. Bernard S. Levy and Paul E. Szarmach (Kent, Ohio, 1981), pp. 1–24, and 'The Alliterative Revival: Origins and Social Backgrounds', in *Middle English Alliterative Poetry and its Literary Background*, ed. David Lawton (Cambridge 1982), pp. 34–53. For attempts to characterize the poetry of the Alliterative Revival, see Geoffrey Shepherd, 'The Nature of Alliterative Poetry in Late Medieval England', *Proceedings of the British Academy* 56

(1972), 57–76, and David A. Lawton, 'The Unity of Middle English Alliterative Poetry', *Speculum* 58 (1983), 72–94; and for an endeavour to define 'alliterative romance', see Arlyn Diamond, '*Sir Gawain and the Green Knight*: An Alliterative Romance', *Philological Quarterly* 55 (1976), 10–29.

2 The following examples are taken from Jean Ritzke-Rutherford, 'Formulaic Microstructure: The Cluster', in *The Alliterative Morte Arthure: A Reassessment of the Poem*, ed. Karl Heinz Göller (Cambridge 1981), pp. 70–82; pp. 72–3.

3 'Loose collocational word groups' is the phrase used by Ritzke-Rutherford, art. cit., p. 73; the term 'grammetrical' derives from P. J. Wexler, 'On the Grammetrics of the Classical Alexandrine', *Cahiers de Lexicologie* 4 (1964), 61–72. Ritzke-Rutherford, p. 74, claims that in my discussion of formulaic style in *The Gawain-Poet*, p. 21, I 'confused the collocation or cluster with the idea of the formula'; I would argue that I simply made a different and equally valid division of the same conceptual field; but the disagreement at least illustrates the difficulty of the whole area.

4 *The Siege of Jerusalem* is quoted from the edition of E. Kölbing and Mabel Day, EETS OS 188 (London 1932).

5 *Beowulf* 259

6 Cf. Chapter 2, pp. 53–4, above

7 *Landscapes and Seasons of the Medieval World* (London 1973), pp. 177–8, quoting the *Parliament*, ed. M. Y. Offord, EETS OS 246 (London 1959), line 42

8 The general similarities between the *Morte Arthure* and the *chansons de geste* have been widely accepted since being pointed out by John Finlayson, ed. *Morte Arthure* (London 1967), pp. 11ff. More recently backing of a different kind for the parallel has been supplied by Valerie Krishna, who notes the similarity between the two in the density of their use of formulas, strictly defined: see her 'Parataxis, Formulaic Density, and Thrift in the *Alliterative Morte Arthure*', *Speculum* 57 (1982), 63–83.

9 Juliet Vale, 'Law and Diplomacy in the Alliterative *Morte Arthure*', *Nottingham Medieval Studies* 23 (1979), 31–46; pp. 39–40

10 S. L. A. Marshall, *Men Against Fire* (New York 1947), quoted by John Keegan, *The Face of Battle* (Harmondsworth 1978), pp. 71–2. Marshall repeats the paradox implicit in the phrase 'dredde ay schame': it is the *fear* of loss of reputation, quite as much as courage, that enables men to overcome the natural fear induced by battle.

11 *Ricardian Poetry* (London 1971), pp. 103, 110, 128

12 The C-text of *Piers Plowman* is quoted from *Piers Plowman by William Langland: An Edition of the C-text*, ed. Derek Pearsall (London 1978).

13 Arguments for a later date, at least for the completion of the poem, are put forward by Larry D. Benson, 'The Date of the Alliterative *Morte Arthure*', in *Medieval Studies Presented to Lillian Herlands Hornstein*, ed. Jess B. Bessinger and Robert K. Raymo (New York 1976), pp. 19–40, and by Mary Hamel, ed. *Morte Arthure* (New York 1984), pp. 53–8.

14 William Matthews, *The Tragedy of Arthur* (Berkeley 1960), p. 178; Larry D. Benson (ed.), *King Arthur's Death* (Indianapolis 1974), p. xv; John Gardner (trans.), *The Alliterative Morte Arthure, the Owl and the Nightingale, and Five Other Middle English Poems* (Carbondale 1971), p. 240; Turville-Petre, *The Alliterative Revival*, p. 102

15 Cf. the remarks of Elizabeth Salter in her 'Medieval Poetry and Visual Arts', *Essays and Studies* ns 22 (1969), 16–32, p. 23, comparing the *Gough Map* (c. 1360) with Chaucer's road to Canterbury:

> It provides fairly accurate information on the road-network of medieval England, based, it is thought, on well-tried itineraries between main cities; it also includes stylised "vignettes" for towns and important castles, with spires, towers, crenellated walls and a few houses. Chaucer's references to particular places on the way to Canterbury are brief, but deliberate; the background is only empty in the same way as the background to a mapped-itinerary might be called "empty". It is to common knowledge of a map that he appeals.

Derek Pearsall, 'Rhetorical *Descriptio* in *Sir Gawain and the Green Knight*', *Modern Language Review* 50 (1955), 129–34, comments on the rhetorical functions of some of the apparently realistic details of the landscapes in *Sir Gawain*.

16 Mary Hamel, 'The Dream of a King: the Alliterative *Morte Arthure* and Dante', *Chaucer Review* 14 (1979–80), 298–312, p. 303; cf. my completely misleading statement in *Medieval to Renaissance in English Poetry*, p. 139. Despite Hamel's interesting argument, I am not convinced that the poet knew Dante's work, though the possibility is certainly intriguing.

17 Lee W. Patterson, 'The Historiography of Romance and the Alliterative *Morte Arthure*', *Journal of Medieval and Renaissance Studies* 13 (1983), 1–32, p. 14, quoting *Convivio* I.5

18 Jill Mann has some interesting remarks about the body and blood in Malory in her 'Malory: Knightly Combat in *Le Morte D'Arthur*', in *The New Pelican Guide to English Literature*, vol. 1, Part I, pp. 331–9; pp. 338–9.

19 Krishna rightly remarks that lines 1162–5 'are obscure, very likely because of the wordplay' (ed. cit., p. 179). A possible translation might be: 'Now indeed it seems, by God, that he can seldom go in search of saints, and so he grips all the more fiercely as he thus drags this sacred body out of these high cliffs, carrying out such a churl so as to enclose him in silver [as a relic]'.

20 Rosalind Field, 'The Anglo-Norman Background to Alliterative Romance', in *Middle English Alliterative Poetry*, ed. Lawton, pp. 54–69; p. 68

21 Matthews, *The Tragedy of Arthur*; Finlayson, ed. *Morte Arthure*, Introduction

22 I quote the views of several contributors to *The Alliterative Morte Arthure*, ed. Göller, including Göller himself, 'A Reassessment of the *Alliterative Morte Arthure*', p. 16 and passim; Manfred Markus, 'Language and Style: The Paradox of Heroic Poetry', p. 62 and passim; Jörg A. Fichte, 'The Figure of Sir Gawain', p. 116; and Göller again, 'The Dream of the Dragon and Bear', p. 139. The concept of 'anti-romance', which appears quite often in recent discussion of medieval romances, seems of dubious validity, since it is not clear that there existed a sufficiently definite contemporary concept of 'romance' to which it could be opposed.

23 Markus, op. cit., p. 62

24 See especially the excellent article by Elizabeth Porter, 'Chaucer's Knight, the Alliterative *Morte Arthure*, and Medieval Laws of War: a Reconsideration', *Nottingham Medieval Studies* 27 (1983), 56–78.

25 Göller, 'A Reassessment of the *Alliterative Morte Arthure*', pp. 26, 28

26 Anke Janssen, 'The Dream of the Wheel of Fortune', in Göller, *The*

Alliterative Morte Arthure, entirely misrepresents the situation in arguing that Arthur is exactly the same as the first six of the Worthies (each of whom, according to the dream, laments that 'derflyche I am dampnede for ever' [3277]), and that he therefore 'foregoes salvation' (p. 151). The first six are pagans and Jews and hence (according to the commonest medieval view) cannot be saved; Arthur is a Christian.

27 Janssen, ibid. As we have seen, whatever Arthur's spiritual state may be, the poet does not in fact indicate that he is claiming 'things to which he is not entitled'.

28 Cf. Matthews, *The Tragedy of Arthur*, pp. 112–13

29 A. I. Doyle, 'The Manuscripts', in *Middle English Alliterative Poetry*. ed. Lawton, pp. 88–100; p. 93. For evidence suggesting that the *Morte Arthure* poet may have been among the readers of *The Siege of Jerusalem*, see *Morte Arthure*, ed. Hamel, pp. 47–52.

30 See Phyllis Moe, 'The French Source of the Alliterative *Siege of Jerusalem*', *Medium Aevum* 39 (1970), 147–54

31 Doyle, 'The Manuscripts', p. 95

32 David Lawton, 'Middle English Alliterative Poetry: An Introduction', in *Middle English Alliterative Poetry*, ed. Lawton, pp. 1–19; p. 8

33 Cf. Arthur's plan in *Morte Arthure*, once he has seized Rome, to 'graythe over the grette see with gud men of armes,/ To revenge the renke that on the rode dyede' (3216–7).

34 For a general survey of this theme, see Derek Brewer, 'The Arming of the Warrior in European Literature and Chaucer', in his *Tradition and Innovation in Chaucer* (London 1982), pp. 142–60.

35 For the lines from the *Destruction* and its source, see *Morte Arthure*, ed. Hamel, pp. 54–5 and n. 154; cf. *Aeneid* IV 522ff. Birds are the only example Virgil gives of creatures asleep; his dawn passage comes later at 584ff.

7 *Purity* and danger

1 2nd edn (London 1969)

2 Cf. Larry D. Benson, *Art and Tradition in Sir Gawain and the Green Knight* (New Brunswick 1965), p. 166, on the poet's 'keen awareness of the semantic function of form'.

3 E.g. Charlotte C. Morse, 'The Image of the Vessel in *Cleanness*', *University of Toronto Quarterly* 40 (1970–1), 202–16, and *The Pattern of Judgment in the "Queste" and "Cleanness"* (Columbia MO, 1978); T. D. Kelly and J. T. Irwin, 'The Meaning of *Cleanness*: Parable as Effective Sign', *Mediaeval Studies* 35 (1973), 232–60; S. L. Clark and Julian N. Wasserman, '*Purity*: the Cities of the Dove and the Raven', *American Benedictine Review* 29 (1978), 284–306. What these particular instances have in common is a determination to find a secret, non-literal level of meaning in the poem, an enterprise that seems to me misguided. On feasts, see Elizabeth R. Keiser, 'The Festive Decorum of *Cleanness*', in *Chivalric Literature*, ed. Larry D. Benson and John Leyerle (Kalamazoo 1980), pp. 63–75, and Jonathan Nicholls, *The Matter of Courtesy* (Cambridge 1985), ch. 6.

4 *Purity*, ed. Robert J. Menner (New Haven 1920), p. 103

5 Dorothy Everett, *Essays on Middle English Literature* (Oxford 1955), p. 70

6 W. A. Davenport, *The Art of the Gawain-Poet* (London 1978), pp. 86, 91

7 The examples are discussed by Douglas, *Purity and Danger*, chs. 9 and 3. The camels, rock-badgers and hares are condemned as unclean in Leviticus 11:4–6 and Deuteronomy 14:7 (the Authorized Version has 'coney' for rock-badger); the belief about contact with a menstruating woman is held by the Mae Enga of New Guinea (and is also much more widespread).

8 This phrase is the title of the first chapter of Claude Lévi-Strauss, *The Savage Mind* (London 1966).

9 'The Chinese Written Character as a Medium for Poetry', in Ezra Pound, *Instigations* (New York 1920), pp. 357–88; pp. 380, 383, 363

10 Henceforward, page-references in this chapter are to *Purity and Danger*, as in n. 1 above.

11 Keiser, 'The Festive Decorum of *Cleanness*', pp. 68–9

12 Cf. the remarks of Julia Kristeva in *Powers of Horror*, trans. Leon S. Roudiez (New York 1982), a book which is partly concerned to reinterpret the thought of Mary Douglas in terms of a feminist semiotics:

> . . . no matter what differences there may be among societies where religious prohibitions . . . are supposed to afford protection from defilement, one sees everywhere the importance, both social and symbolic, of women and particularly the mother. In societies where it occurs, ritualization of defilement is accompanied by a strong concern for separating the sexes, and this means giving men rights over women . . . It is as if . . . two powers attempted to share out society. One of them, the masculine, apparently victorious, confesses through its very relentlessness against the other, the feminine, that it is threatened by an asymmetrical, irrational, wily, uncontrollable power . . . That other sex, the feminine, becomes synonymous with a radical evil that is to be suppressed. (p. 70)

This is an accurate description of attitudes widespread within the 'official' culture of the Middle Ages, dominated as it was by a caste of celibate males. In the *Gawain*-poet, such attitudes are perhaps reflected in the treatment of Sir Bertilak's wife in *Sir Gawain and the Green Knight* or, in *Purity*, of Lot's wife; but they are not found throughout his work, nor, where they are found, is it usually in crude forms. His ability to see sex as a matter of divinely devised play rather than simply as sin must surely help to explain this difference.

13 See O. F. Emerson, 'A Note on the M.E. *Cleanness*', *Modern Language Review* 10 (1915), 373–5. Emerson noted that salt 'causes slight fermentation', and suggested that the poet might have been 'directly acquainted with the Hebrew commentaries on the Bible' (pp. 374, 375).

14 *Implicit Meanings* (London 1975), p. 269, with reference to Leviticus 11:41–4 and Deuteronomy 14:19

15 *Cleanness*, ed. Sir Israel Gollancz (London 1921), pp. xvi–xvii. On *cortaysye* in the poet's work, see D. S. Brewer, 'Courtesy and the *Gawain*-poet', in *Patterns of Love and Courtesy*, ed. Lawlor, pp. 54–85, and Nicholls, *The Matter of Courtesy*.

16 *Powers of Horror*, pp. 69, 74–5

17 Cf. Nicholas Jacobs, 'Alliterative Storms: a Topos in Middle English', *Speculum* 37 (1962), 695–719

8   The *Gawain*-poet's sense of an ending

1 The phrase is borrowed, of course, from Frank Kermode's thought-provoking and influential book, *The Sense of an Ending* (New York 1967), to which anyone who writes about literary endings must owe a debt. For an interesting attempt to apply Kermode's ideas to some medieval poems, including *Pearl*, see Margaret Bridges, 'The Sense of an Ending: the Case of the Dream-Vision', *Dutch Quarterly Review* 14 (1984), 81–96.

2 *New Readings vs. Old Plays* (Chicago 1979), p. 114

3 Albert B. Friedman and Richard H. Osberg, 'Gawain's Girdle as Traditional Symbol', *Journal of American Folklore* 90 (1979), 301–15, p. 309; and Ralph Hanna, 'Unlocking What's Locked: Gawain's Green Girdle', *Viator* 14 (1983), 289–302, p. 291, n. 4.

4 I am especially indebted to the penetrating article by Ralph Hanna noted above, which also includes some interesting thoughts about endings. Hanna lists in p. 289, n. 1, other articles which have 'drawn out the connections' (p. 289) between the girdle and the pentangle.

5 Robert W. Hanning, 'Poetic Emblems in Medieval Narrative Texts', in *Vernacular Poetics in the Middle Ages*, ed. Lois Ebin (Kalamazoo 1984), 1–32, p. 25

6 John Stevens, 'The *granz biens* of Marie de France', in *Patterns of Love and Courtesy*, ed. Lawlor, 1–25, p. 21; *The Lais of Marie de France*, trans. Robert Hanning and Joan Ferrante (New York 1978), p. 2.

7 L. T. Topsfield, *Chrétien de Troyes* (Cambridge 1981), suggests that the portraits of the four arts of the quadrivium on Erec's robe

> . . . symbolise Erec's *savoir* and *science*, his wisdom and practical knowledge of life, and his promise as a future king. On a higher level, the way in which the four arts are described may indicate that the robe is also intended as a symbol of the divine ordering of the universe. (p. 60)

8 Cf., however, Gerald Morgan, 'The Significance of the Pentangle Symbolism in *Sir Gawain and the Green Knight*', *Modern Language Review* 74 (1979), 769–90:

> . . . we need to recognize that the pentangle is not by definition a perfect unity; it possesses greater unity than a quadrangle but less than a circle. We do not therefore expect of Gawain perfection that is appropriate to an angelic being or to God himself . . . (p. 782).

Morgan derives his interpretation of the pentangle from Dante and Aquinas, and assumes that the *Gawain*-poet's participation in 'the habits and presuppositions of Scholastic philosophy' (p. 779) would have led him to share it; the poet himself, however, gives no indication that he sees the pentangle as symbolizing only a limited perfection.

9 'Poetic Emblems in Medieval Narrative Texts', p. 1. Hanning goes on to propose that the fish covered in *sleye* sauce, served to Gawain on Christmas Eve (*Gawain* 893), can be regarded as a reflexive emblem of 'the problematic relationship between appearance and reality, or act and interpretation, throughout *Sir Gawain and the Green Knight*' (p. 27) – a suggestion I find it hard to take seriously. See also his article 'Sir Gawain and the Red Herring:

The Perils of Interpretation', in *Acts of Interpretation*, ed. Carruthers and Kirk, pp. 5–23.

10 *A Book of Showings to the Anchoress Julian of Norwich*, ed. Edmund Colledge and James Walsh, vol. 2 (Toronto 1978), ch. 5, p. 303

11 *The York Plays*, ed. Richard Beadle (London 1982), p. 49. In the following stanza God uses the word *endeles* about himself.

12 Cf. A. Kent Hieatt, '*Sir Gawain*: pentangle, *luf-lace*, numerical structure', in *Silent Poetry*. ed. Alastair Fowler (London 1970), pp. 116–40. Hieatt suggests further that it is significant that *lace* also means 'snare', and that the lady uses the *luf-lace* to ensnare Gawain. J. A. Burrow, however, in his *A Reading of Sir Gawain and the Green Knight* (London 1965), writes:

> Unlike the pentangle, the belt is not, so far as the poem is concerned, a "natural" symbol. It does not, that is, have any particular symbolic value on the strength simply of its intrinsic natural properties. (p. 158)

My own argument is that the girdle *is* a natural symbol of imperfection, but that it has a different symbolic value assigned to it in the course of the poem.

13 *The Gawain-Poet*, p. 236

14 See, for example, Derek Brewer, 'The Interpretation of Dream, Folktale and Romance with Special Reference to *Sir Gawain and the Green Knight*', *Neuphilologische Mitteilungen* 77 (1976), 569–81; and *Symbolic Stories*, pp. 84–91.

15 Cf. Benson, *Art and Tradition in Sir Gawain and the Green Knight*, p. 32

16 Cf. Loretta Wassermann, 'Honor and Shame in *Sir Gawain and the Green Knight*', in *Chivalric Literature*, ed. Benson and Leyerle, pp. 77–90, and J. A. Burrow, 'Honour and Shame in *Sir Gawain and the Green Knight*', in his *Essays on Medieval Literature* (Oxford 1984), pp. 117–31

17 Here I restore the manuscript reading, in place of the emendation *ledes* proposed by Burrow and adopted by Andrew and Waldron.

18 See Hanna, 'Unlocking What's Locked', p. 290

19 On the secular orders of chivalry, see Maurice Keen, *Chivalry* (New Haven 1984), ch. x. On the founding of the Order of the Garter, see Juliet Vale, *Edward III and Chivalry* (Woodbridge 1982), ch. 5. On the Band and its possible influence on the Garter, see Richard Barber, *The Knight and Chivalry*, 2nd edn (London 1974), Appendix I.

20 *Sir Gawain and the Green Knight*, ed. Sir Israel Gollancz, EETS OS 210 (London 1940), p. 132.

21 Keen, *Chivalry*, p. 193

22 Ed. Colledge and Walsh, vol. 2, ch. 39, pp. 451–3. The passage is also quoted in this connection by Burrow, 'Honour and Shame in *Sir Gawain and the Green Knight*', pp. 128–9.

23 B XVIII 48: 'And bigan of grene thorn a garland to make'. The B-text of *Piers Plowman* is quoted from *The Vision of Piers Plowman: A Complete Edition of the B-text*, ed. A. V. C. Schmidt (London 1978). Colledge and Walsh, annotating the passage of Julian referred to in the previous note, cite a passage from *Ancrene Riwle* in which crucifixion is seen as turning 'schome to menske'.

24 *Pearl, Cleanness, Patience, Sir Gawain and the Green Knight*, ed. A. C. Cawley and J. J. Anderson (London 1976), p. xiv. For discussion of numerical patterns, see, e.g., P. M. Kean, 'Numerical Composition in *Pearl*', *Notes and*

Queries 12 (1965), 49–51; Maren-Sofie Røstvig, 'Numerical Composition in *Pearl*: a Theory', *English Studies* 48 (1967), 326–32; John MacQueen, *Numerology* (Edinburgh 1985), pp. 97–8.

25 Cf. Otto von Simson, *The Gothic Cathedral*, 2nd edn (Princeton 1962), pp. 34–5 and n. 37

26 '*Pearl*'s "Maynful Mone": Crux, Simile, and Structure', in *Acts of Interpretation*, ed. Carruthers and Kirk, pp. 159–72

27 It is an intriguing fact that the word *rawe*, like *lyne*, could also refer to a line of verse (see *The House of Fame* 448, discussed above in Chapter 4, p. 93).

28 Cary Nelson, *The Incarnate Word: Literature as Verbal Space* (Urbana 1973), notes the applicability of Christ's saying to the poem's 'outer structure' (p. 27).

29 Cf. Robert W. Ackerman, 'The Pearl-Maiden and the Penny', *Romance Philology* 17 (1963–4), 615–23, to which I am generally indebted.

30 Cf. Barbara Nolan, *The Gothic Visionary Perspective* (Princeton 1977), p. 157: 'A secret "cnawyng," veiled and hidden, implied rather than demonstrated in the literal story, appears to be the poem's central organizing principle'.

31 Rosalind Field, 'The Heavenly Jerusalem in *Pearl*', *Modern Language Review* 81 (1986), 7–17; pp. 13, 15

32 *York Plays* I 98, p. 52

33 'A Note on *Pearl*', in *The Middle English Pearl: Critical Essays*, ed. John Conley (Notre Dame 1970), pp. 325–34

34 *The Book of Vices and Virtues*, ed. W. Nelson Francis, EETS OS 217 (London 1942), pp. 99–101. The same exposition of the Lord's Prayer (widely read in other translations of its French original besides this) also identifies the daily bread with 'the sacrament of the auter' and with the penny that the Lord gives to the workers in his vineyard (p. 111).

35 I would thus go somewhat further than Ackerman, 'The Pearl-Maiden and the Penny', who writes that the final stanza 'is a miracle of compression, yet it epitomizes the main argument of the entire poem' (p. 622). By contrast, see Jörg A. Fichte, 'The End of an Age Reflected in its Poetry', *Poetica* 8 (1977), 6–22, p. 7:

> . . . the end of *Pearl* is tagged on by its author because of his conviction that a poem demands formal closure. The work could very well have ended abruptly with line 1200, as the additional stanza cannot bring about the originally hoped-for conclusion.

Fichte makes no attempt to analyse the relationship of the final stanza to the rest of the poem.

9 *Piers Plowman*: allegory and verbal practice

1 It has recently been persuasively argued that the version of the poem found in MS Bodley 851 represents a stage in its composition earlier than the A-text: see *Piers Plowman: The Z Version*, ed. A. G. Rigg and Charlotte Brewer (Toronto 1983).

2 I have in mind Schmidt's B-text and Pearsall's C-text, but above all *Piers Plowman: The A Version*, ed. George Kane (London 1960), and *Piers Plowman: The B Version*, ed. George Kane and E. Talbot Donaldson (London 1975).

3 In lines 181–2 I have adopted the punctuation of Kane and Donaldson in preference to that of Schmidt.

4 Elizabeth Salter, *Piers Plowman – An Introduction* (Oxford 1962), pp. 21, 22, 35, 37–40, 41

5 See ibid, p. 29, and my 'Verbal Repetition in *Piers Plowman* B and C', *Journal of English and Germanic Philology* 62 (1963), 722–37, and *Criticism and Medieval Poetry*, 2nd edn (London 1972), pp. 127–31

6 Cf. George Kane, 'Music "Neither Unpleasant nor Monotonous"', in *Medieval Studies for J. A. W. Bennett*, ed. P. L. Heyworth (Oxford 1981), pp. 43–63

7 Noted in *The Vision of William Concerning Piers the Plowman*, ed. W. W. Skeat, vol. II (Oxford 1886), pp. 28–9

8 James 2:25; Joshua 2

9 Compare for example the supreme enactment of release from prison in the Harrowing of Hell in B XVIII, supported by metaphors such as *unspered* (86) and 'unjoynen and unlouken' (257).

10 Jill Mann, 'Eating and Drinking in *Piers Plowman*', *Essays and Studies* ns 32 (1979), 26–43, writes well about the relationship of this passage to other food images and about the difficulty of separating the literal from the metaphorical in Langland's references to food. See also A. V. C. Schmidt, 'Langland's Structural Imagery', *Essays in Criticism* 30 (1980), 311–25; p. 316.

11 John Holloway, *The Proud Knowledge* (London 1977), p. 65. In context the passage concerns Wordsworth, with special reference to the early books of the 1805 *Prelude*, but the description is remarkably apt to Langland.

12 So Elizabeth Salter and Derek Pearsall, ed. *Piers Plowman* (London 1967), p. 82, with reference to Wrath's confession. Pearsall, however, in his edition of the C-text, p. 109, notes that much of the circumstantial detail in Langland's personification of the sins as sinners 'goes beyond the possible experience of a single individual'.

13 Pearsall, ibid., p. 114

14 Priscilla Jenkins, 'Conscience: The Frustration of Allegory', in *Piers Plowman: Critical Approaches*, ed. S. S. Hussey (London 1969), pp. 125–42; p. 128. However one judges Langland's conscious intentions, this article, and the fuller account of the poem by the same author, Priscilla Martin, *Piers Plowman: The Field and the Tower* (London 1979), offer a convincing account of the outcome: an allegorical narrative that criticizes and deconstructs itself.

15 E.g. by J. A. W. Bennett, ed. *Piers Plowman* (Oxford 1972), p. 161, and Schmidt, p. 316

16 For a valuable discussion of certain features of punning in Langland, see A. V. C. Schmidt, '*Lele Wordes* and *Bele Paroles*: Some Aspects of Langland's Word-Play', *Review of English Studies* ns 34 (1983), 137–50.

17 S. T. Coleridge, *Table Talk*, 5 March 1834

18 The phrase is used by Barbara Palmer, 'The Guide Convention in *Piers Plowman*', *Leeds Studies in English* ns 5 (1971), 13–27; p. 24. I believe this article to be fundamentally mistaken, but it is of value in its forthright criticism of Langland's work for failing to operate according to the criteria by which we might expect to be able to judge it. Palmer concludes that the poem is a failure; I conclude that we must rethink our criteria.

19 Among the many studies of this part of the poem, I am variously indebted to: Nevill Coghill, 'The Pardon of Piers Plowman', *Proceedings of the British*

Academy 30 (1944), 303–57; Robert W. Frank, *Piers Plowman and the Scheme of Salvation* (New Haven 1957), ch. 3; John Lawlor, 'The Pardon Reconsidered', *Modern Language Review* 45 (1959), 449–58; J. A. Burrow, 'The Action of Langland's Second Vision', *Essays in Criticism* 15 (1965), 247–68; Rosemary Woolf, 'The Tearing of the Pardon', in *Piers Plowman: Critical Approaches*, ed. Hussey, pp. 50–75; Mary C. Schroeder, '*Piers Plowman*: the Tearing of the Pardon', *Philological Quarterly* 49 (1970), 8–18; Elizabeth D. Kirk, *The Dream Thought of Piers Plowman* (New Haven 1972), pp. 80–100; Susan H. McLeod, 'The Tearing of the Pardon in *Piers Plowman*', *Philological Quarterly* 56 (1977), 14–26; Maureen Quilligan, *The Language of Allegory* (Ithaca 1979), pp. 64–79; Ruth Ames, 'The Pardon Impugned by the Priest', in *The Alliterative Tradition in the Fourteenth Century*, ed. Levy and Szarmach, pp. 47–68; Janet Coleman, *Piers Plowman and the "Moderni"* (Rome 1981), pp. 99–107; Margaret E. Goldsmith, *The Figure of Piers Plowman* (Cambridge 1981), ch. V; D. A. Lawton, 'On Tearing – And Not Tearing – the Pardon', *Philological Quarterly* 60 (1981), 414–22; Judson Boyce Allen, 'Langland's Reading and Writing: *Detractor* and the Pardon Passus', *Speculum* 59 (1984), 342–62. Among the more extreme views expressed recently should be mentioned those of Lawton, that in tearing the pardon *atweyne* (115) Piers is simply confirming its own separation of the sheep from the goats, so that the omission of this tearing from the C-text makes no difference to the meaning, and of Allen, that 'the pardon passus is not about pardon, but about Psalm 22, as understood by Hugh of St-Cher' (art. cit., p. 353, n. 22).

20 Cf. *Morte Arthure* 3497, quoted on p. 164 above
21 For a thought-provoking discussion of the conflict within Langland's attitude towards economic activity, see David Aers, *Chaucer, Langland and the Creative Imagination* (London 1980), ch. 1.
22 Rosemary Woolf, 'The Tearing of the Pardon', p. 54
23 Janet Coleman, *Piers Plowman and the "Moderni"*, loc. cit.
24 Cf. Margaret Aston, 'Huizinga's Harvest: England and *The Waning of the Middle Ages*', *Medievalia et Humanistica* ns 9 (1979), 1–24; p. 16
25 Cf. Geoffrey Shepherd, 'The Nature of Alliterative Poetry in Late Medieval England', pp. 19–20
26 Peter Dronke, *Poetic Individuality in the Middle Ages* (Oxford 1970), ch. VI, writes well about this, referring in passing to the Pardon scene, of which he asks,

> Is it not possible that what is enigmatic in such moments may be deliberately so, that the poet is demanding of his audience not the simple acceptance of the situation as he tells it to them, but a response that embraces it as intrinsically problematic? (p. 200)

27 'Change the Object Itself', in *Image-Music-Text*, pp. 165–9; p. 167
28 Anne Middleton, 'Narration and the Invention of Experience: Episodic Form in *Piers Plowman*', in *The Wisdom of Poetry*, ed. Larry D. Benson and Siegfried Wenzel (Kalamazoo 1982), pp. 91–122; p. 109
29 In addition to the general works on *Piers Plowman* cited in note 19 above, I am particularly indebted to Peter Dronke, 'Arbor Caritatis', in *Medieval Studies for J. A. W. Bennett*, pp. 207–53, and to David Aers, *Piers Plowman and Christian Allegory* (London 1975), pp. 79–109; also to E. Talbot Donaldson, *Piers Plowman: the C-text and its Poet* (New Haven 1949), pp. 180–96, and *Piers*

Index

265

Index

Index

Index

Index

269

Index